A VIETCONG MEMOIR

TRUONG NHU TANG

WITH DAVID CHANOFF AND DOAN VAN TOAI

HARCOURT BRACE JOVANOVICH, PUBLISHERS

SAN DIEGO   NEW YORK   LONDON

Requests for permission to make copies of any
part of the work should be mailed to:
Permissions, Harcourt Brace Jovanovich, Publishers,
Orlando, Florida 32887.

The publisher wishes to thank The Indochina Archives, Institute of East Asian Studies, University of
California at Berkeley for permission to print the
photographs on pages 8, 15, 74, 88, 121, 132, 139,
148, 149, 150, 151, 152, 153, 172, 238, 256, 276, 281.

Library of Congress Cataloging in Publication Data
Truong, Nhu T'ang.
    A Vietcong memoir.
    Includes index.
    1. Truong, Nhu T'ang.   2. Vietnam—Politics
and government—1945–1975.   3. Vietnam—Politics
and government—1975–   .   4. Vietnamese
Conflict, 1961–1975—Personal narratives, Vietcong.
5. Mặt trận dân tộc giải phóng miên nam Việt Nam—
Biography.   6. Revolutionists—Vietnam—
Biography.   I. Chanoff, David.   II. Doan, Van Toai,
1946–   .   III. Title.
DS556.93.T78A38 1985   959.704'38   84–25132
ISBN 0–15–193636–6

Designed by Jacqueline Schuman

Printed in the United States of America

First edition

A B C D E

To my mother and father.

And to my betrayed comrades,
who believed they were
sacrificing themselves for a
humane liberation of their people.

▲▲▲▲▲▲▲▲▲▲▲▲▲▲▲▲▲▲▲ Contents

A VIETNAM VOCABULARY   *xi*

FOREWORD   *xii*

1   The Family Cocoon   *1*

2   An Afternoon with Uncle Ho   *9*

3   My Personal Liberation   *18*

4   Going Home   *25*

5   Opposing Diem   *33*

6   Albert Pham Ngoc Thao: Master Spy   *42*

7   The Birth of the NLF   *63*

8   Strengthening the Front   *81*

9   The Urban Struggle   *88*

10   Prison Once More   *102*

11   Tet and a Secret Exchange   *11*

12   The Alliance, South Vietnam's Third Force   *130*

13   The Provisional Revolutionary Government   *145*

CONTENTS

14 Life in the Maquis *156*

15 Race against Death *176*

16 First Troubles with the North *186*

17 1972: The Watershed *200*

18 The Aftermath of Paris *219*

19 The Ideologues Claim a Victim *234*

20 PRG Ambassador *240*

21 Joys and Sorrows *258*

22 Concord and Reconciliation *271*

23 One Nation *283*

24 Exile *291*

EPILOGUE *309*

GLOSSARY OF NAMES *311*

APPENDIX *317*

INDEX *341*

Maps appear on pages ix, 169, 184, and 306.

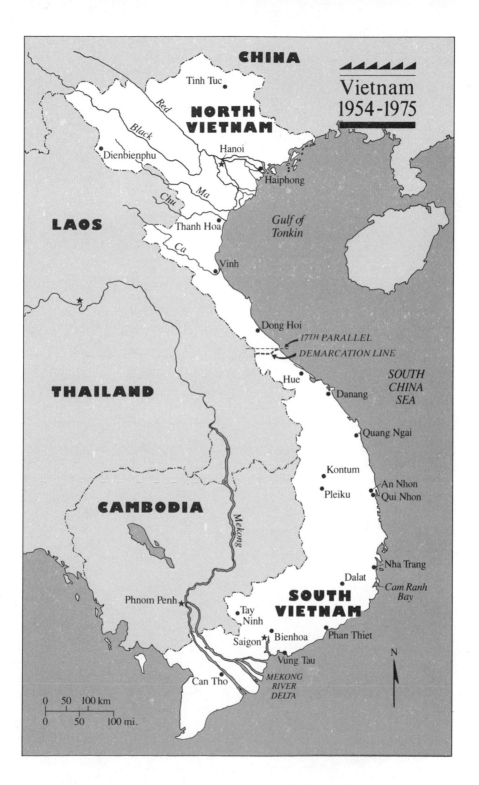

CHINA

Tinh Tuc

NORTH VIETNAM

Vietnam 1954-1975

Red

Black

Dienbienphu

Hanoi

Ma

Haiphong

Chu

LAOS

Thanh Hoa

Gulf of Tonkin

Ca

Vinh

Dong Hoi

17TH PARALLEL

DEMARCATION LINE

Hue

THAILAND

Danang

SOUTH CHINA SEA

Quang Ngai

Kontum

Pleiku

An Nhon

Qui Nhon

CAMBODIA

Mekong

Nha Trang

Dalat

Cam Ranh Bay

Phnom Penh

SOUTH VIETNAM

Tay Ninh

Saigon

Bienhoa

Phan Thiet

Vung Tau

N

Can Tho

MEKONG RIVER DELTA

0   50   100 km

0   50   100 mi.

Vietminh The resistance front against the French formed in 1941 by Ho Chi Minh. The term is short for Viet Nam Doc Lap Dong Minh, or Vietnam Independence League.

Vietcong A term used since the late 1950s and applied generally to the insurgent forces in South Vietnam; the fighting arm of the NLF. The name is short for Viet Nam Cong San, or Vietnamese Communist. Many of the non-Communist revolutionaries initially considered the term insulting.

NLF The National Liberation Front for South Vietnam. Established in 1960 as the formal organization of the South Vietnamese revolution.

PLAF People's Liberation Armed Forces. The NLF army.

Alliance of National, Democratic, and Peace Forces A Southern opposition front organization established under the auspices of the NLF in 1968.

PRG Provisional Revolutionary Government of South Vietnam. The Southern revolutionaries' political organization, established as an alternative government in 1969.

DRV The Democratic Republic of Vietnam. The official name of North Vietnam. After the formal unification of North and South in 1976, the name of the country as a whole became the Socialist Republic of Vietnam.

NVA The North Vietnamese Army. Officially it was known as the People's Army of North Vietnam, or PAVN.

Lao Dong The Vietnamese Communist Party. Literally, the Vietnamese Workers' Party (Dang Lao Dong Viet Nam). The Communist Party assumed the name in 1951, six years after it was ostensibly disbanded by Ho Chi Minh. In 1976 the name was changed officially to The Communist Party.

COSVN Central Office South Vietnam. The Lao Dong (Communist Party) headquarters branch for most of South Vietnam.

GVN Government of Vietnam. The common term for South Vietnam's government. Officially, the South was called the Republic of Vietnam.

ARVN Army of the Republic of Vietnam.

FCP The French Communist Party.

PRC The People's Republic of China.

ICC The International Control Commission. A three nation group (Canada, India, and Poland) set up by the Geneva agreement in 1954 to monitor the armistice. In 1973 the Paris Accords established a similar four nation group.

These memoirs are the story of my life as a revolutionary. There is little in them about some of the Vietnam War's events best remembered in the West: the clash of arms at Khe Sanh, the surprise offensive of Tet Mau Than, the POWs, or the last American helicopters darting from the embassy roof as Saigon fell to the North Vietnamese army. There is, I know, a great deal of interest in the military side of the war. But that was not my side. I was never a warrior and took no part in what we called the *Dau Tranh Vu Trang* ("the Violence Struggle"), though in the course of things I experienced a fair share of violence myself, in prison and in the jungle under the great B-52 deluges of 1969 and 1970. My own role as a Vietcong urban organizer, then as a cabinet member, was narrowly defined, and in the nature of our struggle I kept (and was kept) away from the dimensions of confrontation that did not closely concern me.

But there was another side of the war as well, one that the Vietnamese revolutionaries considered primary—the political side. My own direct involvement, over almost two decades, was on this front. For years I lived a double (occasionally a triple) life in Saigon, proselytizing and organizing for the revolution among Saigon's upper classes and youth. After my imprisonment and eventual exchange, I lived in the jungle, at the headquarters of the Provisional Revolutionary Government (whose minister of justice I was), then—briefly —as a diplomat visiting Eastern Europe and Third World countries.

Because my view of the Vietnam War is a partial one, the picture I can draw of the revolution needs to be filled out by other accounts: from those who were involved in areas of the political arena different from mine, and of course from those whose memoirs and histories might candidly illuminate the military side of the conflict. Unfortunately, given the compulsion in present-day Vietnam to keep history the handmaiden of ideology, prospects for such memoirs and reports ever emerging from my country are not bright. Still, it is only through understanding the Vietnamese who fought on the other side that Americans will have anything like a complete portrait of a war upon which they have been reflecting so deeply—the only war they have ever lost.

The West knows, I think, extraordinarily little about the Vietcong: its plans, its difficulties—especially its inner conflicts. The circumstances of war and the great care taken to conceal its workings combined to mask the revolution in secrecy. But the Vietcong was no monolith; the motives of its members often clashed—violently. And many of us who composed its political core have felt that its goals were, in the end, subverted. The human motives, the internal struggle, the bitter resolution—these are the things I have attempted to record here.

Tr. N. T.
Paris, 1984

The Family
Cocoon

You . . . you will be a pharmacist." It was my father speaking to me. I was thirteen. "Your older brother will be a doctor, number three brother a banker, numbers four, five, and six engineers."

Blessed with six sons (and no daughters), my father was exercising his god-given right as a Vietnamese paterfamilias to build a world out of his children's talent and obedience. It would be a world blessed in every way—with money, position, well-chosen wives, virtue—a rich, harmonious family organism, bonded together by filial piety. Somewhere in this vision my older brother Quynh (the doctor) and I (the pharmacist)* would work together, supporting each other and enhancing each other's careers and fortunes. For the three youngest there would be a family-owned factory, with Bich (the banker brother) providing the financing. I had no reason to question my father's judgment in any of this, nor any desire to. Life was, after all, already rich and harmonious in the many-roomed three-story house on Saigon's rue d'Espagne where we lived.

My father had come from wealth and had married wealth. His own father was a self-taught man of letters and a Confucian scholar, also an official in the French colonial administration, who had made sure that his son had the best French schooling available to a Viet-

---

* The pharmacist in French colonial Vietnam had far more prestige and affluence than his counterpart in contemporary America.

namese. Educated to French culture, my father had become a professor at the French College Chasseloup Laubat (later to be renamed the Lycée Chasseloup Laubat). Teaching, however, he did only for pleasure. His business was the rubber plantation in Thu Dau Mot and the printing house in Saigon, whose offices comprised much of our first floor. It was these *affaires* that allowed him to nurture his numerous offspring properly.

If my father's pleasure was teaching, his children were his passion. It was our care, training, and futures that absorbed his attention. Everything requisite for studies and good health was brought into our home. It was our job, as we grew up, simply to use these resources wisely, according to the plans he had so enthusiastically and meticulously laid out to bring us (and him) happiness. The French education in which he had been raised, less severe than the native Vietnamese variety, encouraged him to forgo the corporal punishment and dictatorial manner inflicted by most fathers on their children in that time and place. By nature gentle and patient, by profession a teacher, he spent countless hours explaining the world to his six inquisitive fledglings.

To assist my father in this great task of bringing us up, my mother brought an equally sweet and reasonable character. Among her other cares was the supervision of six Chinese nurses (one for each of us), who lived on the first floor behind the printing offices and were our daily companions until the age of thirteen. It is an article of faith in Vietnam that all Chinese women love children—indiscriminately, it seems—and so the Truongs, like other rich families, had as many as circumstances required and their wealth could support. Our amahs would accompany us to school and escort us home afterward, constantly chatting with and admonishing "their" children, as well as each other, so that it seemed as if we were always part of a familiar and noisy crowd. Even after we outgrew our amahs, several of them had become so much a part of the family that they stayed on, helping more generally with household duties and still keeping a fond and vigilant eye on their former charges.

The amahs, however reluctantly, were often forced to share their guardianship with a variety of tutors and pedagogues whom my father had also retained. The moment any of us displayed a weakness in one or another of our school subjects, an appropriately learned individual would appear to help dispel the confusion. Although all six brothers were good students, the numerous courses in our school curriculum guaranteed that at any given time several of these specialists would be on the premises. More welcome were the music teachers, who came to instruct each of us twice a week. My father had by no means neglected the artistic side of our development: Quynh and I had played the violin from quite an early age; Bich (the third) was a pianist, while the three engineers-to-be were trained to the mandolin. We were taught Western music exclusively, and playing was our love and our sport. I often wondered when I was young if my father's talk about family harmony was not perhaps meant to be taken literally.

But though family harmony was one of my father's favorite subjects, I was aware that this concept, as well as the other ethical principles of life, were in the special keeping of my grandfather. His house was on the outskirts of Saigon, in Giadinh. For us, as for our near and distant relatives, it was the place where we gathered on all the feasts, holidays, and anniversaries of deaths, to mourn or celebrate, to venerate the ancestors and to reassert our own identity as a family, the family Truong. My grandfather was the head of this clan, just as my father was the head of our particular branch of it. Having so many souls in his care, though, he was only able to concern himself with the most significant dimension of their well-being, their moral lives.

Each Sunday we would gather at my grandfather's house to visit and also to listen as he taught us the precepts of Confucian ethics. He would remind us of our duty to live virtuous lives, lives of personal rectitude and filial piety. And he would talk about the five cardinal ethical principles: *nhon, nghia, le, tri, tin* ("benevolence, duty, propriety, conscience, and faithfulness"). There was nothing abstract or dry about his exposition. Instead he would weave his story around the adventures and exploits of ancient Chinese heroes and sages, whose lives illustrated one or another of these virtues. For boys especially, he would tell us, there are two unshakable necessities: protection of the family's honor and loyalty to the nation. And we would sing together the moral songs that we all knew by heart: *"Cong cha nhu nui Thai Son,"* "Your father's sacrifice in raising you is as great as Thai Son Mountain/ Your mother's love and care for you is a never-ending source." We were sure that particular song had been written about our own father and mother.

My mother's side of the family offered a somewhat different religious experience. My maternal grandfather had been one of the founders of the Cao Dai religious sect; in fact, he had given the three hundred hectares of land in Tay Ninh where the Cao Daists had built their "Vatican." Cao Dai is a syncretic religion, combining elements of Buddhism, Christianity, Islam, and Confucianism with heavy overtones of Vietnamese nationalism. My grandfather's second wife was the leader of the Cao Dai women. My mother (also a high-ranking member of the sect) often took my brothers and me to Tay Ninh for visits. During prayer we were obliged to bow for an hour, which I found a great annoyance.

We lived our lives surrounded by a soft envelope of warmth, moving between our second-floor sleeping and working quarters, our school, and our grandfather's house. During our early years we were not permitted out to visit friends, and friends could not come to visit us. Our days were full of studies and music, the ministrations of our teachers, and the company we provided for each other. For diversion, besides the trips to Tay Ninh, we had a house in the mountains at Dalat and another on the beach at Cap St. Jacques (Vung Tau). To one or another of these establishments the entire household would repair each summer—nurses, cook, tutors, music teachers, and all— as if all by ourselves we constituted some minor nomadic migration. Amidst this spiritual and material abundance, I passed my youth and adolescence, bundled up in the security of a well-established order.

Our school was Saigon's Lycée Chasseloup Laubat (where my father taught), reserved for children of the French colonial administrators and the most privileged Vietnamese. I enjoyed it from the very first. Whatever the other consequences of my father's approach to child rearing, he and my grandfather had instilled in all of us a powerful thirst for knowledge, and the Chasseloup teachers matched our need to learn with their own compulsive determination to teach. From an early age we knew that the goals of life were to study, to become good, and to become rich. Study was the means, goodness and riches the ends. School was another one of the resources that had been provided to help us along the way.

At the Chasseloup Laubat we spoke and wrote exclusively French, and we learned, along with mathematics, science, and literature, all about the history and culture of *nos ancêtres les Gaulois*. We learned by heart the geography of France; we knew her literature, her people, her art. We read of France's great political and military heroes, her men of science and of letters. We felt at home in the great worldwide civilization that these illustrious "ancestors" of ours had created. About our own country we remained profoundly ignorant, except for what we read in the final chapters of our history books, the ones on France's colonial empire, *France outre-mer*. But our ignorance did not disturb us; in fact, we were not even aware of it. It wasn't until after I had begun secondary school that I began to realize that I was—in some ways at least—different.

The scene of my initiation into the mysteries of colonialism was the lycée schoolyard during recess. As the games we played became rougher and more competitive, my Vietnamese friends and I learned that we, in contrast to our French schoolmates, were part of a racial entity sometimes called *nhaques* (peasants), sometimes *mites* (a derogatory abbreviation of *Annamite,* the French term for Vietnamese). Completely unprepared for attacks of this kind on my amour propre, I was first shocked by the insults. Soon shock gave way to anger, and recesses were occasionally punctuated with brawls, which mirrored the hatreds felt by many of our elders. But given the thick protective armor that still encased me, I had no way of knowing about any of that. Nor, as I began to feel the first stirrings of my Vietnamese identity, was I in the least aware of how the French had come to master Vietnam or of the history of Vietnam's dealings with previous masters.

Stinging as they were, these schoolyard encounters and the feelings they engendered remained a distinctly minor chord as I went about preparing for my future as a pharmacist. Despite the fact that I loved history and felt little warmth for chemistry, in 1943 I began pharmaceutical studies at the Grall Hospital and the following year left for further training in Hanoi. Hanoi University, the single institute of higher learning the French had seen fit to establish in Vietnam, was (to my father's way of thinking) a solid step on the road to a university education in France. Quynh had already embarked on his medical studies in Paris, and I was to join him there at the end of my year of seasoning in the North.

It was a year that passed quickly and pleasantly enough. Though I did not feel at all unhappy about my cloistered upbringing, I was delighted to discover and explore the novelties made available by life beyond the circle of family, school, and close friends. The only discordant note in the experience was my growing conviction that I had no calling to be a pharmacist. How would my father react to this news? I was not yet ready to find out. But the first hints of this potential for filial disloyalty—previously unsuspected—were already causing me trouble when I returned to Saigon in the summer of 1945. Almost immediately, however, the personal qualms I was experiencing were engulfed in events of real moment.

On August 15 Japan's surrender to the Allies was announced in a radio broadcast by the Emperor Hirohito. Whatever joy that event may have brought in the rest of the world, in Vietnam the surrender brought confusion. By the seventeenth, guerrillas in Tonkin (northern Vietnam) had entered Hanoi, and a mass uprising was under way that would wrest power from the defeated Japanese and Vichy French colonial regime. Within days a National Liberation Committee had taken control, and on September 2, Ho Chi Minh, its president, was reading the Vietnamese declaration of independence to an immense throng that overflowed the city's Ba Dinh Square. "All men are created equal," he began. "They are endowed by their creator with certain inalienable rights. . . . Do you hear me distinctly my fellow countrymen?" As Ho moved quickly to create a solid base of mass

support, the Allies—Americans, British, Chinese, and Free French—
were each deciding how best to pursue their own interests in Vietnam
and how to deal with the new self-proclaimed president in Hanoi.

For me, just back from my year of pharmacy, the events in Hanoi
and all the accompanying international agitation might as well have
been happening on another planet. What I did know was that
Saigon too was seething. The August Revolution was erupting all
around me in a constant stream of meetings and street demonstrations.
The air was charged with excitement and anticipation, fueled by
leaflets proclaiming "Vietnam for the Vietnamese," banners, flags, and
inflammatory speeches. During one stormy march a Vietnamese student was shot, and his death triggered a citywide outpouring of anger.
In each neighborhood bands of *Jeunesse d'Avant-Garde* ("Vanguard Youth") were being organized. Caught in a tide of emotional
patriotism and excited by danger and the idea of independence, all
of Saigon's young people seemed to be joining. I was filled with
exactly the same passions, and I hadn't a moment's doubt about what
to do. Without any knowledge about (or concern with) the fierce
political maneuvering going on between the various nationalist
groups, I marched down to the *Jeunesse* office to enlist, carrying my
father's bird rifle proudly over my shoulder. There I found that the
gun (though I hadn't located any ammunition for it) and my high
school education automatically made me chief of our neighborhood
contingent, the rest of whom were armed with bamboo sticks. Together with my friend Albert Thao, who had a motorcycle, I was fully
prepared to lead them into battle.

The order wasn't long in coming. On August 21 all of Saigon took
to the streets. Huge crowds marched from one end of the city to the
other, groups from the political parties, the mass organizations, religious sects together with swarms of ordinary citizens, chanting their
feelings—"*Da Dao de quoc, Da Dao thuc dan phap*" ("Down with the
Imperialists, Down with the French Colonialists"). Scattered knots of
French were set on and beaten. In a few places the mass hysteria broke
out in lynchings. I saw a nearby group of *Jeunesse* attack a Frenchman
who struggled desperately to get away from their sticks and fists. I

Street demonstration during the August 1945 revolution in Saigon. A group of Vanguard Youth is at center.

ran forward to try to pull him away. This wasn't the patriotism I wanted, this brutal flailing out at some innocent stranger. Frightened and disgusted by the frenzy of hatred, I handed my rifle to Albert and walked home in dejection. Back in the calm protection of the family milieu, I would be able to think over this brief brush with revolutionary "glory," and be properly thankful for the opportunity to get on with my life soon—in Paris.

2

An Afternoon
with Uncle Ho

But in the unsettled year of 1945 nothing was certain, not even Father's plans for my schooling. Back in March Japan had formally terminated the nominal Vichy French government in Saigon, and the United States had responded by bombing the city. With hostilities of this sort going on and good prospects for continued violence, Father had decided to evacuate the entire family to the provinces. So instead of embarking for Paris, I found myself in Ben Tre, taking long walks in the rice fields with the beautiful daughter of one of my father's close friends, a doctor and large landowner at whose house we had taken up residence.

The country idyll I now began to enjoy contrasted starkly with the chaos that was erupting throughout the South. In Saigon, September was a bloody month. Anti-French riots had exploded on the second. The British expeditionary force, whose mandate from the Allies was to maintain order, pursued this end by freeing French legionnaires imprisoned by the Japanese since March. On the twenty-second the legionnaires, leading crowds of French civilians, sacked and murdered their way through downtown Saigon, taking over the city hall, prisons, and police stations. They were answered on the twenty-fourth by a general strike and a dawn assault on several French suburbs that left hundreds of people dead or injured. It was mid-

October before the new colonial administrators were able to impose a semblance of order in the city. Driven into the provinces, the Vietminh and other nationalist groups settled down to a grim guerrilla war against the regular French divisions, which now began to push out from Saigon.

Sequestered in Ben Tre Province and involved in a deepening affair of the heart, I was not touched by any of this. I had participated in the hysteria and violence of August, and as far as I was concerned, that experience was more than sufficient. From time to time I biked to Saigon with several friends in order to check the rue d'Espagne house (maintained in our absence by two of the Chinese nurses), but except for these trips I lived in a world apart, happy with the slow pace of life and the pleasures of falling in love.

It was a pleasant limbo that lasted until March, when Ho Chi Minh and the French negotiator, Jean Sainteny, worked out a tentative agreement on Vietnamese independence within what was being called the French Union. Satisfied that calm and reason were once more prevailing, my father moved us all back to Saigon, and I took up the plans for school in Paris that had been dropped the previous fall. The period was enlivened by the formal engagement my girlfriend and I now entered into, with the full approbation and benediction (not to say collusion) of our two families. Shortly afterward I embarked on the long sea voyage to France, together with other Vietnamese students also blessed with privilege and farsighted parents.

From Toulon where we finally landed, our group traveled by train to Paris. A student reception committee welcomed us at the Gare du Nord and took us out to the university, where we were given rooms in the Maison de l'Indochine, the Indochinese student residence. Two days later we all received invitations from the Maison president to a get-together, where we would be introduced to several Vietnamese delegates to the conference being held at Fontainebleau to finalize the Ho–Sainteny agreement.

At the stipulated time, several men in business suits were on hand to tell us that they had been sent by President Ho Chi Minh "to convey his warmest regards and welcome you to France"—also to invite us to meet with the president the following morning at eleven.* This un-expected announcement caused a murmuring in the group. Some-body sitting behind me whispered, "Who's Ho Chi Minh?" Another voice answered, "I don't know; never heard of him." Someone else, more politically aware, said, "Look, he's the president. He's negotiating with the French for equality. We've got to see him."

The next morning, promptly at ten, a number of cars arrived at the Maison to drive us to Montmorency where a country house had been provided for Ho. The house belonged to Raymond Aubrac, the World War II resistance chief in Marseilles, who was close to the French Communist Party. His wife, a member of the National Assembly, was on cordial terms with Ho. As our caravan pulled to a stop in front of the house, we could see a group of people gathered on the steps to greet us. Standing in the middle was a frail-looking, older man, who was introduced to us as President Ho. With him were Pham Van Dong and other leading figures of the revolution, not a single one of whom was familiar to any of us.

Looking on with a kind of confused interest, I was immediately struck by Ho Chi Minh's appearance. Unlike the others, who were dressed in Western-style clothes, Ho wore a frayed, high-collared Chinese jacket. On his feet he had rubber sandals. In contrast to the tense-looking younger men around him, he gave off an air of fragility, almost sickliness. But these impressions only contributed to the im-

* Despite the fact that few of us knew anything about Ho, by the time of the Fontainebleau negotiations he was already fifty-six years old and had been a revolu-tionary for thirty of those years. In 1911 Ho had left Vietnam for a variety of jobs in Western Europe and (according to some accounts) the United States. He spent a number of years at sea, worked as a laborer and a gardener, and was for a time assist-ant pastry chef at London's Carlton Hotel under the great French chef Escoffier. By 1917 he was settled in France where he began to agitate for Vietnamese rights. Originally allying himself with the French Socialists, he became in 1920 one of the founders of the French Communist Party which he saw as more active on colonial issues. Within a few years he was in South China, sent there by the Comintern to organize among Vietnamese students and dissidents. His activities as pamphleteer, recruiter, editor, and organizer were as varied as his pseudonyms. Born Ngugen Tat Thanh, he called himself by various names: Nilovsky, Wang, Nguyen O Phap (Nguyen Who Hates the French), and Nguyen Ai Quoc (Nguyen the Patriot). Ho Chi Minh was the name that stuck. It wasn't until 1941, thirty years after he had left the country, that Ho returned and established a guerrilla movement to fight the Japanese occupiers and their Vichy French puppet administration.

perturbable dignity that enveloped him as though it were something tangible. I had never thought of myself as a person especially sensitive to physical appearances, but Ho exuded a combination of inner strength and personal generosity that struck me with something like a physical blow. He looked directly at me, and at the others, with a magnetic expression of intensity and warmth.

Almost reflexively I found myself thinking of my grandfather. There was that same effortless communication of wisdom and caring with which my grandfather had personified for us the values of Confucian life. I was momentarily startled when Ho reached his arm out in a sweeping gesture, as if he were gathering us in. "Come, my children," he said and sat down on the steps. We settled around him, as if it were the most natural thing in the world. I sat next to him, already infusing this remarkable person, who seemed so like Grandfather, with the schoolboy reverence I had felt toward the personal heroes adopted from my reading of history: Gandhi, Sun Yat-sen, and especially Abraham Lincoln. Lost in thoughts like these, I was not observing my comrades closely, but my impression was that their attention too was riveted on Ho. He told us to call him Bac Ho—Uncle Ho—instead of Mr. President. Then he began asking each of us in turn about our families, our names, our studies, where we were from, how old we were. He wanted to know too about our feelings toward Vietnam's independence, a subject on which most of us had only the vaguest thoughts. We certainly hoped our country would be free. But beyond that we had little to contribute.

When Ho realized that among our group there were students from the North, South, and Center of the country, he said gently, but with great intensity, "*Voila!* the youth of our great family of Vietnam. Our Vietnam is one, our nation is one. You must remember, though the rivers may run dry and the mountains erode, the nation will always be one." To Western ears such phrases may have sounded artificial. To ours the simple sentimentality was evocative. It was the language of slogan and poetry that Vietnamese leaders had always used to rally the people to a political cause. Ho went on to say that, when he was born, Vietnam was a nation of slaves. Since his own adolescence, he had been struggling for liberty, and that now we had the fortune to be free and independent citizens, a fortune that our parents and grandparents had not enjoyed. Eighty years of slavery had diminished the nation; now it was time to reestablish the heritage given to us by our ancestors and recover from our backwardness. If our people were to gain an honorable place among the peoples of the world, it would depend largely on us, on our efforts to study and learn and to contribute to the national family.

It was a message that combined ardent and idealistic nationalism with a moving personal simplicity. Ho had created for us an atmosphere of family and country and had pointed to our own role in the great patriotic endeavor. Before an hour had passed, he had gained the heart of each one of us sitting around him on those steps in front of Aubrac's house.

A week later a presidential secretary came back to the Maison de l'Indochine to announce that Uncle Ho would like to invite two representatives of our group to spend an afternoon with him—two students from the South, a boy and a girl. When we asked why he wanted two Southerners, the secretary answered that it was the people of the South who were suffering most severely in the struggle to resist the French reconquest. After some discussion, I was chosen along with a Miss Ly, another pharmacy student, to go and have tea with Uncle Ho.

Again we were driven out to the house in Montmorency, and this time shown into a living room, furnished with heavy, dark furniture. Most prominent was a large table, which we decided was where the delegation had done its work. As there was no one in the room, we stood around for a few minutes, looking at the furnishings, then sat down at the table. A moment later I felt a hand rest lightly on my head, and a voice behind me said, "My children, I'm so pleased you have come to bring me a breath of warmth and comfort from the heroic South. Let's talk a bit and have some tea together." With this Ho Chi Minh sat down across from us. "Remember," he said, "I want you to call me Bac Ho."

With one stroke he had put us at ease, as if we were sitting around a table in our own homes. We hardly noticed when tea appeared and was poured. We were already too busy telling him all about our families and ourselves. Before I had gone very far in this personal history, Ho interrupted me, saying that he would bet my grandfather had been educated in the Chinese tradition and was a Confucian scholar. As for me, I had probably been stuffed with Confucian learning myself and was no doubt an expert in manipulating Chinese characters. My father, he would guess, had been educated in French culture and was more comfortable writing French than *Quoc Ngu* (the Roman alphabet developed for Vietnamese by the priest Alexandre de Rhodes in the nineteenth century). All of this I confirmed with admiration.

"*Eh bien, mon enfant,*" he said, "your name doesn't sound right to me. It seems to me that your grandfather must have named you, just as he named all your brothers." (In Vietnam it is traditionally the grandfather's place to name grandsons.) "You have told me your brothers' names, and the Chinese characters for them all have the 'jewel' radical. I am positive that your grandfather wanted to name all of you for precious stones—the jewels of the family Truong. So your name must really be 'Toan' not 'Tang.' *Tang*, you know, only means a block of stone, but *toan* is a kind of gem." Then Bac Ho asked me to draw the Chinese characters for my name, and looking at them together, we confirmed the accuracy of his comments.

From talk about our families, Ho led us into talk about the country. He spoke to us about the proud traditions and history of our ancestors' struggles against the Chinese and Mongols, about our great heroes who had defeated these invaders: Tran Hung Dao, Le Loi, Nguyen Trai, and Quang Trung. Then he explained that the French had used Vietnam as a slave state, keeping the people in a state of underdevelopment for the benefit of France. Our country, he said, was doubly exploited, by feudalism as well as colonialism, but that now the people had come together in a great struggle for national liberation.

He discussed the uprising of the previous August, explaining it in a way that made me understand something about the events I had seen. Right now he was negotiating with the French. But the fight would be a long and difficult one, and our only strength was in our own courage and willpower and love of our nation. He emphasized that our struggle was not only against aggression, but against the ignorance and poverty that afflicted our fellow countrymen. "Nothing," he said, "is more precious than independence and liberty." (It was the first time I had heard this phrase, ultimately to become the best known of all Ho Chi Minh's slogans.)

That afternoon was a short course in the history of Vietnam taught to us over tea by Uncle Ho. He had done it all in the traditional Vietnamese manner with which we felt so comfortable, with touches

Ho Chi Minh.

of light humor, legends, anecdotes, and moral tales to amuse and instruct at the same time. It had been another Sunday with my grandfather at one of his educational sessions, but with a difference. Grandfather's text had always been morality. Ho's was politics and revolution.

At the end of the visit, he advised us to apply ourselves to our studies so that we could build our own futures and happiness. "But it will be even better if you use your knowledge to build the future of our country and the happiness of our people. The South," he added with obvious emotion as he embraced us, "is always in my heart." To each of us as we left, he gave an autographed photograph. Written across the bottom of mine was "An affectionate remembrance to my nephew 'Toan'—Ho Chi Minh."

From that afternoon I was Ho Chi Minh's fervent partisan. I had been won by his simplicity, his charm, his familiarity. His culture and burning patriotism offered me a model that I could follow in my own life. That afternoon had brought together the separate fibers of my training and emotions, whose unity I had never before been able to see clearly. The values of learning and virtue and loyalty to the nation had somehow been crystallized for me into a whole. I could see how they fit together, and I began to make out, however dimly, the shape of my own future as a fighter for independence. Although I knew nothing of his past, his politics, or his actions, the force of Ho's personality had by itself created a turning point in my life. I was hardly alone. Ho had had a galvanizing effect on almost all the Vietnamese students in France. When September 2 came, we enthusiastically celebrated the anniversary of Vietnam's independence. And when Ho left Paris for Vietnam, I was among the devoted crowd that saw him off at the Gare de Lyon.

Since that time I have not lacked for opportunity to reflect on the paradoxes of Ho Chi Minh's nature. Nationalist, humanist, Marxist-Leninist, Machiavellian, Confucianist—these were just some of the aspects of his remarkable character. One undeniable element in his success, though, was his ability to affect people with his humility and personal warmth. My encounter with him at Montmorency was just one example of the impression he conveyed in many far more significant situations. But that occasion exemplified the value he placed on cultivating personal relationships, and it also suggested something about his habitual determination to look toward the future. At the time Ho invited Miss Ly and myself for afternoon tea, he must have been a man in deep despair. The Fontainebleau negotiations for Vietnamese independence were ending in a personal disaster. Reneging on the promises they had made to him in Vietnam, the French had in the end given him nothing. When our group from the Maison de l'Indochine was introduced to the Vietnamese delegation, they were already on their way home, leaving Ho behind to try to salvage at least some face-saving concessions on his own. When even these were not forthcoming, Ho knew he faced at least the possibility of his own political demise and at best a bloody uphill war. It was with these thoughts oppressing his mind that he set aside an entire afternoon for two young students from the South. It is hard to think of another world leader who under similar circumstances might have done the same.

My Personal
Liberation

Even as I began getting down to my pharmaceutical studies, I was thinking feverishly about my country in a way that was altogether novel to me. Everything that I knew and that I had seen in Vietnam— the French administrators, the privileged position of French families, the poverty of the countryside, the racial bigotry—all began to appear in a new light. It suddenly dawned on me that these things were *not* part of the natural order of the universe. On the contrary, there was a single cause, a comprehensible pattern that was amenable to analysis. The subordination of the Vietnamese nation to France could be understood as a historical and social phenomenon, and it could be fought— if one had the right tools. Before long I was spending the better part of my days in the library of the National School of Political Science (soon to be renamed the Institute of Political Studies), devouring everything I could get my hands on about political philosophy in general and colonialism in particular.

As my eyes opened to Vietnam's political situation, I also began to see France in a new light. For a young man brought up to the strict order and stagnant oppressiveness of colonial rule, Paris in 1946 was a bracing north wind. I was living right in the middle of the wild political ferment of the Fourth Republic. With my understanding of politics expanding each day, the ideals of the French Revolution seemed to be taking life before my eyes. At the very moment I had become addicted to reading political theory, the French, possessed by their own political demons, were thrashing out a new constitution. Socialists, Communists, Republicans, and a variety of lesser enthusiasts were embroiled with each other in a display of political contentiousness amazing to anyone not born to it. The entire apparatus of democratic politics was laid bare, as government succeeded government and one unlikely coalition dissolved before another even more wondrous. Already in love with French culture, I was now utterly fascinated by the spirit and vitality of French political life. I wished ardently that a fraternal cooperation between my country and France would grow out of the modus vivendi that Ho and Colonial Minister Marius Moutet had just signed. Meanwhile, I decided to join the movement for Vietnamese independence that was beginning to percolate in the Paris streets and debating halls.

In the midst of this excited awakening to my new life, I received a letter straight out of my old one. It was from my father. In courteous tones of paternal affection, he announced his decision: My conjugal happiness was not to be indefinitely delayed. My fiancée would arrive in Paris, along with her father, the following summer. All that remained (he wrote) was for me to finish my pharmaceutical studies. Then, with diploma in hand, I could step immediately into the golden future that awaited me.

His announcement filled me with confusion. I was hardly ready to jettison all the expectations I had grown up with, and filial obedience had laid very deep claims on my soul. But neither was I prepared to abandon the changes I had undergone since my arrival in France. Whatever my father's thoughts on the subject, marriage was not foremost in *my* mind, and this marriage threatened to bring with it overwhelming pressures to live a quiet and civilized life—the kind of life I was just now learning to live without. It seemed to me an almost Shakespearean quandary: to be or not to be. And I was not sure which life I really wanted.

I still hadn't resolved the confusion when I took my first steps into politics. I started to attend meetings of the Association of Vietnamese in France, then to participate in its activities. I took part in the demonstrations, conferences, and debates that were beginning to mobilize opposition to the breakdown of peace in Vietnam. Against what I knew to be my father's deepest wishes—not to mention his explicit orders—I was now on my way to becoming a rebel. To compound matters, as the semester advanced, I abandoned my pharmaceutical studies and enrolled at the École Nationale des Sciences Politiques, where I avidly attended lectures and seminars that complemented the reading I was more and more immersed in. In my mind's eye, I began to envision a radical westernization of Vietnam along the lines of Japan's miraculous industrialization of the late nineteenth and early twentieth centuries. There seemed to me no reason that Vietnam, newborn to independence but full of hard-working, intelligent citizens, could not adopt the best from the world's political and economic cultures: the American approach to economics, the German scientific spirit, the French fervor for democracy.

But as I groped passionately, if awkwardly, toward a concept of Vietnam's future, actual conditions inside the country were deteriorating quickly. The cease-fire between French and Vietminh forces that Ho and Moutet had agreed to fell apart on November 20, 1946, when a bloody street battle was fought in Haiphong. A few days later the French renewed their assault with tanks, air attacks, and a naval bombardment from their ships anchored in Haiphong harbor, causing many civilian casualties and a flood of refugees out of the city. By December there seemed little hope for conciliation. Even when the Socialist Leon Blum (an old friend of Ho's) came to power, there was no stopping the inexorable march toward war. Ho's last appeals for negotiation were received in silence. (It is likely that these messages to the government in Paris were purposely delayed by the French high command in Saigon.) On December 19, pushed to the brink, Ho issued an appeal to the people:

Compatriots throughout the country!
Out of love for peace we have made concessions. But the more concessions we made, the further the French colonialists went because they are resolved to invade our country once again. No! We

would rather sacrifice everything than lose our country, than return to slavery.

Compatriots! Rise Up!

Men and women, old and young, regardless of creeds, political parties, or nationalities, all the Vietnamese must stand up to fight the French colonialists to save the Fatherland. Those who have rifles will use their rifles. Those who have swords will use their swords. Those who have no swords will use their spades, hoes, and sticks. Everyone must endeavor to oppose the colonialists and save his country.

Soldiers, self-defense guards, militiamen!

The hour of national liberation has struck! We must sacrifice to our last drop of blood to save our country. Whatever hardships we must endure, we are ready to endure them. With the determination to sacrifice, victory will be ours!

Long live an independent and unified Vietnam!

Long live the victorious resistance!

In Paris I became more and more involved in the agitation against the war. At the same time my reading began to focus on military and diplomatic subjects and especially on what was for me the great theme: colonialism. I raced through Machiavelli's *Discourses,* Talleyrand's *Mémoires,* Clausewitz, histories of the First and Second World Wars. The vogue for Marxism then current among French intellectuals led me to Lenin and to Stalin's *Book of Contradictions. Lenin's Imperialism, the Highest Stage of Capitalism* impressed me as an excellent justification for Vietnamese nationalism. I was beginning to understand in my own right the economic background to French intransigence and why the British, fearful for their own colonial empire, had been so eager to reestablish French colonial claims after the war. I began for the first time to explore the contradictions between France's democratic ideals and her imperialistic motives. And I was struck by the complete absence of support among the democracies for the colonized and oppressed peoples.

My father, already deeply upset by my political activities and my desertion from the pharmacy school, began to threaten a cutoff of funds. In an attempt to induce me to return to the path of filial duty, my fiancée (accompanied by her father) was dispatched to Paris to formalize our marriage—the idea being that mature responsibilities, combined with her gentle suasions, would rekindle my sense of propriety. Indeed, by this time I had not the least opposition to these arrangements. I had already begun to feel secure in my understanding of events and in my politics, but separation from home and family had not been easy for me, and memories of my fiancée often vied with thoughts about the national struggle. My parents' attempt to use this marriage to steer me away from what I considered was the right path no longer troubled me greatly, while the prospect of sharing my finacée's love and companionship exerted a powerful attraction.

When they arrived, the three of us left for a tour of France, Italy, and Switzerland, returning to celebrate the wedding in the office of the mayor of Paris' Fifteenth Arrondissement (at the same time the ritual ceremonies were performed by the two families in front of the ancestral altars in Saigon). To my father's way of thinking, of course, the peace and sweetness of conjugal life and obvious prospects for a family and established career could hardly fail to snap his son out of the spell that had strangely transformed him into a political sorcerer's apprentice. But nothing in my father's experience or training had prepared him for the earthquake that was now swallowing up the old familial and colonial order of things. As for me, my heart had embraced the patriotic fire, and my soul was winging its way toward the empyrean of national liberation. I was already well on the far bank of my personal Rubicon. Nor did he recognize the fiery spirit that lived beneath my new wife's outwardly respectful demeanor. The happiness we were now discovering together was unmarred by political discord. Instead of bringing with her the irresistible attractions of a quiet and traditional life, once in Paris she responded as willingly as I had to the call of Vietnamese independence.

As the war intensified in Vietnam, so did the antiwar movement in Paris. I was now a regular in the fight against what was now becoming known as *la sale guerre* ("the dirty war"), throwing myself into the drive to mobilize the overseas Vietnamese community as well as

French public opinion. In this work, my militant friends and I found our chief allies among progressive intellectuals and especially in the French Communist Party. Though the FCP had an undeniably schizophrenic outlook on Vietnamese independence (Maurice Thorez, the secretary general, had once announced, "If we can't reach an agreement with them [the Vietnamese nationalists], we'll talk to them with cannons"), they provided almost the only organized French opposition to the war, and we did everything we could to assist them.

At one particularly large and well-publicized meeting held by the Party to rally French opinion, the Vietnamese Association chose my wife to present a bouquet of flowers to Madame Jeannette Versmersch, Thorez's wife and a member of the FCP Central Committee. My parents heard about this affair, and the news that I had now succeeded in involving my wife with the French Communists spurred them to take action. Both her father and mine, speaking with their combined authority and utilizing every imprecation at their disposal, now issued a direct and explicit order for us to return to Saigon immediately.

My wife did not want to go. She was ready to defy the immense authority wielded by her father. I had broken the chains of my own obedience well before this. But she was now six months pregnant, and our parents had promised to cut off every penny of the allowances we were living on. We agonized for days over what to do. How would we live? If it were just myself, I was sure I could find a way to get along. But how could I possibly support my wife and a baby as well? We desperately wanted to stay together. But my wife too was afraid for our child. Had she not been pregnant, we would have both stayed. As it was, we finally decided that she should go back by herself. We hoped that our parents' feelings would be softened by the arrival of a grandchild and that eventually they would accommodate themselves to my disobedience and forgive it. This reasoning, though, did not give us great comfort, and it was with the deepest foreboding that we embraced each other for what we secretly feared might be the last time.

So my wife went back alone. When my father realized the irrevocable nature of my disobedience, he flew into a rage that dwarfed his previous displays of anger. I quickly found myself not only completely cut off from the parental love that had enveloped me for my entire life, but also without a sou for food or rent. I longed for my wife and found myself in anguish over the estrangement from my parents (though I hoped both would be temporary). Money was a different story. Within a few days I had a job as a *plongeur,* dishwasher and assistant potato peeler, at the university restaurant. It was the first manual labor I had ever done. But before long I felt I had been at this kind of work forever.

Perhaps my parents had thought that destitution, in addition to the separation from my wife, would eventually work the desired reform. But when they heard that I was now supporting myself as well as persisting in my incomprehensible political agitation, they had had enough. My father and my wife's father now ordered my wife to stop communicating with me altogether. Then they moved to break up our marriage. In her last letter, my wife wrote that she would always love me. But she was unable to stand up alone against both sets of parents. She was just twenty. We had been married two and a half years.

When I received her letter, I went into a state of mental shock. I locked myself up in my room. I had never believed that our darkest forebodings would really come true. It just wasn't possible that my parents would go so far, that they might really consider me a lost son and cast me out of their lives for good. That they and my parents-in-law would decide that my wife should remake her life with someone who better conformed to their ideas of propriety—no, I could not accept such an idea. But they had done exactly that. I lived like an automaton in a dark fog, my soul hovering between going home and trying to remake my life, on the one hand, and continuing my resistance activities in Paris on the other. After several months of violent inner turmoil, I decided that I had to stay.

Going Home

I was not to hear from my father again for a year and a half, a period that was for me one of great sadness but also of immense personal growth. By 1951 I had completed my studies, earning a master's degree in political science and going on to take a licentiate in law at the University of Paris. Meanwhile, the war in Vietnam had become a protracted, vicious affair, with Ho Chi Minh's resistance forces operating with increasing effectiveness in both North and South against the modern French army. In 1948 the Soviet Union had begun to take an active interest in the Vietminh's efforts, and the 1949 Chinese Communist victory over Chiang Kai-shek opened up a direct pipeline for arms and equipment to the guerrilla army.

Recognizing the power of Ho's appeal to Vietnamese nationalism, the French had attempted to establish credence for their own version of a native government under the hereditary emperor Bao Dai. They had also managed to obtain support from the United States. As the conflict became internationalized, the level of internal violence steadily heightened. In Paris I began to consider seriously whether I shouldn't enlist in the resistance.

But though to me it seemed that the time had come for this move, my friends in the Vietnamese Association counseled against it. They argued that I had no experience with combat or any taste for it. They couldn't imagine how I might fare as a guerrilla. Without question, they maintained, I would be more a burden than a help as a jungle fighter. On the other hand, I had already demonstrated a talent for organizing. My place was clearly on the political front in France, helping to arouse overt public resistance to the war.

After mulling over this candid advice, I reluctantly decided that my friends were probably right. I would continue with the work of political agitation in Paris, helping to plan conferences and demonstrations, writing open letters, distributing literature, propagandizing in every way I could for French withdrawal. I cannot say that I altogether regretted the decision to remain in Paris. The city had been the scene of my rebirth. I recognized that my political activities over the last five years, together with my studies, had decisively changed the person I had been. I had arrived in France a superb product of the French colonial system and its *mission civilisatrice*. Paradoxically, life in the French capital had imbued me with an understanding and a love for my own country far deeper than I had previously known. After five years I was at one with my Vietnamese identity, with the history, the national culture, the Asian soul of my country. I felt Vietnam's humiliation, its misery, and its backwardness as my own. The words Ho had spoken to us in 1946 were my constant companions: "We must fight a war against foreign domination, a war against hunger, a war against ignorance. To gain 'victory, victory, great victory,' we must have 'unity, unity, great national unity.' "

Perhaps I should not have been surprised that my plans to stay in France would fall victim to circumstance. Toward the end of 1951, I received an unexpected letter from my father. In it he told me that the businesses were not going well. The fighting in Thu Dan Mot had badly damaged the rubber plantation, and the printing house was struggling for life in Saigon's harsh economic climate. It had become a great financial effort for him to support my five brothers (all of whom were now studying in European universities). He was unable to be as active as he once was, and he was deathly afraid that my brothers would be forced to terminate their studies. He asked me— with dignity but also with a hint of desperation—to return home to help him.

At this point my older brother, Quynh, was in his last year of medical school at the University of Paris. Bich, the third, was a year away from his degree at the London School of Economics. Like my father, I simply could not stand the idea that they and the others might have to quit. Since I was the only one who had completed his studies, it was my duty to return. I no more questioned that than my father had questioned his own responsibilities, or than my brothers would have questioned theirs if they had been in my position. This time there was no choice to be made. At the end of 1951 I embarked for Saigon.

I had not been back more than several days before I received my draft orders from the Bao Dai government. The playboy king's army was badly in need of recruits, and I had now put myself within reach. Faced with the need to contribute to the family and at the same time to avoid enlistment in the French puppet army, I took the only available path—an alternative service job in one of the distant provinces. I enrolled as a teacher available for work anywhere there was a need.

It so happened that just then the government was opening a secondary school in the province of Chau Doc on the Cambodian frontier, about two hundred miles west of Saigon. The bad roads and worse communications meant that this job would be a real exile. But with no other options available, off I went to become a teacher. Not just a teacher, as it turned out, but the senior teacher. Just as during the August Revolution my high school diploma (along with my gun) had automatically made me the leader, here my Paris degrees qualified me as the senior teacher, entitled to be addressed as "professor." But the reverence accorded to teachers in the South Vietnam countryside, as I quickly discovered, in no way lessened the demands made on them by a people starved for education. Before long I was bearing up under a teaching load that included courses in French, mathematics, history, chemistry, physics, even English.

Each week my salary went directly to my family, and whenever I had three days or more off, I would return to Saigon to help my father with the businesses. In addition to the financial and organizational assistance I could give, I knew I was also becoming increasingly important to my parents emotionally, with all the other children away and beset as they were by unfamiliar money worries and anxieties about the war.

Still, as I got to know my colleagues and people in the town where I was teaching, I became aware of how truly national the war against the French was. Almost everyone sympathized with the Vietminh and either had relatives who were fighting or were themselves supporting the struggle in some practical way. As I adjusted to the new job and new people, I began to fall into my old habits of agitating and organizing support, as well as lending a hand in sending badly needed medicines to the guerrillas. Yet, I was keenly aware that my contribution was meager. I wanted to do something more.

With this thought in mind, during the Easter holidays I made contact with a Maquis unit operating in the Cai Lay region southeast of the capital and arranged to join them on a temporary basis. I was anxious to see how the guerrillas lived—to understand their motivations. I wanted to know how they survived the hardships and how their aspirations enabled them to persevere against the French, year in and year out. For the first time I would see what combat was like.

Despite a severe hemorrhoid problem complete with hemorrhaging and considerable pain, I managed to get to my contact point at the given time. In a good deal of physical discomfort but with a light heart, I began to share the dangers of guerrilla life.

During the week I was with the unit, its chief mission was an ambush they had planned for a French detachment that would be moving down the Chau Van Tiep Canal, a minor branch of the Mekong. Just beyond a bend in the river, the guerrillas set obstacles made of logs and branches bound together and camouflaged with thick bunches of aquatic plants. A good distance before the bend they prepared other obstacles, and poised them on the banks ready to slide into the water behind the French riverboats, to prevent them from escaping. At the expected time, the French appeared—maybe a dozen boats altogether—carrying nearly four hundred soldiers. As they reached the barrier, the guerrillas, hiding on either side of the river, opened fire. Downstream, others pushed the escape barriers into place, trapping the flotilla. Caught in a deadly cross fire and unable to move, many of the French were simply mowed down. Even their machine guns and heavier firepower were ineffective against the guerrillas, who moved unseen behind the high reeds that choked the banks. One boat began to sink, then another. By the time the French planes arrived to drive the guerrillas off, a number of the riverboats lay half submerged in the water; others had disappeared below its surface.

I watched all this from relative safety, hunched in the reeds next to the Maquis chief. I realized, not without some surprise, that I could stomach the sight of death. I was full of admiration for the guerrillas, for the skill and bravery with which they carried out their attack, though they were facing greater numbers and superior weapons. After we had retreated and regrouped, I found I wanted to stay with them, but I knew that in my condition (not to mention my family responsibilities) it would be impossible. I understood instinctively that I would never make a soldier myself. Nevertheless, I was equally sure that I could play a role in the propaganda and psychological war which, as I was already beginning to understand, was as important as the actual fighting. At the end of the week, I was still quite sick, and the guerrilla commander advised me to go back and get my condition taken care of before I made any decisions.

But whatever I might have been thinking in the heat of the moment, once I got back to Chau Doc it was clear that there was no way for me to join the resistance actively. Soon school got under way again, and I once more found myself heavily involved with my students and administrative duties, reconciled after a fashion to what I had to do. Before long, another unforeseen event was to complicate my thoughts about the future still further. In July of 1952 I was serving as an examiner for the high school graduation exam in Can Tho, when one of my colleagues introduced me to an extremely attractive girl, a cousin of his who lived in the city. Our friendship ripened quickly, and within six months we were married. A year later, in December of 1953, our daughter Loan was born.

By this time it was clear that the war was coming to something of a head. As early as November 1953, France put out negotiating feelers, and contacts were initiated that would eventually result in the Geneva Conference. But the growing possibility of serious talks in no way diminished the level of warfare. On November 20, the first French paratroopers landed at Dienbienphu, and by December Ho's chief of staff, General Vo Nguyen Giap, had decided to wage a major battle there if the French commanders would let him. At the same time, more American aid than ever was flowing into France's efforts, allowing her to raise and equip large additional numbers of troops.

These events had direct personal consequences for me. As a new recruitment drive scoured the country for able bodies, the Bao Dai government decreed that alternative service was no longer acceptable. Once more I received a draft notice. Surveying my options, I decided to join the national navy that was just then being established. Training as an officer in this new service would take me back to France for an extended period, and by the time I was finished, the war might well be over. If it weren't, I could always avoid combat by making arrangements to remain in France. Since I had the necessary master's degree, I was accepted by the French School of Naval Supply in Toulon, for which I left at the beginning of 1954, my wife and daughter following a short time later.

I was in Toulon when Vietminh and French negotiators met at Geneva along with representatives from the Bao Dai government, Laos, Cambodia, the Soviet Union, China, Great Britain, and the United States. On May 7, the day before the conference opened, General Giap's forces raised their flag over the shattered French command post at Dienbienphu. With the grim recognition that seven years of effort had brought them defeat on the battlefield and demoralization at home, the French were now ready for concessions. Still it took over two months—until July 20—to work out a compromise. In the end, Vietnam was granted independence, but in the process the country was temporarily partitioned at the seventeenth parallel. Ho Chi Minh's government would take power in the North, while the South would remain in the hands of the Bao Dai regime and its French sponsors. It was also decided that, within two years, there would be a nationwide

As a naval cadet at the School of
Naval Supply in Toulon, 1954.

election to reunify the two zones.

Although disappointed by this outcome, I took great pride in our victory over France and in the fact that the struggle had given Vietnam a sense of unity and nationhood. On the other hand, the Geneva agreement was like a warning shot, signaling that Vietnamese nationalism had now become hostage to the ideological and geopolitical conflicts of the great powers. The partition of the country had been agreed to by Russia's Molotov and China's Zhou En-lai for reasons of their own national interest. Most ominously, the United States had refused to become a signatory to the Accords. Though some Vietnamese nationalists were livid about Ho's acceptance of even a temporary partition, everyone was aware that behind the French loomed the

Americans, and that if the war were extended, American intervention was a distinct possibility.

Watching these developments from some distance, I completed my schooling, then immediately resigned from the navy. In Vietnam Ngo Dinh Diem had taken power as Bao Dai's new prime minister and was working to establish a credible government in Saigon. To me as to most other Vietnamese, Diem was an unknown quantity. I decided that the wisest course would be to wait in France until the situation in Saigon became clearer. But in the middle of 1955 my father once again wrote, asking me to return. Having finished their studies, my brothers Quynh, Bich, and Khue (who had graduated as an engineer from Zurich's Polytechnion) were now back in Saigon, contributing part of their own salaries to my father's efforts to educate the last two brothers. The plantation, however, had been totally destroyed, and the printing house had fallen on especially hard times. I was needed at home.

Opposing Diem

There was nothing quiet about the political atmosphere in Saigon when I returned in July of 1955. Having been named prime minister by Bao Dai, Ngo Dinh Diem had now launched a campaign to get rid of his royal patron. Leaflets were being distributed all over the city by an organization called the Revolutionary Committee, made up of a number of nationalist parties which were anxious to overthrow the hereditary monarchy and create a republic in South Vietnam. This group was agitating for Diem's appointment as head of the new government and for the removal of all remaining French troops. No one had any question that Diem himself was orchestrating the "Revolutionary Committee's" efforts.

As the committee's rhetoric heated up, Bao Dai's own Imperial Council raised its voice in favor of a new republic. Under the tutelage of one of Diem's brothers, the most powerful political personage in Hue, the council announced unequivocally that the king should be deposed. Power, it declared, should now be transferred to Diem, upon whom the responsibility had devolved "to protect the interests and the future of the people." At almost the same time, the government declared that, "according to the people's desires," a national referendum would be held in October to choose between the old monarchy and the proposed republic.

It was evident that Ngo Dinh Diem and his American advisers had done a good job of organizing the coming transition. But if that much was clear, very little else was, and the foremost enigma was Diem himself. On the one hand, his ties with the Americans were a source of real concern. Diem's backers were deeply committed to a world-wide struggle against communism, a "cold war" that was producing a series of local hot wars. Their reaction to the Berlin blockade in 1948, the Chinese civil war in which the United States attempted to contain the Chinese revolution, the three-year war in Korea (only recently ended), and support for French Indochinese colonialism all indicated the seriousness with which the Americans viewed their post-war geopolitical role, and the strident anticommunist tone of their commitment.

Although I felt no animosity toward the United States on ideological grounds, I could see that American activities had already proved hostile to Vietnamese nationalism. The Americans had underwritten a good deal of the French military effort, and their attitude at Geneva had been frigid, threatening. But the moral and philosophical conflict between the United States and its communist adversaries was not then a major issue for me, nor, certainly, was the global clash between Russian and American national interests. I thought of the United States only insofar as it related to Vietnam, and in this area the danger was substantial. The American goal would clearly be to erect an un-bridgeable wall between North and South and to back the strongest anticommunist policies in the South. All this augured a permanent division of the country and a high level of internal political repression.

There was nothing secret about the American orientation or about what her policies intended. But as of yet no one had taken the personal measure of Ngo Dinh Diem. Foreign attempts to manipulate Vietnam were hardly a novelty, but manipulation was always a two-way street. The classic example of this was Ho Chi Minh himself, who had used Chinese and Soviet support in pursuit of his own goals, but had done this without relinquishing his stature as a nationalist. Similarly, United States objectives were one thing, but so far it was impossible to tell to what extent Ngo Dinh Diem might merely be using the Americans as a stepping-stone to help him build a viable South Vietnamese government, or to what extent he truly shared the American vision of Vietnam.

Trying to gauge the temper of the man was not easy. Diem was from both a mandarin and a Catholic family—which suggested both a feudal and parochial cast of mind. His personal connections with American public figures such as Francis Cardinal Spellman also indicated a rigid and narrow political outlook. On the other hand, Diem had resigned from the French colonial administration before the war in protest over France's unwillingness to move toward Vietnamese autonomy. Sketchy stories about his life in an American seminary hinted at a streak of asceticism and inner strength. He was a mystery, and as he worked to establish his regime, I found myself watching carefully for signs of what I considered patriotism and independence.

Specifically, I was looking for a government that would strive to reconcile the former pro-French Vietnamese (among whom were my own parents), the various groups of nationalists, and especially the former Vietminh fighters and sympathizers (the overwhelming preponderance of people in the countryside, if my experience in Chau Doc was any indicator). In my opinion, domestic policies were needed that would move toward building a broad-based, inclusive government, along something like French democratic lines. Also, I was not willing to accept a permanent, hostile confrontation between North and South imposed arbitrarily, either by the major powers (as had happened at Geneva) or by a domestic politician subservient to them.

The fact was that at this point two Vietnams existed: one already socialist, and one still struggling to be born. What relationship might evolve between them was open to question. There was little doubt that no reunification elections would be held in 1956, though a referendum had been stipulated by the Geneva Accords. But if Diem were able enough, if he had sufficient stature, he might succeed in establishing a political identity for the South while also seeking to open various types of economic and political ties to the North. It seemed to me that the sentiment for national unity was so powerful that some way would have to be found to accommodate it. On the other hand, there were substantial economic, social, and cultural distinctions between South and North (let alone the ethnic minority regions) that argued for a regional rather than a centralized approach to unity. Strength and imagination would be required of the Southern leadership on this issue, together with the ability to mobilize wide popular support. But polarization of the domestic political scene would surely turn the fundamental aspiration for unity into a loaded pistol aimed directly at Diem's head.

Though I hoped that the South would undergo a democratic political development, it would be misleading to say that I was firmly opposed to what was happening in the North. The wholehearted nationalism that had consumed me in France (and that I shared with so many others) was in essence far more a diffuse patriotism than a political philosophy. My personal struggle had been one to realize my Vietnamese identity against the cultural and psychological backdrop of French colonialism. Compared to this, adopting a systematic political philosophy was for me an important but secondary endeavor. My years of struggling to understand the character of Ho Chi Minh had convinced me that at heart his motivations were similar, that the Leninism he espoused was an accretion that served the cause of Vietnamese nationalism. Whatever my personal inclinations, I would have been willing to accept almost any regime that could achieve real independence and that had the welfare of the people at heart. I was quite prepared to give Ho's Northern government the benefit of the doubt on this score, knowing that the restoration of nationhood would be a long and difficult process.

Reports of what was happening in the North were also very hard to come by. A mass of refugees had fled from above the 17th Parallel after the Accords.* But most of them were Catholics with an ingrained hatred of communism in any form. Consequently, the stories they told about collectivization and "people's justice" were not especially credible. Moreover, Ho Chi Minh himself had already been crowned

---

* The 1954 Geneva Accords had provided for a period of free movement either North or South, so that individuals could live in whichever zone they preferred. Nine hundred thousand Northerners, many of them Catholics, came South. About a hundred thousand Southerners moved to the North.

as a national hero, by Southerners as well as Northerners, and the entire Hanoi government was bathed in his immense prestige. Under these circumstances, my attention was absorbed by the political developments going on under my nose in Saigon, rather than by suspicions about motives and conduct in Hanoi.

As a certified member of Saigon's small French-educated elite, I was sure I would not remain a passive observer forever. Sure enough, very little time passed before old classmates began getting in touch. One evening shortly after my return, as I was having dinner with my parents in Cholon (Saigon's Chinese area), the familiar face of Vo Van Hai appeared over my shoulder with a cheery exclamation of surprise that I was back in town. "Tang," I heard, "we haven't seen each other for so long! What are you up to these days?" Hai had studied with me at the Institute of Political Science. He had joined the Diem entourage in Brussels a year and a half earlier, and had now become Diem's private secretary, his "shadow," and a power in the new government.

"Oh, I've only been back a couple of days. No particular plans yet. What about you?"

"You know I'm in the administration, don't you? Brother Tran [Tran Te Duong, another fellow alumnus from the institute] is director of foreign trade. Some others are working with me too. We should really all be together, don't you think? Give me a call, and we can talk about it."

But Hai's upbeat enthusiasm for Diem was not part of a universal chorus. Another Paris graduate I ran into shortly afterward had gotten himself onto the wrong side of the administration. Au Truong Thanh, who was teaching law now at Saigon University, had participated in the Movement in Defense of Peace, formed the previous year to press for compliance with the Geneva-mandated unification elections.* Made up primarily of intellectuals who had returned from France, together with some well-known Saigonese personalities, the group had been crushed by Diem and his chief American adviser, Colonel Edward Lansdale. Afraid that the movement might become an

---

* Thanh was later to become economics minister under Nguyen Cao Ky.

obstacle to his consolidation of power, Diem had accused the largely moderate or vaguely leftist members of being communists and had jailed some, expelled others, and sent a number into internal exile—including Nguyen Huu Tho, later to become the NLF's first president.* Other friends had also had bad experiences with Diem, some minor, some not. One, an American-trained dentist, Nguyen Van Tho, who Diem believed had slighted him in the United States, found himself blackballed from government and university positions, despite the fact that his education and intelligence qualified him eminently.†

But the petulant and unforgiving side of Diem's personality paled before the ruthless brutality with which he was treating the former anti-French guerrilla fighters. (I had known some of these men in Paris, and I was again beginning to talk to them.) Though Diem had established his own patriotism in years past, he had never been actively engaged in the French war and had spent the last four years of it outside Vietnam. As a result, he viewed the resistance veterans as rivals for power who had to be crushed. Labeling them all communist or procommunist, he was using the secret police and the blue-shirted Republican Youth to hunt down these people—people who were considered by almost everyone else as freedom fighters.

It was a disastrous tactic. Fired by the compulsion to eliminate any potential opposition, Diem was irrevocably alienating himself from the emotional nationalism that had been the most potent force in Vietnam for a decade. Instead of unfurling the banner of patriotism and rallying the country behind it, he had chosen to rely on his ability to cow or destroy everyone who might get in his way. In exercising power, he had resurrected the old feudal methods of closed government, complemented now by the advice and training provided by his American supporters. It was quickly becoming evident to me that Diem

---

* Contrary to the assertions of several historians of the period, there was no organizational relationship between this peace movement (sometimes called the Saigon-Cholon Peace Committee) and the NLF. Though a number of the group's members, in addition to Tho, later joined the Front, the idea that the movement was somehow an embryonic NLF has no validity.

† Ky was later to appoint Tho minister of education.

had an instinct for isolation and autocratic control and that he could only hope to make this approach to government work through brute force. In this endeavor the Americans would necessarily have to become full partners. The United States was thus blithely assuming for itself the mantle of the newly departed French colonialists—in a country whose simmering xenophobia had just exploded in an eight-year-long revolution. Diem's inability to conceive of himself as a popular leader meant that he would have to put his regime in permanent thrall to American aid and protection.

At least so it seemed to me. I was just then reaching my own decision not to cooperate with my friend Hai and the others who had joined the regime. The only question now was what form my opposition would take. As I mulled this problem over, the country officially became a republic—and Diem the first president. The 98.2 percent vote in favor was achieved through a variety of contrivances, including the use of voter-identification cards. These cards were stamped at the polls, and people with no stamp to show were likely to find themselves in trouble with the police later on. There was nothing special about Diem's cynical and blatant manipulation of the election. But it was both peculiar and disheartening to watch this unreconstructed mandarin utilizing the forms of democracy in order to placate his American protectors. By this time I had no doubts left that we were in for what I considered the worst case: a despotic regime, continued subservience to foreigners, a politically polarized people, and an iron curtain between North and South.*

But with all this, I was also beginning to think that the democratic facade Diem felt compelled to adopt might possibly be used to establish an open opposition to his policies. At that time a team from Michigan State University was in the country consulting with the government on the implementation of democratic political procedures. Whether these academic experts actually believed that the man who had just been elected president by a 98.2 percent vote could be reborn

---

* Diem had been exposed to the McCarthy-Spellman brand of anticommunism during his years in the United States. His own attitude, it became clear, was every bit as hard-line.

as a democrat, I don't know. But Diem was at least showing a temporary zest for the approved parliamentary forms—among which was a constitutional assembly he had scheduled for the coming March.

Together with two friends whose thinking was in accord with my own, I now began making plans to go into legal opposition. Meeting at my grandfather's house in Giadinh (to where my parents and now my own family had moved after Grandfather's death), Tran Huu The, Ngo Khac Tinh, and I collaborated on a program for a liberal party and started devising an election strategy.* But while we were in the middle of these deliberations, the government announced that only members of the National Revolutionary Movement led by Diem's brother, Ngo Dinh Nhu, would be allowed to participate in the Assembly. Despite his willingness to use the democratic vocabulary pressed on him by his American advisers, Diem was obviously not the man to risk a particle of control in some Western-inspired electoral process. No opposition would be tolerated.

In light of this unwelcome (though not especially surprising) development, Tinh suggested our strategy should be to join Ngo Dinh Nhu's movement, then consider our options once we were elected. My conclusion was different. "If we join," I told Tinh and The, "we won't have any maneuvering room at all. What's worse, we'll lose every shred of our credibility. That's my opinion anyway. Of course everyone has the right to do what he wants, but I'm not going to have any part of it." In the end both my colleagues decided to join, and both were elected. In all, only two members of other parties won places; but even those elections were subsequently declared irregular, and movement candidates took their places. Understandably, the established nationalist parties were furious. Diem had now made it absolutely clear that their fight for a strong, democratic Southern government that could face up to the Northern challenge was to be suppressed rather than enlisted. In the coming months he would reinforce this message through a series of repressive decrees that effectively shut off the possibility of a loyal opposition. For this scion

---

* Later, The became Diem's minister of education, while Tinh subsequently received an appointment in the Thieu cabinet.

of the Hue imperial court, the very concept was a most improbable contradiction in terms.

Shaken by these developments, various nationalist party figures began contemplating a different mode of opposition. My path too turned in other directions. As I moved toward a decision, I took a job as chief comptroller for the Industry and Commerce Bank of Vietnam. It was a position that would protect me from unwanted government attention while I decided on my next step.

6

Albert Pham Ngoc Thao: Master Spy

One bright January morning in 1956, not long after I had started the comptroller's job, I got a phone call from someone who refused to give his name to my secretary. When I picked up the receiver, a voice said, "Is this really Tang? This is Albert—Albert Thao."

"My God, Albert!" I shouted. "Where in the world are you? What are you doing? Come right over—now, if you can. I'd love to see you."

Albert Pham Ngoc Thao had been my dearest friend at the lycée. Together we had gone out with girls and had spent endless hours talking about everything under the sun. We were closer than brothers. I had last seen him eleven years earlier during the August Revolution, careening through the streets on his motorcycle, sporting a red-and-yellow revolutionary armband. The morning of the uprising he had come for me and my hunting rifle, and we had ridden off through the crowds to lead our friends into the glorious, independent future. When the street violence turned out to be more than I had bargained for, it was Albert to whom I had given my gun, and Albert who took my place at the head of the district's Vanguard Youth.

When I embarked for Paris and the life of a French university student, Albert had stayed behind, taking an administrative post in the Department of Transportation. That much I knew. I also knew that Albert's brother Gaston, a highly regarded lawyer, had joined the

Vietminh and finished the war as vice chairman of the Resistance Committee for the South. Despite the family's ardent Catholicism, in 1954 Gaston had rallied to the North and had been appointed the new government's ambassador to East Germany. What Albert had been doing during the war I didn't know. But I was aching to find out and to hear his views on the current situation.

Albert couldn't get away immediately, so I left the account books on the desk and took a pedicab over to the National Bank, where it turned out he was working. We embraced wildly. The years hadn't changed him a bit—still slim and quick moving, still the soft-spoken humorist, one walleye distracting your attention. With Albert, you never quite knew which eye was looking at you, just as you were never quite sure when he was serious and when he was joking. As well as I had known him, there had always been an enigmatic quality about Albert Thao, some hidden level of thought that defied probing. But that wandering eye of his gave this secretiveness a humorous cast, in keeping with his easygoing, mocking nature.

We began immediately to make up for lost time, recalling our days at the Chasseloup Laubat and the fights we had gotten into with French students who enjoyed baiting the school's *nhaques* and *mites*. Albert told me that the August Revolution had awakened him politically. As his story unfolded, I marveled at what he had been through.

"I followed the call," he said. "I didn't know the first thing about Marx or Lenin. But I did know about Ho, and I thought that he was the right person to lead us. He had sacrificed his entire life, a real patriot. That seemed to me the kind of thing I wanted to do. So I joined the Maquis.

"In 1946 the Resistance Committee ordered me to go to the Delta to help with organizing things there. But on the way I was arrested by a group of local guerrillas in Mytho. Of course they didn't know me, and with my French suit and identity papers, they thought I must be come sort of French agent. So they decided to get rid of me. They tied my hands behind my back and attached a block of stone to the ropes. Then they threw me into the river. I was sure I'd had it. Somehow, as I was going down, I managed to get my hands free so that I could swim to the opposite bank and scramble out. Boy, were they pissed off!

"Finally I found my way to Vinh Long, where I thought I would at least be safe, with all my family in the province. But before I could make my contacts, I was caught again—by another group of locals. It was like a bad dream. I couldn't believe what was happening to me. These men didn't want to take any chances either, and they began trussing me up, just as the others had. But just before they threw me in, one of the leaders recognized me and sent me on to my brother Gaston. After a bit, I was ordered to help organize and train the 410th Battalion. When that was finished, we did a lot of fighting around Ca Mau; then in 1952 they sent me back to Saigon under cover to report on troop movements there."

At this I looked at Thao and asked, only half in jest, if he was still an agent. He just laughed.

"After Geneva I was assigned to the Joint Cease-Fire Commission. When that work was done, I decided I didn't want to go North. So I stayed here. I was afraid there wouldn't be any unification election, and I certainly didn't want to get stuck in Hanoi. Now that I know what the Americans are up to, I can tell you that there isn't a chance in the world that Diem will hold elections. These people are fanatical anticommunists. You know, at first I didn't understand Diem. It seemed as though he might be a patriot, no matter what else he was. There couldn't be anything better than some kind of peaceful unification, and somebody with stature could pull it off. I would cooperate with anyone who wanted to move in that direction. I'm just sorry Diem isn't the man for it—he's too tied in with the Americans. But who knows, maybe I'll still be able to influence things a bit."

I told Thao that I had shared his initial thoughts about Diem. "But what I've learned since is that he's nothing but a small-minded autocrat. There's no way to change him; he doesn't have the breadth for it. He's stubborn, and he's going to go his own way, no matter how many people don't like it. From what I can see, the Americans are steering the boat, and Diem is doing the rowing. Try and oppose that!

What makes you think you or anyone else will have a chance to influence anything?"

"Well," said Thao, "You may be right. But I've joined the government anyway. I've got my own methods."

I had no idea what he meant by that—a typical Albertism, with its suggestion of some deeper meaning. Exactly what meaning I was only to find out eight years later, after Diem was dead and Albert had become chief of military security for the South. For the present, though, I knew there was no use in even trying to follow up this tantalizing tidbit. I changed the subject.

"Listen, Albert, if you were so involved, how have you managed to avoid this To Cong business?* How come you've got this job?"

Thao's face lit up. "Now that," he said, "is an interesting story. After the Joint Commission, I got out of Saigon as fast as I could. I knew the secret police and Youth Movement people were after me, but I had developed a pretty good underground network here during the war, and I was able to get away to Vinh Long.

"You know my family—most of them except Gaston and me were scared to death of the Communists. You remember what churchgoers they were? Well, they hid me and put me in touch with the parish priest—I was the black sheep finally come home to the fold. You knew that my parents were followers of Bishop Thuc,† didn't you? Between them and the priest, they persuaded Thuc to meet with me. It couldn't have gone better. Father Thuc liked me so much that he decided to protect me. He's the one who arranged this situation for me."

Albert and I continued our reunion a few days later over dinner at my house. It turned out that not only had Father Thuc protected Albert and arranged a job for him, he had also introduced him to secret police chief Tran Kim Tuyen as well as to Ngu Dinh Nhu and to Diem himself. Albert did not describe in detail just how he had

---

* The To Cong Campaign was Diem's attempt to jail or eliminate those Vietminh who were suspected of communist sympathies.

† Ngo Dinh Thuc was Diem's older brother, and perhaps the most influential member of the family.

captivated the bishop. But clearly Thuc had come to believe that this former Vietminh guerrilla, with his intelligence, energy, and intimate knowledge of communist tactics, could be important to the regime. He undoubtedly considered that Thao's Catholic and family loyalties were stronger and more durable than his youthful enthusiasm for revolution. Though the Ngo family were bitter enemies of the Vietminh, they had also opposed the collaborationist government of Bao Dai. With this inbred understanding of Vietnamese nationalism, Thuc could conclude that Albert Thao's participation in the anti-French war had been a genuine, if misguided, expression of the patriotic feelings that Thuc himself knew well. He was apparently willing to believe that after the war, Thao had come to regret his association with the Communists. Playing brilliantly on Thuc's predisposition to think of him as a repentant son of faithful retainers, Albert Thao had carved an identity for himself as a man of ability, who could be trusted.

In any event, the next time I saw Albert, he was wearing an army uniform with major's insignia on the shoulders. He had just been assigned by Diem to train the civil militia.

By now I was increasingly in touch with former Vietminh and other unhappy elements in Saigon society. Before long I found myself part of an informal network of people who opposed Diem. Slowly, we were beginning to form the underground resistance that would eventually evolve into the National Liberation Front, the political organization of the Vietcong. For his part, Albert stayed in the army, winning the confidence of his superiors and widening his circle of contacts.

Over a period of time, Albert grew closer to Diem and Nhu and was able to impress them with his ideas about antiguerrilla strategy and rural pacification. As a result, in 1957 he was sent to Malaysia to study the counterinsurgency techniques that had been used so successfully against the Communist guerrillas there. Among these was the strategic-hamlet program, which became a special interest of Diem and his American advisers. The British had developed this concept as a way of separating the insurgents from the rural population by concentrating peasants in large, well-defended villages. In such places, government control was facilitated and opportunities for the guerrillas to exert political and military influence minimized.

But the idea had a rough time of it in South Vietnam. In 1959 Diem attempted to implement a homegrown version through an ambitious, countrywide plan to construct self-contained, modern villages called Agrovilles. From the start the peasants reacted angrily. First they were forced to contribute their labor to building these ill-conceived communities, which had nothing whatsoever to do with their ordinary patterns of social and economic life. Then they were forced to leave their old homes and live in these compounds. After a year or so, peasant outrage reached such a pitch that the government was forced to abandon the project. None of the objectives were achieved, and a great many country people were alienated.

Nevertheless, the idea kept simmering, reappearing in 1962 as the strategic-hamlet program. This time Albert was put in charge. He told me that among the American advisers he was working with there were two trends of thought. Some wanted to proceed quickly, taking the initiative and bulling through the construction and re-location, afraid of getting bogged down in the innumerable details and difficulties. Others were more sensitive to the dangers involved in such a drastic social-engineering project. These more cautious Americans wanted to move step by step, setting up models and carefully analyzing performance before going ahead with large-scale implementation.

But Ngo Dinh Nhu, Diem's nervous, calculating younger brother, was anxious to fence the countryside from the guerrillas, and he wanted to see rapid progress. Albert more than fulfilled his boss's wishes in this; construction moved fast. He did not share his inner thoughts with me at the time. But in retrospect, it is probable that Albert's real goal was to sow confusion. It is certainly a fact that under his supervision the strategic hamlets created even more hostility among the peasants than had the Agrovilles before them. After a short time this program too withered away, adding to the government's record of failure.

Both before and during this period, Nhu was also using Albert to investigate army officers he suspected of disloyalty. Anxious about their own increasing unpopularity, Diem and Nhu were constantly scrutinizing those around them for signs of disaffection. Officers with field commands drew special attention from the ubiquitous Albert Thao, whose bloodhound position made him the object of universal fear and respect. Albert capitalized on his role by developing relationships with many of the most prominent military figures. Among those he was closest to were Generals Nguyen Khanh and Tran Thien Khiem. Khiem was then commander of the 7th Division with headquarters in Mytho, about thirty miles southwest of Saigon. Later to become chief of staff, then defense minister and prime minister under President Thieu, Tran Thien Khiem was an ambitious and acquisitive individual, whose uncomplicated motives and vital field command recommended him to Albert's attention. Nguyen Khanh, who was to engineer a successful coup in 1964, was another character whose voracious ambition and lack of scruples spotlighted his potential as a troublemaker.

During this entire period Albert and I kept in close touch. As his importance to the Ngo brothers increased, a coherent opposition to the regime had also taken shape and was now absorbing more and more of my attention. By the fall of 1960 we [the NLF] were only months away from our first full-scale organizational meeting. But even as his external opposition solidified, Diem himself remained preoccupied with thoughts of internal disloyalty.

On November 11, 1960, his fears were realized. Early that morning several battalions of paratroops seized key points in Saigon and surrounded the Palace. The colonels leading this revolt had support from a number of opposition political figures representing moderate parties. Their aim was to force Diem into broadening his government and eliminating the corrupt individuals around him, especially the detested Nhu. Setting up a telephone link with the Palace, they pressed Diem for a commitment to allow opposition nationalists and even former Vietminh into the Assembly. While they talked, Nguyen Khanh—who opposed the coup—drove up to the embattled Palace, found an unguarded stretch of wall, and vaulted over. As Diem engaged the colonels in long discussions over the details of a new, liberalized regime, Khanh stiffened the courage of the Palace guard and deployed them for a last-ditch defense. At the same time, Albert Thao was speeding down highway Number 4 toward Mytho to describe the situation to Khiem personally and urge him to intervene. By ten o'clock the next morning, lead elements of Khiem's division were engaging rebel paratroopers, and the coup leaders were fleeing toward Cambodia.

Diem and Nhu took advantage of the suppressed revolt to carry out mass arrests of people who had aroused their suspicions or irritated them for any reason. Thousands were interned. As for Thao, he rose even higher in the brothers' regard, and his intimacy with Khiem and Khanh ripened.

In 1961 Diem rewarded the former guerrilla with the job of province chief of Ben Tre. Located in the Delta south of Saigon, Ben Tre was known as a dissident outpost. During the French war it had been a stronghold of the Vietminh, and in 1959 and 1960 guerrilla attacks there had grown in frequency and violence. Because of its location and resistance to government control, the province had become something of a hideout for Diem's enemies.

But shortly after Albert arrived, the atmosphere in Ben Tre began to change. I visited him there several times and was able to drive around without fear, even at night. There were no more ambushes, no sabotage, little fighting of any sort. Many years later I heard reports that Albert and the guerrillas had had a secret understanding to stabilize the region so that it could be used as a Vietcong rest and staging area. Whether this was true, or whether Albert had simply arranged a pause in local activity to enhance his own credibility with Diem, I don't know. But as long as he was chief, Ben Tre was pacified, becoming perhaps the most peaceful of South Vietnam's provinces. After Albert's departure, it quickly regained its reputation as a violent place, once more unsafe for Diem's soldiers.

Albert's remarkable success in Ben Tre won him praise from both his American advisers and Diem. As a consequence, he was moved up to a position on the general staff, working with his old friend Nguyen Khanh, who had meanwhile been named to head the army. The ambitious General Khiem also had been promoted and now held the position of executive officer of the joint chiefs of staff. Another of Albert's aquaintances, Tran Van Don, was named acting general chief of staff. This impressive title masked a meaningless job with no real responsibility for a man whom Diem secretly distrusted. The president was again seeking to allay his fears by keeping his generals off balance, rotating them in and out of field commands, and keeping them under the surveillance of trusted lieutenants. Meanwhile, Albert Thao was spinning a web of relationships and influence that included general staff officers and extended down to the Young Turk colonels whose units guarded Saigon.

New acting chief Tran Van Don was not a happy man. With plenty of time on his hands to contemplate his own isolation from power and the general botch Diem and Nhu were making, he began seeking remedies. First he enlisted the help of several generals who had been similarly isolated. Then he turned to Khiem and Khanh, and to other dissatisfied senior officers and colonels, whose field commands would be vital to the success of a coup. But as South Vietnam's domestic life declined into riots and factionalism during the summer of 1963, he found he was not alone. Other plots were afoot, some serious. At the center, with links to the various groups of conspirators as well as to the field commanders, was Albert Thao, a man who, moreover, had the implicit trust of the president and his brother.

At this delicate stage, Albert was faced with the complex question of how best to pursue his overall goal of destabilizing the Saigon regime. For its part, the National Liberation Front was not at all anxious to see Diem overthrown. His intolerance and brutality had alienated whole segments of South Vietnamese society and were daily contributing to NLF strength. The government's anti-Buddhist campaign had even snapped the patience of United States Ambassador Lodge. Exasperated beyond endurance by Diem's feudal mentality, the Americans unsuccessfully sought to pressure him to liberalize his policies and get rid of Nhu, whom they had come to regard as his evil genius. As their frustration burgeoned, so did Diem's resentment. It was not a situation the NLF was eager to alleviate.

Adding flavor to this broth, Nhu had opened contacts with NLF representatives in Hanoi, using the Polish member of the International Control Commission, which had been set up at Geneva to monitor the accords, as intermediary. We quickly concluded that these overtures were not serious, that Nhu's main object was to blackmail the Americans. But of course we continued to encourage these so-called talks, with the intention of further muddying Diem's relationship with his American allies.

Beyond all this, we believed that a military coup would likely bring to power a group of generals completely beholden to the United States, presaging a more effective cooperation between Washington and Saigon. Consequently, we had no orders to assist in Diem's downfall. I didn't, and I strongly doubt that Albert did. His task was simply to foment trouble and to stay as close as possible to whatever strongmen might emerge from the confusion.

Although at this point we had not yet revealed our NLF identities to each other, our friendship and the sympathy of our views allowed us to discuss matters freely. It was in some ways a bizarre and not altogether comfortable situation. Albert was a friend, a confidant, but also a source of valuable information about the inner struggles of the Saigon military. He must have had similar feelings about me—an intimate with whom he could share doubts and problems, but also a man with potential to help the cause. The secrecy our positions demanded forced us to regard each other through two eyes, one of friendship, one of calculation. No doubt there were many relationships between friends, and even relatives, similarly affected by the war.

As General Tran Van Don's plot gathered steam, Albert began to weigh his options with great care. Diem, he said, was monumentally arrogant. He took advice from no one outside his family, not even from the Americans. As his policies aroused more and more angry opposition, he cut himself off from any criticism, tolerating around him only corrupt sycophants. He faced serious challenges at all levels—from the peasants, the urban factions, most importantly from the Buddhists, whose riots and self-immolations had caught the world's attention. Amidst it all, Diem seemed impervious and unresponsive. Even the Americans, Albert judged, had begun to think of him as a lost cause. Under these circumstances, there seemed to be no way to try to save him, and Albert concluded that the time had come to ally himself in earnest with Tran Van Don's group of plotters, in order to insure ties with the next government in power. Ironically, as October wore on, the Americans were coming to somewhat similar conclusions.

On October 28, 1963, Albert arrived unexpectedly at my house with a look of concern on his face. He told me he was afraid that the secret police were laying a trap for him. In fact, as I found out later, Nhu had been warned of the plot and had prepared an elaborate scheme to ensnare the plotters and reestablish his and Diem's credibility with the Americans. This plan involved the staging of a phony coup, which would actually be carried out by loyal forces, the subsequent suppression of this "coup," and a massive roundup of dissident civilians and suspected officers. Careful as always, Albert did not want to sleep at his own house, afraid that the devious Nhu might arrest him there. For the next three days Albert stayed with me. In the evenings I drove him to meetings with various generals who were involved in the final stages of planning. Nights we slept in my room, going over the details of the arrangements.

Albert told me that the Tran Van Don group had won over the young colonels who commanded in the vital Third Military Region (around Saigon), and that they would be able to isolate any generals who might oppose the coup. In addition to Don, generals Kim, Xuan, and Minh were the organizers, and Do Mau, chief of military security, had been brought in. Don was sure that the key generals, whom he had promised to reward, would go along—especially since it was the junior officers who would be taking responsibility for most of the military action.

The major obstacle had been General Dinh, the overall commander of the Third Region. Dinh was known as a Diem loyalist, but he also had close ties with the conspirators. Without his coopera-

Albert Pham Ngoc Thao
prior to the 1963 over-
throw of Ngo Dinh Diem.
(*AP-Wide World Photo*)

tlon, the carefully worked out plans would have been worthless.
According to Albert, Security Chief Do Mau had been given the job
of persuading the unpredictable and volatile Dinh (they were both
natives of Hue). Mau succeeded, but not before actually getting down
on his knees to plead with Dinh to go along "for the sake of the
country."

With General Dinh committed, the only regular forces remaining
that could cause trouble were those in the Delta south of Saigon. To
forestall any rescue attempt from that direction, Dinh posted a subordinate to command the 7th Division, which was positioned to
block the access routes from the south. With these arrangements in
place, the plotters were ready to strike.

At dinner on the night of the thirty-first, Albert warned me that
the coup was scheduled for one o'clock the next afternoon. I might

be wise, he said, to stay at home. After breakfast the following morning, he was off. The coup went off exactly as planned, with Albert taking personal command of a tank unit during the final stages of the fighting. The following night news spread that Diem and Nhu had been killed outside a Cholon church, where they had taken refuge. Albert Thao had not missed a step. He was now the trusted colleague of South Vietnam's new rulers.

About a week after the coup, Albert invited me and my wife to dinner at his home. We were joined there by a paratroop commander and his wife, and also by a young air-force major, who had with him a rather exotic-looking dance-hall girl. This major, with flashing eyes and a thin mustache, turned out to be Nguyen Cao Ky, and much of the talk over dinner was about him—specifically, how to arrange for his promotion to commander of the air force. Clearly, the flamboyant flyer had caught Albert's attention as a potential comer— indeed he was being noticed by others as well. Albert, with his close ties to the coup leaders, felt he could manage the business of having the current commander removed and skipping Ky up the ranks into the job. Then, of course, beholden to Thao's silken manipulations, Ky would become an important link in the agent's network of influence.

Not long afterward, Albert's efforts bore fruit. The air force commander, Colonel Mai, received a sudden and unwelcome posting as military attaché to the Vietnamese embassy in Bonn, and the career of the mustached thirty-three-year-old Ky began its meteoric rise. As for Albert himself, he became spokesman for the Revolutionary Council and took over Do Mau's old post of chief of security for South Vietnam's armed forces.

By this time I had left my bank comptroller's job to become director general of the Société Sucrière, Vietnam's national sugar company. With its plantations, mills, refineries, distilleries, and import/export operations, the Société was the South's largest conglomerate. But even with the heavy schedule my work now demanded, I made it a point to stay in regular touch with Albert, and I became a frequent visitor at the military security headquarters. During one of our discussions, Albert expounded his reading of the American position in South Vietnam.

"You must understand," he told me, "that United States strategy in Southeast Asia is to maintain South Vietnam as an anticommunist bastion, especially to keep the Chinese contained. That's why they will have to find a government they can count on not to negotiate with the Front. They suspect that Tran Van Don is tainted by his French ties and might be concocting some kind of neutralist strategy. My own feeling is that they'll throw their support behind Khanh—Taylor* especially. I think Taylor sees him as a pro-American bulwark."

It was common knowledge at this time that Charles de Gaulle was promoting the concept of a neutral Southeast Asia as part of France's recent accommodation with China. Such a policy was not at all congenial to the Americans, and there was quite a lot of local speculation about whether this conflict would have an effect on Saigon politics. Don, who had been born in France and had won a commission in the French army, was easy to suspect of harboring lingering Francophile sympathies.

My response to Albert was that, regardless of what might happen, the masses, especially the Buddhists, would intensify their fight for a neutral South and that the NLF would undoubtedly use the masses in its struggle for political participation. Despite his ruthlessness, Diem had failed in suppressing popular feeling, and no other dictator was going to have any more success than Diem. I suppose it was my language and tone that encouraged Albert at that point to interrupt my monologue. He fixed me with his good eye.

"Ba," he said, in a deliberate voice, using my family nickname, "I've recognized your smell for quite a while now. You're Maquis, aren't you?"

"Albert," I answered, "I've been picking up the same aroma on you."

Each of us had been sure for some time that the other was working for the NLF. But up until that moment we had avoided any men-

* At the time, General Maxwell Taylor was United States ambassador to South Vietnam.

tion of the subject. The fact was that the nationalist and anti-American sentiments that colored everything we said were common among many Southerners who were not necessarily associated with the "Front" at all. There had been no special need to probe each other on this point, and—given the dangers of this kind of knowledge— there was good reason to remain ignorant. Despite our closeness, we had both managed to maintain a facade of indifference for seven years.

After that day, there was a special sense of irony about our visits in the military security offices. I had been one of the original organizers of the Front in 1958 and had been elected a secret member of the Central Committee in 1962; Albert had been leading an even more hazardous double life since 1954. We were not by any means the only NLF people in the Saigon government, but there was a good deal of satisfaction in knowing that the two of us were sharing risks as well as convictions.

On January 30, 1964, the unwieldy ruling council of the anti-Diem plotters fell before another group of conspirators—led this time by the opportunistic Khanh and the ambitious Khiem. With two of his cronies now in power, Albert was promoted to colonel and became one of Khanh's closest advisers. There followed a period of governmental instability and confusion startling even by South Vietnamese standards. It was marked by bitter rivalry between Khanh, who was acting as chief of state, and various politicians and generals who either wanted more power for themselves or who were simply opposed to Khanh's leadership. Conspicuous among the rivals was Khiem himself, with whom Albert continued to maintain the closest of relations. For his part, Khanh took energetic measures to consolidate control, and in doing so infuriated many of his political allies as well as important social and religious factions. Buddhists, Catholics, and students took to the streets, each group loudly proclaiming its grievances and demanding changes. Mob violence became a common occurrence in Saigon's streets. As the summer began, people were gripped by a sense of impending chaos.

In an attempt to retrieve the situation, at the end of August Khanh dissolved his government and created a new ruling committee, consisting of himself, Khiem, and the popular "Big" Minh, who had been one of the principal anti-Diem plotters. But within a month, this triumvirate had fallen apart, bedeviled by the continuous intriguing of its members. To replace it, a civilian government was established, headed by the ancient Pham Khac Suu, but in fact controlled by Khanh. To relieve himself of his unpleasant rivals, Khanh arranged an extended overseas goodwill tour for "Big" Minh and appointed Khiem ambassador to Washington. Albert was not spared the rod this time—caught in the middle of the infighting between his two associates, he found himself exiled to the American capital as military attaché, in company with his frustrated friend.

One morning in late December 1964, three months after these frenzied doings, Albert showed up at my door with a suitcase in his hand. I was flabbergasted. *"Troi Oi!"* ("My God!"). I shouted. "What in the world are you doing here?"

"Oh," Albert replied nonchalantly, "I just got in from the airport. Khanh's people almost had me."

Nguyen Khanh had apparently reconsidered the advisability of keeping two such potentially dangerous individuals as Albert and Khiem together, even half a world away, and had ordered Albert back to Saigon, planning to arrest and (so Albert thought) execute him. Despite the risks, Albert had decided to come back, making arrangements to elude Khanh's police and take the offensive himself. He had thought to hide with me while preparing his campaign against Khanh. But in late December I was busy organizing the Committee to Defend the Peace, and my house was a thoroughfare for opposition-minded activists and a fair bet to attract police attention eventually. Uncomfortable with all the activity, Albert asked me to contact a mutual friend, a woman pharmacist who owned a drugstore on Le Loi Street. Shortly afterward he moved into a hidden room behind her store, safe for the time being from the police dragnet that had been thrown out for him.

General Khanh was nervous, as well he should have been. Albert had contacts everywhere—among the armed forces officers he had so meticulously cultivated (including Nguyen Cao Ky, who was now air force vice marshal), the politicians and Catholic leaders, and of course in the extensive underground network he had been developing since the French war. To Khanh, Albert was a dangerous schemer with a score to settle, a type he knew intimately and feared. What he didn't suspect was that Albert's true motives went far deeper.

On August 4, 1964, four and a half months prior to Albert's surprising return, the U.S. Seventh Fleet had launched its first raids against North Vietnamese targets. Several days later, the American Congress had passed the Gulf of Tonkin Resolution, authorizing President Johnson to "take all necessary measures." While Albert was in Washington, the United States government was intensely assessing its options, and in early February McGeorge Bundy,* known as a proponent of intervention, arrived in Saigon to confer with General Maxwell Taylor (who had succeeded Lodge as ambassador) and examine the situation at first hand.

For us, the escalation of American military involvement and the heightened activity of the United States government were signs that pointed ominously toward intervention by American ground forces. To the NLF, this eventuality was a living nightmare. No one, as 1965 dawned, had any illusions about our ability to gain a military decision against the immensely powerful American war machine. Thoughts of direct intervention filled us with sick anticipation of a prolonged and vastly more brutal war.

It was not a question of any lack of determination or confidence in our ultimate victory. But the war we were fighting in South Vietnam we saw at that point chiefly as a political struggle with a subordinate military dimension. Our strategy was to achieve a political revolution. To this end, armed violence was a means, but the political front was primary. If the Americans were to intervene in force, the scale of violence would increase geometrically. As a different set of priorities emerged, the armed struggle would most likely take center stage. The scenario laid itself out with some clarity—the country and its people would be subjected to a new level of destruction and suffering

* Head of the National Security Council under Presidents Kennedy and Johnson.

over a prolonged period. We contemplated this prospect with great foreboding.

But if some of the consequences of American involvement were evident, the way to preclude intervention was not clear at all. Military action such as the successful attack on the Bienhoa air base in October or the occupation of Binh Gia at the end of December could demonstrate our strength and determination, and might stimulate the American leaders to consider deeply before committing themselves. But those very actions might equally well dramatize the inadequacies of the Saigon military and give more leverage to proponents of escalation within the Johnson administration.

Against this background, several factors stood out. First, time was very short. Second, although the balance of military forces between ourselves and the regime was steadily improving, our true strength and the enemy's true weakness was on the political front. Nothing illustrated that better than the events that had plagued Saigon since Diem's overthrow. The unrestrained irresponsibility and incompetence of the generals had led to apathy and disgust among people at every level. South Vietnam was a society without leadership and without direction—and these essentials the Americans could not provide. They could not impose order on chaos. And without a government in Saigon that could claim at least some tatters of legitimacy and effectiveness, how could the United States dare commit its troops and its all-important prestige? Overt anarchy in Saigon might force the Americans to look once again at their assumptions, to begin thinking about what they might salvage in Vietnam instead of how they might win.

But General Khanh's regime, as inept and shaky as it had proved to be, was still a government. One more push, though, might bring about the conditions for a general uprising—the political revolution that was our goal. At the very least, it would flash another conspicuous warning signal at the Americans. Albert Thao intended to provide that push. "Khanh," he told me as we talked in his room behind the Le Loi pharmacy, "will suppress all the opposition. We are going to have intervention and more bloodshed than you or I can imagine. I'm going to get rid of him no matter what the price."

"Albert," I said, "you're alone. You're hiding. You can't do it. Even if you could, the Americans will just create another Khanh."

"No, Tang. You're wrong. At this point there's no one else the Americans trust. Khanh is the only one they have. With him gone, the field is empty. Don't worry so much. I know how to pull off this sort of thing."

"Listen," I told him, "if this doesn't work, you'd better take yourself off to the jungle. They'll be happy to have you there."

As we talked, Albert put on the straw hat and dark glasses he wore on the rare occasions he ventured out.

"Come on," he said. "Give me a lift to the phone booth on Ham Nghi Street. I've got to call someone."

The booth on Ham Nghi was one of the big blue wooden phone boxes, and both of us were able to squeeze inside. I listened as Albert put through a call to Nguyen Cao Ky, now one of the most powerful men in the military. Huddled next to Albert, I heard most of the conversation. Indeed, one of his reasons for bringing me along was to alleviate my obvious fears for his safety, and to show me that he was very much in control.

"Hello, Ky? This is Pham Ngoc Thao."

Even through the static on the line I could make out Ky's surprise: "Thao! Where are you calling from? How can you be so brave?"

"Ky, listen to me. Khanh is screwing things up royally. I'm going to get rid of the son of a bitch. I want to know what your position is on it?"

Ky's initially emotional greeting gave way to more cautious tones.

"Khanh's treated me well. Between you and him, I'm neutral. I consider you both good friends."

Ky at any rate was not going to make any commitments before he understood the odds thoroughly, regardless of what favors who might owe whom. Experienced plotter that he was, Albert no doubt had anticipated this. But he could not have anticipated the complicated and self-serving role that Ky would actually play some weeks later as the coup hung between success and failure.

After the call to Ky, Albert methodically began to line up his backing—field commanders, politicians, Catholic leaders—pulling in the whole network of support he had so carefully laid for himself over a decade of tireless effort.

I did not see Albert's plans come to fruition. Ten days before he made his move, I was arrested and interned in the Chi Hoa Central prison. Afterward the cells began filling up with Albert's coconspirators, and it was from them I heard the details of what had happened.

On February 19, 1965, troops commanded by Albert's supporters took over the radio station and post office and surrounded the military headquarters and Khanh's residence. Khanh himself, however, managed to escape and contacted Air Marshal Ky at Bienhoa. At first Ky offered to protect Khanh and threatened to bomb the rebel troops in Saigon. Later that night a meeting was arranged between Ky and his old benefactor, Albert Thao, along with Albert's colleague, General Phat. In an attempt to resolve the impasse, Albert and Phat offered to give up the coup, but only if Khanh was forced to resign. It was an offer that appealed to Ky, and he agreed to go along. With Khanh gone, Ky himself, with one or two other military chiefs, would become the dominant figure on Saigon's political horizon. Whether Ky had cleverly turned Albert's coup to his own advantage, or whether Albert, caught in a standoff, had manipulated events to achieve his purpose is still open to debate. I never saw Albert again. As forces loyal to the military command (though not to Khanh) moved into Saigon, he disappeared. Weeks later I got a message from him through my mother, whom he had taken the time to visit. Sooner or later, he said, he would be able to get me released.

I was still at Chi Hoa in July when I read about Albert's death in the newspapers. He had been hiding in a Catholic refugee area north of Saigon, and one report had it that he was betrayed to the government by a priest. There were also rumors that General Thieu (later to be president) trapped him, and that in the skirmish Albert was wounded, then brought back to military headquarters and tortured to death.

Whatever the facts of his death, Albert Thao was a man who throughout his life fought single-mindedly for Vietnam's independence.

He was a nationalist, not an ideologue, one whose attitudes and goals were shaped at a time when Vietnam was a politically suppressed and economically exploited colony of France. A talented and vibrant personality, he was also a consummate actor, who played a leading role in the struggle for the South. Looking back at his life, it is hardly an exaggeration to say that he personally changed the balance of political power between the Saigon government and the NLF. He helped weaken Diem and Nhu by assisting in the debacle of their rural-pacification schemes, and he was a major figure in the whirlwind of plots that undermined and eventually destroyed them. For a while he was a key political adviser to the scheming Nguyen Khanh, during whose troubled year and a half of power the government abandoned its last vestiges of credibility. Then he brought Khanh down, leaving the South with a leadership vacuum that was eventually filled by the architects of ultimate defeat, Nguyen Cao Ky and Nguyen Van Thieu. When his end came, Albert was still spreading discord—intriguing this time against Khanh's inept successors. With his cover still intact, he had refused to leave the political arena for the relative safety of life as a guerrilla—as I had pleaded with him to do when we last talked.

Thao's great failure—and indeed the great failure of the NLF during the early sixties—was that all his efforts did not deter the United States from its decision to intervene. He can hardly be blamed, though, for insufficiently pointing out the shabby incompetence of the South Vietnamese political system—the system upon which America's new strategy ultimately depended.

7

The Birth
of the NLF

Between the appearance of Albert Thao at my door that bright January morning in 1956, and his death in 1965, the events that molded my own life—that led me down my own road to insurgency—unfolded only gradually.

By the time 1957 merged into 1958, Ngo Dinh Diem had exhausted the patient hopefulness that had initially greeted his presidency. From the first he had moved ruthlessly to consolidate his personal power, crushing the private army of the Binh Xuyen,* then subduing the armed religious sects. From there he attacked those suspected of communist sympathies in what was called the To Cong ("Denounce the Communists") campaign, jailing and executing thousands who had fought against the French. Each of these moves was carried out with surprising energy, and in their own terms they succeeded. As he surveyed the political landscape three years after assuming power, Diem could see no well-organized centers of opposition to his rule. The National Assembly was wholly dominated by his brother's National Revolutionary Movement, the troublesome private armies had been severely handled, the Communist-dominated resistance veterans were cowed and in disarray.

But Diem's successes had all been of a negative sort. Though he

---

* A tightly run organized crime syndicate that controlled underworld activities in Saigon and Cholon and was not averse to injecting itself into politics.

had asserted his authority and gained time, he had done nothing about establishing positive programs to meet the nation's economic and social needs. He had not used the time he had gained. After three years it was apparent that the new president was a powermonger, not a builder. For those who could see, the fatal narrowness of his political understanding was already evident.

In the first place, Diem's armed enemies had for the most part only been mauled, not destroyed. Elements of the defeated sect armies went underground, licking their wounds and looking for allies. Gradually they began to link up with groups of former Vietminh fighters fleeing from the To Cong suppression. The core of a guerrilla army was already in the making.

Even as old enemies regrouped, Diem was busy adding new ones. In the countryside he destroyed at a blow the dignity and livelihood of several hundred thousand peasants by canceling the land-redistribution arrangements instituted by the Vietminh in areas they had controlled prior to 1954. He might have attempted to use American aid to compensate owners and capitalize on peasant goodwill; instead he courted the large landholders. Farmers who had been working land they considered theirs, often for years, now faced demands for back rent and exorbitant new rates. It was an economic disaster for them.

In 1957 Diem promulgated his own version of land reform, ostensibly making acreage available, though only to peasants who could pay for it. But even this reform was carried out primarily on paper. In the provinces it was sabotaged everywhere by landowners acting with official connivance. The result of all this was a frustrated and indignant peasantry, fertile ground for anti-Diem agitation.

Meanwhile, the city poor were tasting their own ration of misery. In Saigon the government pursued "urban redevelopment" with a vengeance, dispossessing whole neighborhoods in favor of modern commercial buildings and expensive apartments, which could only be utilized by Americans and the native upper classes. Not a few times, poorer quarters were completely razed by uncontrollable fires (Khanh Hoi and Phu Nuan were particularly calamitous examples). Few thought these fires were accidental; they were too closely followed by massive new construction. The displaced moved onto sampans on the river or to poorer, even more distant districts. In the slums and shanty villages resentment against the Americans mixed with a simmering anger toward the regime.

In the highland regions of the Montagnards too, Diem's policies were cold-blooded and destructive. Attempting to make the tribespeople more accessible to government control, troops and cadres forced village populations down out of the mountains and into the valleys—separating them from their ancestral lands and graves. In Ban Me Thuot and other areas, the ingrained routines of social life were profoundly disrupted by these forced relocations, which seemed to the tribespeople nothing more than inexplicable cruelty.

By the end of 1958, Diem had succeeded brilliantly in routing his enemies and arrogating power. But he had also alienated large segments of the South Vietnamese population, creating a swell of animosity throughout the country. Almost unknown at first, in a few short years he had made himself widely detested, a dictator who could look for support only to the Northern Catholic refugees and to those who made money from his schemes. Most damning of all, he had murdered many patriots who had fought in the struggle against France and had tied his existence to the patronage of the United States, France's successor. To many nationalist-minded Vietnamese, whose emotions were those of people just emerging from a hundred years of subjection to foreigners, Diem had forfeited all claims to loyalty.

In light of Diem's conduct of the presidency, two facts were clear: First, the country had settled into an all too familiar pattern of oligarchic rule and utter disregard for the welfare of the people. Second, subservience to foreigners was still the order of the day. We had a ruler whose overriding interest was power and who would use the Americans to prop himself up—even while the Americans were using him for their own strategic purposes.

As far as I was concerned, this situation was intolerable. Replacing the French despots with a Vietnamese one was not a significant advance. It would never lead to either the broad economic progress or the national dignity which I (along with many others) had been brooding about for years. Among my circle of friends there was anger and profound disappointment over this turn of events. We were living, we felt, in historic times. A shameful, century-long era had just been violently closed out, and a new nation was taking shape before our eyes. Many of us agreed that we could not acquiesce in the shape it was taking. If we were not to be allowed a say about it from within the government, we would have to speak from without.

By the end of 1958, those of us who felt this way decided to form an extralegal political organization, complete with a program and plan of action. We had not moved toward this decision quickly; it was an undertaking of immense magnitude, which would require years of effort before giving us the strength to challenge Diem's monopoly on power. To some, that prospect seemed quixotic at best. But most of us felt we had little choice.

From casual discussions, we began to meet in slightly more formal groups, sometimes only a few of us, sometimes eight or ten together. Two doctors, Duong Quynh Hoa and Phung Van Cung, took active roles, as did Nguyen Huu Khuong, a factory owner, Trinh Dinh Thao, a lawyer, and the architect Huynh Tan Phat. We were joined by Nguyen Van Hieu and Ung Ngoc Ky, who were lycée teachers, and other friends such as Nguyen Long and Tran Buu Kiem. Our first order of business was to identify and make contact with potential allies for what we knew would be a long and bitter struggle.

To do this we formed what we called the mobilization committee, whose members were myself, Hieu, Kiem, Ky, Long, Cung, and architect Phat. Through friends, relatives, business and political contacts we began to establish a network of people who felt as we did about Diem and his policies. Phat and a few of the others were old resisters and had kept their ties with fellow veterans of the French war, many of whom were hiding with friends and family from the To Cong hunters. They too were beginning to organize, and they had colleagues and sympathizers in every social stratum throughout the country. They were natural allies.

Among us we also had people with close ties to the sects, the legal political parties, the Buddhists. In each group we made overtures, and

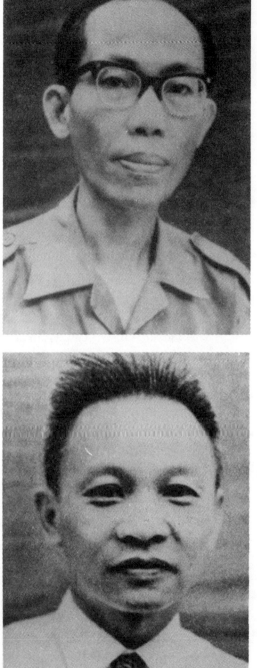

Three of the seven members of the mobilization committee of the National Liberation Front: Dr. Phung Van Cung (*above, left*), Ung Ngoc Ky, (*above, right*) and I.

everywhere we discovered sympathy and backing. Sometimes individuals would indicate their desire to participate actively. More often we would receive assurances of quiet solidarity. At the same time, we sent Nguyen Van Hieu to Hanoi to begin working out a channel of support from our Northern compatriots.

At each stage we discussed carefully the ongoing search for allies, wary about how to gather support and still retain our own direction and freedom of action. It was a delicate and crucial problem, of the utmost complexity. The overwhelming strength of our enemy urged us to acquire whatever assistance we could, from whatever source. In addition, the anticolonial war had not simply ended in 1954; a residual Vietminh infrastructure was still in place and was beginning to come alive again. For better or worse, our endeavor was meshed into an ongoing historical movement for independence that had already developed its own philosophy and means of action. Of this movement, Ho Chi Minh was the spiritual father, in the South as well as the North, and we looked naturally to him and to his government for guidance and aid. . . . And yet, this struggle was also our own. Had Ngo Dinh Diem proved a man of breadth and vision, the core of people who filled the NLF and its sister organizations would have rallied to him. As it was, the South Vietnamese nationalists were driven to action by his contempt for the principles of independence and social progress in which they believed. In this sense, the Southern revolution was generated of itself, out of the emotions, conscience, and aspirations of the Southern people.

The complexity of the struggle was mirrored in the makeup of our group. Most were not Lao Dong ("Workers' Party"—the official name of the Vietnamese Communist Party) members; many scarcely thought of themselves as political, at least in any ideological way. Our allies among the resistance veterans were also largely nationalist rather than political (though they had certainly been led and monitored by the Party). But we also had Party activists among us, some open, some surreptitious. Tran Buu Kiem, the architect Phat, and the teachers Hieu and Ky I knew as politically-minded individuals, who had been leaders of the New Democratic Party during their student years at

Hanoi University in the early forties. This militant student union had been absorbed by the Lao Dong in 1951, some of its members enrolling in the Party, some defecting altogether, some simply accepting the change in leadership without themselves becoming Communists. What I didn't know was that Phat had been a secret Party member since 1940 while Hieu, Ky, and Kiem had rallied to the Party in 1951.

But I was not overly concerned at that point about potential conflicts between the Southern nationalists and the ideologues. We were allies in this fight, or so I believed. We needed each other, and the closest ties of background, family, and patriotism united us in respect for each other's purposes. This was my reading of the situation in 1959 as the yet-to-be-named National Liberation Front gathered momentum. I was not alone in drawing this conclusion. And I was not the only one whom time would disabuse.

In addition to making contacts and setting up working relationships with supporters, we also began searching for a leader. Our requirements were clear: someone who was well known and who had a reputation for integrity, someone associated with neither the French nor the Communists. This person had to strike a note of moderation and goodwill, attracting support from all sides and alienating no one. Several names kept surfacing in our discussions about this, and finally we drew up a list of four candidates.

Our first choice was Tran Kim Quan, a pharmacist who had been president of the South Vietnamese Student Association at Hanoi University and chairman of the Peace Movement in 1954. Quan met all the criteria; he had an established reputation as a patriot and was widely respected as a man of principle. Kiem was delegated to approach him for us. But though Quan turned out to be sympathetic to our goals, he was unwilling to accept our offer. Perhaps he had a premonition of the tortuous course this struggle would take.

There were two second choices, Trinh Dinh Thao, already one of our colleagues, and Michael Van Vi. Thao was a high official of the Cao Dai sect and had been a minister in the old imperial cabinet. Accordingly, he was conspicuously free from any Communist taint. Van Vi, director of the Franco-Chinese Bank, was likewise distant from leftist ideology. His nonprofessional interests ran largely to culture; he chaired the Society for the Propagation of the Vietnamese Language. I was appointed to sound out Thao and Van Vi, but my luck was no better than Kiem's had been. They were willing to play a supporting role, but would not assume the leadership.

By elimination our list now was narrowed to Nguyen Huu Tho, a lawyer who, with Quan, had been cochairman of the Peace Movement, a vaguely leftist group of Saigon intellectuals who had tried to encourage Diem to hold reunification elections as stipulated by the Geneva Accords. But talking to Tho would be a complicated matter. His peace activities had landed him under house arrest in Tuy Hoa, a town in the center of Vietnam. Phat, who had contacts with the resistance veterans in the area, was assigned the job of stealing Tho away from his guards.

As Phat was making his plans, we began to refine our working procedures. Up to this point we had not been terribly afraid of the police. Ours could easily be construed as just another circle of talkative Saigon intellectuals engaged in the national sport of arguing about politics. There was nothing we had actually done. But by the fall of 1959 our organization had grown considerably. As we began working toward a first large-scale general meeting, the time had come to shift over to more formal, security-conscious methods.

Now we divided up our more numerous membership into many small working groups of three, four, or five people, no single group knowing who belonged to the other groups. This cell structure is sometimes thought of as a communist innovation, but for the Vietnamese, with their long history of secret societies, it is practically second nature. Each cell included people from different classes and backgrounds to insure a wide range of thinking. I found myself working with three others: Sau Cang, a small businessman; Le Van Phong, a resistance veteran; and Truong Cao Phuoc, a schoolfellow of mine who had also fought with the Vietminh and whose family owned a large rubber plantation.

The mobilization committee also appointed a leadership group made up of Phat, Hieu, and Kiem—responsible for overseeing the details of organization and bringing together input from the different working groups. After two months or so of intense activity throughout the organization, the leadership was ready to circulate a consensus of the ideas that had been generated. General agreement had been reached on the following objectives:

1. Bring a sense of unity to the different classes of people in the South, regardless of their position in society or their political or religious views.

2. Overthrow the Diem regime.

3. Achieve the withdrawal of American advisers and an end to American interference in the self-determination of the South Vietnamese people.

4. Defend and protect the rights of Vietnamese citizens, including democratic freedoms and respect for private property rights.

5. Carry out a "land to the tiller" policy.

6. Build an independent economy.

7. Establish an educational system that will protect Vietnamese traditions and culture.

8. Establish a pluralistic national government, nonaligned and neutral.

9. Unify the North and the South on the basis of mutual interest through negotiations, without war.

As we finished shaping our broad objectives and began grappling with their ramifications, we also set a tentative date for the first general meeting: December 19 and 20 of the following year. We decided too on a name for our movement: the National Liberation Front of South Vietnam. We devised a flag (later to become famous as the flag of the Vietcong) and an anthem, "Liberate the South." At the same time, Hieu was sent North again, this time for guidance from Uncle Ho on the platform we had enunciated. By the end of 1959, work was complete on transforming these general principles into a manifesto and a formal political program. (See Appendix.)

Reading through the finished documents, I was impressed by the analysis they presented of the South's political situation and the balance of forces within the country as well as in Southeast Asia and throughout the world. It was clear that these works had been finely crafted to appeal to the broadest spectrum of people in the South and to marshal the anticolonial emotions that animated almost everyone. At the same time, the manifesto and program responded forcefully and specifically to the interests of the various elements of South Vietnamese society—the intellectuals, students, middle class, peasants, and workers.

As I read, I had the distinct sense that these historical documents could not have been the work of just the leadership group. They had too much depth, they showed too expert a grasp of politics, psychology, and language. I suspected I was seeing in them the delicate fingerprints of Ho Chi Minh. There seemed nothing strange about this. Ho's experience with revolutionary struggle was not something alien, to arouse suspicion and anxiety. It was part and parcel of our own background.

We were now, in the winter of 1959–1960, ready to move into the next phase of the struggle. In early March, as internal tension grew, the Resistance Veterans' Association suddenly launched an appeal to the people of the South. Spread through leaflets and posters, broadcast by Hanoi Radio, it called for an armed struggle to begin. It was a signal that the political action, which had been our focus for the past two years, would now acquire a coordinated military dimension. With this step, the Northern government had reinforced the Front's credibility and had flashed its own readiness for a wider conflict.

I felt a hint of trepidation at this. For several years there had been violence in the countryside; indeed, violent conflict had been a fact of life since Diem's suppression of the sects and the former Vietminh fighters. But the struggle we were now embarked on would involve military confrontation on a different scale altogether. My colleagues and I had known from the start that moving Diem into any serious negotiations regarding political participation would require the sustained use of force. Regardless of our personal predilections, there was no choice in this. But our priorities had always been distinctly political. We envisioned as our goal a political settlement that could be brought about largely by political means. Military victory was seen neither by us nor by anyone else as a serious possibility. Diem's own army was vastly superior to any forces we might deploy—and behind Diem were the Americans. A high level of warfare would bring with it the grave danger of direct American intervention, which we wished at all costs to avoid. What all this meant was that violence was called for, but a carefully controlled violence that would serve political ends. In addition, I believed that the core group of the NLF, men who felt much as I did, would act as an effective brake against those who might be tempted to look for a military solution. Nevertheless, now that the engagement was opened, there was occasion for a surge of doubt.

But events quickly pushed trepidation aside. The signal given by the Resistance Veterans' Association was loudly confirmed by the Third National Congress of the Workers' Party, which met in Hanoi during the second week of September. Proclaiming the liberation of the South as a major priority, the Northern government was formally announcing its readiness in the most unambiguous fashion. The stage was now fully set.

Meanwhile Huynh Tan Phat had organized a raid to liberate President-designate Tho from his detention in Tuy Hoa. The region around this town had been a center of Vietminh activity in the French war and was crawling with former guerrillas. From these Phat had put together a commando unit whose job was to grab Tho and spirit him away to a safe area on the Laos/Cambodia/Vietnam border. Here he could hide until preparations were completed for the general meeting scheduled for December 19. Phat's deadline was approaching fast.

Along with a number of other peace activists, Tho was being held in a loosely guarded house, looked after by local soldiers. Neither he nor his fellow detainees were considered high security risks, their crimes having consisted of some relatively innocuous agitation for elections several years earlier. No one, neither Tho nor his wardens, suspected that he was about to become a prime object of guerrilla attention. Taking advantage of the relaxed atmosphere, Phat's commandos were able to lure the guards away by having relatives call

Nguyen Huu Tho (*center*) and two other members of the Peace Movement under arrest in Tuy Hoa.

them with various family emergencies that required their immediate presence. With the guards out of the way, the kidnappers simply walked into the house. Unfortunately, so unaware was Tho that anything was brewing that he had requested (and had received) permission for a private visit with his family. At the moment his would-be rescuers began looking through the house, the object of their search was in a government compound on the other side of town, enjoying a reunion with his wife and children.

In a series of comic-opera mistakes, none of the commandos—all of whom were from the Tuy Hoa area—had ever actually seen Tho, though they had been provided with a picture of him as an aid to identification. Now they paraded through the house asking questions and trying to match up the various prisoners with the face in the photo. Unsure as to who was who and skeptical of the story about Tho's outing, they decided to take along the two candidates who most nearly resembled their quarry. These two quickly found themselves transported to the border hideout, where their protestations of mistaken identity were finally confirmed, much to the discomfiture of the commandos.*

Having liberated the wrong men, the commandos were now forced to launch a second operation, organized a little more carefully this time, and including someone who could recognize Tho by sight. But because of the first mix-up, we were still without a president as the December 19 meeting came on.

Early on the morning of December 17, 1960, I left my house for the Saigon bus station, where Le Van Phong, one of my work-group colleagues, was waiting for me. After a few minutes we were approached by a woman whom Phong introduced as Ba Xuyen ("Woman Number Three"). "Ba Xuyen," he told me, "will take you where you have to go." My guide and I bought tickets for Tay Ninh, about seventy miles from Saigon and the home province of the Cao Dai sect, a place I knew intimately from my childhood visits to the sect's "Vatican." On the bus, Ba Xuyen gave me explicit instructions. "If any security people stop us," she said, "let me do the talking. If you have to answer, say that we are going to Can Dang to visit our Uncle Kiem."

The trip was uneventful though, and at Tay Ninh we switched to a Lambretta three-wheel carrier headed for Can Dang, a government outpost village about ten miles from the Cambodian border. At the outpost we stopped for a minute while Ba Xuyen passed a few words with the soldier on duty, slipping something into his breast pocket as she talked. Back on the Lambretta, she directed the driver to follow a dirt path into the jungle. About a mile and a half along this track we arrived at a tiny hamlet, the home, it turned out, of the "uncle" we were visiting. Here we got off, and my guide led me into one of the houses, where old Kiem himself was waiting. As Ba Xuyen slipped out the front door, Kiem showed me to a little

---

* As a footnote to these goings-on, in 1968 I met these two men, both of whom had chosen to stay with the resistance. They had been nicknamed Ba Hoa Binh and Muoi Hoa Binh, that is, Number Three Peaceful and Number Ten Peaceful, referring to their place in family and the fact that they came to the Front through the Peace Movement.

outbuilding behind the house, where I would await my escort for the next stage of the journey.

Here we had lunch, and I dozed off on a cot next to the wall. Sometime later I was awakened to find Kiem gently shaking me, a set of black pajamas in his hand, which he indicated I was to change into. Darkness and fallen. As I put on the pajamas, I became aware that someone was standing in the doorway, a young man also dressed in black. He had come on a bicycle to chauffeur me to the next rendezvous. Sitting on a makeshift seat attached over the rear wheel of his bike, I rode with him through fields of sugarcane and manioc that were barely visible in the last of the twilight. About an hour later we arrived at a small cottage deep in the jungle. Inside, sitting around a table dimly lit by a smoking oil lamp, sat three local guerrillas, drinking tea.

They offered me a cup, and I sat down with them for a few minutes, happy for the rest. Before long, however, another bicycle driver appeared for the next leg. This was turning out to be quite an adventure—and, I realized, quite a meticulously organized one. My new driver pedaled into the heart of the blackened jungle, the invisible trail sloping upward as we came into the foothills of the border region. We drove until well past midnight, stopping every hour or so at a guerrilla cottage for a cup of tea and a brief rest. Sometime in the early hours of the morning we found ourselves among a cluster of small buildings—we had arrived at the meeting site.* I was sore and exhausted from sitting on the back seat for so long, and I marveled at the endurance of my driver. In a minute though, I had been escorted to one of the cottages, and whatever thoughts I was having about this remarkable journey were blotted out in a dreamless sleep.

I awoke refreshed on the morning of the eighteenth, alone in the cottage. As I got up to look around, however, a black-pajamaed guerrilla appeared in the doorway, introducing himself as my escort

* When I returned to the jungle in 1968, I learned that this original meeting had been held at Xom Giua ("Middle Hamlet"), along the Vam Co River near the Cambodian border.

for the next two days. He told me that, like the other secret delegates, I would be staying alone, and that he would take care of my needs. He also described the security precautions. I would be shielded from contact with others and was to use only the code name "Ba Cham" when I talked with anybody. Soon Huynh Tan Phat came by with another man whom he introduced as Hai Xe Ngua ("Brother Two Horse Car"). Brother Two Horse Car was about fifty years old and especially large for a Vietnamese, though trim and muscular. He was, Phat said, in charge of finances for the Front. (I later found out that this personage was Nguyen Van So, a Central Committee member of the Workers' Party.) We exchanged pleasantries, and Brother Two Horse gave me a sheaf of papers that included the meeting agenda, the platform, and various issue papers. If I had any suggestions or comments, I was to write them out, and they would be taken into account at the meeting.

I spent the day poring over these documents, breaking for a light lunch and dinner prepared by my helpful attendant. That evening, I was given a large checkered scarf to muffle my face, and shepherded to a hall with a low stage on one end and a row of curtained boxes along the left side—into one of which I was ushered. Slowly the benches in the middle of the hall filled, and I heard the shuffle of people being shown to the boxes alongside mine. When everybody had arrived, a troupe of entertainers took the stage, a unit of resistance veterans there to put on a rousing variety show. Singers, mimes, and comic acts followed each other, with a heavy emphasis on political satire, which the audience enjoyed hugely. When it was over, my escort led me back to the cottage, taking pains to avoid other members of the audience, some of whom were, like me, carefully attended.

The next morning, December 19, I was again taken to the hall, which now had acquired a different set of trappings. Over the entrance hung a red-and-white banner proclaiming "Welcome General Congress for the Foundation of the National Liberation Front for South Vietnam." Flanking this banner were two flags, red and blue with a yellow star in the center, the flag we had devised during our working meetings the previous year. Inside, last night's stage had become a dais, above which the same banner was draped. On the dais sat Phat, Hieu, and Kiem, our leadership group, together with Ung Ngoc Ky, Dr. Cung, and several others I didn't recognize. These others turned out to be representatives of various groups, youth, peasants, workers, and women—Pham Xuan Thai, Nguyen Huu The, Nguyen Co Tam, and Nguyen Thi Dinh respectively. Again I was shown into one of the curtained boxes along the side, hidden from the public delegates, who were seating themselves on the middle benches and from the other secret members occupying the adjoining boxes.* There were perhaps sixty participants in all, including twenty or so behind the curtains. Over all of us a sense of expectancy began to build, as a spokesman got up to announce the agenda.

After the agenda was read, a security force representative described the safety measures that had been taken and gave instructions about what to do should there be an alarm or an attack by air or land forces. Then Dr. Cung arose for a short inaugural statement, declaring the congress in session and wishing us success in our great undertaking. He was followed by Kiem, who read a report on the political situation in South Vietnam, and Hieu, who presented the manifesto and political program.

The hortatory language of these documents seemed to heighten the drama of what was happening; each individual in the hall was aware that he was participating in a historic event. Sensing the excitement, Hieu went on to explain that the name "National Liberation Front for South Vietnam" symbolized the unity of the Southern people in their struggle to free the country from *My Diem* ("America/Diem"). The flag, he said, red and blue, signified the two halves of the nation, united under the star—in a single purpose. The anthem, "Liberate the South," echoed the appeal with simple clarity.

At midday when the meeting broke for lunch, the delegates were visibly moved by feelings of brotherhood and resolution. For me,

---

* The "public" delegates were people who were living in the jungle as full-time revolutionaries. "Secret" delegates were those who, like me, led open lives in government controlled areas and whose Front identities had to be closely guarded.

though, these feelings were to remain private as, muffled in my scarf, I was led back to the cottage to eat in solitude.

After lunch, the meeting reconvened to hear statements from representatives of various social elements—the sects, the intellectuals, students, peasants—each speaking of the aspirations of his group. When these had been given, we recessed for a dinner of soup, vegetables, and rice, returning to hear statements and suggestions from those who had submitted them in writing the previous day. Near midnight we voted to accept the manifesto, program, flag, everything that was before us. There were no dissenters.

Finally, Huynh Tan Phat moved that we adopt a suggested list of names as a Provisional Committee to carry the movement forward until the next general congress could be held. Specifically, the Provisional Committee would proclaim the creation of the NLF and publicize its manifesto and program not only throughout Vietnam but internationally as well. (The diplomatic front was to open immediately.) The committee would also intensify our proselytizing efforts and make preparations for the next congress, at which a regular Central Committee and organizational hierarchy would be established. It would, in addition, continue to develop our infrastructure throughout the South, with special attention to the Saigon/Cholon/Giadinh zone.

Phat's proposal was passed, again unanimously, and Dr. Cung was elected chairman of the Provisional Committee, with Hieu to serve as secretary general. In the early hours of December 20, we adjourned.

Once finished with our business, the delegates dispersed as quickly as they could, knowing that each moment the danger of discovery increased. I left immediately by bicycle, retracing the arduous trail back to old Kiem's house, where I arrived dead with fatigue but spiritually exalted. In the little outbuilding I changed out of the pajamas into my own clothes and boarded the Lambretta for Tay Ninh. There a bus was waiting to take me back to Saigon. This time I had no need of a guide.

By the following morning I had fully recovered from the lost night's sleep, though my body still ached. From Hanoi that morning a special broadcast reached every corner of the South, announcing the formation of the NLF and offering congratulations from the Workers' Party and the Northern government. It was a time for nourishing the most sublime hopes.

8

Strengthening
the Front

Nineteen sixty was the fifth year of Ngo Dinh Diem's presidency.
Despite a serene demeanor, the man must have felt a mounting
anxiety as the year progressed. Not only had guerrilla activity begun
to step up, it was acquiring a coherent political framework. In general, domestic opposition to Diem was becoming increasingly vocal,
even clamorous. On April 26, after months of continuous ferment,
eighteen leading citizens published an open letter sharply condemning
Diem's repressive policies. The response was characteristic: All eighteen signatories were thrown in jail, and the government clamped a
steel muzzle on Saigon's newspapers, strictly forbidding them to
publish any further criticism. Breeding rancor with each new move,
Diem now found himself facing something approaching a general
conflagration. Among the city's elite there was vitriolic resentment at
his lead-glove tactics. Students, unhappy with the government's educational policies and much else besides, took to the streets, creating a
general din. The newspapers vigorously protested the restrictions that
they felt would now choke them to death.

Inflamed by this angry tide of reaction, Diem's suspicions of disloyalty among his officers ripened quickly, then suddenly burst into
life with the November 11 paratroopers' rebellion. Barely saved by his
own clever stalling and by Albert Thao's dash to Mytho for reinforcements, Diem loosed a shotgun blast at his enemies. Arrests ran

into the thousands, including many political and social figures entirely unconnected with the coup attempt.

Amidst a rising sea of protest, the newly appointed NLF Provisional Committee moved to strengthen its presence in the capital. Plans were quickly developed to establish a Committee for the Saigon/Cholon/Giadinh zone, to exploit the fragility of the Diem regime and give close direction to the Front's efforts in this crucial region. Tet, it seemed, would be a propitious time to set up this committee. Government security would be lax then, and the usual confusion of the Lunar New Year celebrations would mask our gathering.

So it was that on January 30, 1961, I again went down to the central bus station, prepared for another epic journey. This time, though, the trek proved less arduous. With a new guide, I boarded a bus to Bienhoa, twenty miles northeast of Saigon, home base of South Vietnam's air force. From Bienhoa we took a van to the Dong Nai River, where a motorized sampan was waiting to shuttle us upstream to Ben Go, a sleepy little hamlet nestled on the river's northern bank. There I changed into the obligatory black pajamas and at nightfall was driven, again on the back seat of a bicycle, through the local rubber forests to a plantation in the district of Tan Huyen—a place I recognized as belonging to the family of my old friend and work-group comrade, Truong Cao Phuoc.

Here the accommodations were not so luxurious as they had been at Xom Giua, my bed consisting of a hammock slung between two rubber trees, with a plastic canopy stretched overhead in case of rain. Night was uncomfortable in the chilly, mosquito-plagued forest, and I slept fitfully. My escort tried to ward off the cold, lighting a fire in one of the ceramic rubber pails, but the pleasant glow gave off little warmth.

Gradually, though, the restless night gave way to dawn and a breakfast of hot coffee and chicken soup. As my escort and I were sipping the last of it, Huynh Tan Phat appeared out of the forest, accompanied this time, not by Brother Two Horse Car, but by "Sau Dan." Sau Dan was the code name of Vo Van Kiet, a man I knew as a former Vietminh official, who had been hiding in the Saigon area for many years, staying at safe houses and with friends and relatives, moving around often. He had even spent a few nights at my house and was to be my guest again. Though neither of us could then have imagined such a twist of fate, Kiet would also inadvertently provide the cover for my escape from the country seventeen years later.

Kiet was also, though I wasn't to find this out until later, Lao Dong (Communist Party) secretary in charge of Saigon/Cholon/ Giadinh and had been since the French war. After 1954, the Party had retained a skeletal structure in the South, with secretaries for the more important administrative regions. These people, Kiet and his colleagues, had stayed in the South, either living underground or maintaining an elaborate cover for their Party identities. (Sometimes, indeed, they did both.) Kiet himself was a most attractive personality, brilliant, open-minded, with a personal warmth that everyone responded to.*

Kiet greeted me warmly. He had with him, as Hai Xe Ngua had had at the general meeting, the material we would be considering, among which was an appeal to the people of the city urging them to demand their civil rights and intensify their struggle against Diem and his policies. The same routine, Kiet said, was to be followed now as at the earlier congress. Any questions or comments I might have were to be written down and submitted prior to the meeting.

Again I had most of the day to study the agenda material; then as night fell, I muffled my face and followed my escort to the meeting hall. This building was quite similar to the one at Xom Giua, though it seemed less brightly lit by the kerosene lanterns. Here the curtained boxes for the secret delegates lined both sides of the hall, indicating that a good number of the Saigon members would remain unknown to each other.

On the dais sat Phat, Vo Van Kiet, and Mme. Thanh Loan, a famous chanteuse and comedienne, who had joined the guerrillas and was now living in the jungle. With them were three people I did not recognize. The order of business was similar to the proceedings a

* At the time of this writing he is a full member of the Politburo, vice prime minister, and chairman of the State Planning Committee.

month and a half earlier. After the agenda was announced, a security officer gave instructions for any emergency we might face. Phat then made inaugural remarks, and Kiet followed with the political analysis. Then came reports on the mass movements in Saigon, focusing on the recently heated opposition among students and the media. When student and press representatives had been heard, Phat read the appeal to the people of Saigon, together with comments on this proclamation that various delegates had seen fit to make. He then called for a vote, and the appeal was unanimously approved.

Finally, Madame Loan proposed a leadership group for the Saigon/Cholon/Giadinh Committee: Phat for chairman, engineer Le Van Tha for vice chairman (Tha was to become my chief deputy in the PRG Ministry of Justice), and Nguyen Van Tai for secretary general. Thai had been a member of the Saigon Chamber of Commerce, but had been denounced for procommunist leanings and had fled to the guerrillas to avoid arrest.

This list was duly approved, and Phat got up to close the meeting and announce the evening's entertainment, a play to be performed by the Liberation Troupe. The play turned out to be a broad satire on the ineptitude of the Saigon government troops entitled "Primitive Weapons Can Win Against Modern Weapons." Despite the burden of its title, this interlude contained a good deal of wit and slapstick, and everyone got a good laugh out of it. The conviviality of the delegates picked up another notch as a soup dinner was brought in to welcome the New Year.

Biking back through the forest to Ben Go, I was beginning to feel like an old hand at this kind of thing—though I must say that my appreciation for the organizational skills that had gone into this meeting, as well as the first, hadn't slackened a bit. At the hamlet I traded the pajamas for my clothes and began the return trip to Saigon, arriving at the central bus station early in the morning, just as New Year's firecrackers began rattling in the street.

All this while, my family and professional lives were moving along in an orderly and tranquil fashion. I had arranged my work at the bank to give me as much free time as possible for proselytizing activities, which I now plunged into with great enthusiasm. No one suspected my membership in the Front. I was simply an individual with serious concerns about the government, concerns that many shared with me. I would make my approaches gently, talking over current happenings with friends and associates, sounding out their political leanings and the intensity of their convictions. My family background, education, and now my position gave me a wide circle of contacts in the government, business, and intellectual communities, and I planned my overtures with an eye not merely to gaining members for the Front, but to enlisting sympathy or strengthening those strands of opinion that bore an affinity with any of our positions. This was going to be a protracted affair, and support at any level would be significant as the country moved toward what we thought of as a widespread political uprising.

Many of the people I spent time with were not candidates for the Front—with its Northern and communist associations—but nevertheless held strong nationalist views. I did everything I could to reinforce my ties with such individuals, and years later a number of them would join the Alliance of National, Democratic, and Peace Forces, the so-called Third Force, that worked so assiduously for South Vietnamese independence after 1968.

Others were ready to affiliate themselves directly with the Front. We were able, for example, to bring over Commander Vo Van Mon, the leader of the suppressed Binh Xuyen, along with his remaining troops. Major Mung of the Cao Dai sect, and Colonel Muoi Tri of the Hoa Hao* also brought their armed partisans into the movement. These of course were especially welcome, but so were the many others who formally joined at this time, individuals from every echelon within the government and professions, until Saigon society was honeycombed with our people.

Each Sunday during this period I would meet with one of Phat's liaison officers, who would give me the most recent political and military analyses and brief me on developments throughout the country.

* Both the Cao Dai and the Hoa Hao (another quasi-nationalistic religious sect) maintained their own private armies.

I was also kept informed of plans for the First National Congress, which would bring together all of the groups and movements that had affiliated themselves with the Front and would establish a formal and continuous organizational structure. By the beginning of 1962 all the preparations for this meeting were finally completed, and early in February the liaison told me to make arrangements to be away from Saigon for ten days or so. To my chagrin, shortly before the conference was to open, I began experiencing excruciating stomach pains. Before I knew it, I was in the middle of a full-blown ulcer crisis, unable to get out of bed.

Several weeks later I received a complete report on the congress through the usual liaison channels. It had been a great success, attended by people from every social, ethnic, and geographical grouping in the South. We had now regularized our organization at the province and district levels, with sufficient strength to challenge the Saigon government for control in many areas. The Front's claim to being "the sole authentic representative of the South Vietnamese people" had taken a substantial step toward validating itself.

At the upper end of the hierarchy, a presidium had been chosen, with Nguyen Huu Tho as president and Huynh Tan Phat as first vice president. The congress had also created a fifty-two person Central Committee, although only thirty names were made public. Of the twenty-two other places, some were held by secret members, others were reserved for representatives of groups that might affiliate in the future. The liaison officer informed me that I had been named one of the secret members.

With this congress, the strategy of the Front was established on a solid basis and confirmed for the foreseeable future. The overriding goals remained to effect a withdrawal of the United States from South Vietnam and to bring about negotiations between the Front and its adversaries, in order to form a new Southern government. To achieve these political objectives we would pursue the struggle on three fronts: political, military, and diplomatic. We would simultaneously confront our enemy in the field, mobilize our domestic support while

Nguyen Huu Tho addressing one of the early meetings of the NLF. Hanging behind the dais is the Vietcong flag.

undermining Diem's, and gather allies internationally—not forgetting the American people themselves.

This three-pronged strategy was to characterize our approach throughout the war. Every military clash, every demonstration, every propaganda appeal was seen as part of an integrated whole; each had consequences far beyond its immediately apparent results. It was a framework that allowed us to view battles as psychological events and to undertake negotiations in order to strengthen our military position. The Americans seemed never to appreciate fully this strategic perspective, which among ourselves we most often simply called *Danh va dam, dam va danh* ("fighting and talking, talking and fighting"). It was, after all, a traditional Vietnamese approach to warfare, a technique refined over centuries of confrontation with invaders more powerful than ourselves.

The Urban Struggle

Shortly after the overthrow of Diem, I was appointed director-general of the Société Sucrière, the national sugar company, which at the time was the country's largest conglomerate, employing over five thousand people. The company ran four sugar mills, two refineries, and two distilleries, which produced rum and distilled alcohol. In addition, we owned a textile plant for manufacturing jute sugar sacks and conducted a substantial import operation, shipping in approximately two hundred thousand tons of sugar annually.

With this new job, my workday took on vastly different proportions. In the morning I would get to the office between seven and seven-thirty, take a lunch break at home, then return to work until at least seven in the evening, often staying at my desk through the late night hours. Twice a week I'd make a general tour of our plants and refineries, keeping a close eye on production and distribution and supervising the work of the various managers. Occasionally I would find it necessary to go abroad, to Taiwan or Japan, in connection with our import arrangements. Part of my weekly schedule was a meeting with my immediate superior, Nguyen Anh Tuan, undersecretary for economic planning, a session that often would include the minister of economics.

Of necessity there was a good deal less time for the general proselytizing I had been doing earlier. In addition, the Front was now, in early 1964, preoccupied with military and political planning to meet the new circumstances brought on by Diem's fall. Indeed, as the political situation in Saigon deteriorated, our attention was absorbed by an urgent and potentially decisive development, and it was toward this crisis that I now directed my efforts.

We knew that the United States had colluded in the generals' coup de main against Diem out of sheer exasperation. Henry Cabot Lodge, Washington's ambassador in Saigon, had watched with barely concealed despair as the regime alienated one social group after another, finally bringing down the wrath of the country's large Buddhist majority on its head. Despite the indispensable aid the Americans were delivering, Diem persisted in spurning their advice about accommodating his non-NLF opponents. As the Buddhists marched in

As the director-general of the Société Sucrière, the national sugar company.

the streets and immolated themselves in protest (incidents the president's sister-in-law publicly referred to as "barbecues"), Diem wrapped himself in what must have seemed to Lodge an incomprehensible cloak of intransigence and scorn.

Intent on establishing some modicum of stability in the government, Lodge's patience finally caved in altogether and he abandoned support of Diem. Working through CIA agent Lucien Conein, the United States government signaled its willingness to support the army rebellion led by General Tran Van Don. But although the coup succeeded, the events that followed did nothing to fulfill the Americans' cherished hopes. To their immense frustration, Don's government proved to be, if anything, less effective than Diem's. An atmosphere of relief and relaxation had replaced the previous tension, but the ruling Military Council seemed lethargic and without direction. Before many months had passed, drift was to give way to outright confusion.

Early in the morning of January 30, 1964, Don and his colleagues were awakened by the sound of military vehicles rolling into positions around their homes. They had been surprised, in their turn, by one of their coconspirators, the energetic and unscrupulous Nguyen Khanh. Now began a period of riot and political dissension that must have moved Lodge to tears of regret for the departed Diem. By June the ambassador had had enough. He had gotten rid of one impossible dictator only to find himself afflicted with a worse one. With a political campaign back in the United States to attract his interest, he decided to resign from the job he had held for almost exactly one year. To us, how the United States filled the vacancy created by Lodge's departure would tell a great deal about their future intentions. We watched the situation with considerable apprehension.

The nomination of General Maxwell Taylor, chairman of the Joint Chiefs of Staff, was ominous and disheartening news. Alongside Taylor, William Westmoreland was named to head the American military effort. With these new appointees, direct intervention became increasingly probable. All the signs pointed in that direction. Clearly, the American view of South Vietnam's strategic significance had not changed. But at the same time the Southern government had proved itself too despotic, obstreperous, and weak to sustain the role assigned to it. Short of reassessing its fundamental assumptions about the region, Washington would now be forced to take a much greater part in the conduct of Vietnamese affairs, especially on the military front. Taylor and Westmoreland, we felt, were there to provide the leadership and organizational competence for stepped-up American involvement. We could not know the level at which the United States would intercede, but any direct participation of American troops would bring with it the most severe consequences.

Fear of this development haunted the leadership, not just of the Front but of the Northern government as well. Once Americans were involved in the fighting, chances for a negotiated settlement would vanish like a summer shower. Our planning, consequently, revolved around ways to keep this disaster permanently in the wings.

As the crisis ripened during the first half of 1964, we concluded that the key to resolving it lay in vigorously exploiting Saigon's political weakness. This involved no new departures in strategy. Instead we would intensify the political struggle on both the rural and urban fronts. Throughout the countryside, we moved to consolidate our control in liberated areas and accelerate the establishment of NLF governmental entities in disputed regions. The object of this effort was not to take land, but to create a strong and continuous NLF administrative presence, which villagers would accept as their valid government. In the cities we took steps to accelerate pressure for negotiations. If we could substantially weaken the regime's ability to control the rural population and galvanize popular pressure in the cities for talks, we might well precipitate a political crisis which the Americans would be powerless to affect. Depending on our success in generating mass support, we might now bring about a general uprising, which was our strategic objective, or catapult the unstable Khanh (or his successor) into negotiations. Either development would distance, perhaps nullify, the specter of American military intervention.

As Saigon descended toward anarchy under General Khanh's

incompetent rule, all the elements seemed in place for a general uprising. The turmoil infected not just the students and intellectuals, but the still unplacated Buddhists and even the business community. Saigon's influential merchants and industrialists had finally been brought to a precipice. Their vested interests urged them to suspect and fear the Front. But at the same time, they were horrified at the prospect of American intervention and all-out war. At this decisive juncture, our task was to shape this mass of anger and doubt into a coherent force, poised to smash down on the fragile edifice of Nguyen Khanh's government.

Our first step in this direction was to establish an open and legal movement to mobilize opinion and agitate for negotiations and an end to hostilities—a movement with no visible ties to the NLF. To avoid arousing the police prematurely, we planned the initial meeting of what was to be called *Phong Trao Dan Toc Tu Quyet Mien Nam Viet Nam* ("the Movement for Self-Determination") around the funeral anniversary for the grandparents of one of our friends, an optician living in Giadinh. This traditional celebration, the *gio,* would be attended by the many members of his large extended family as well as numbers of the family's friends. On this occasion, the friends would be augmented by forty or fifty specially invited guests, none of whom were NLF but all of whom were deeply concerned about the course events were taking.

The knowledge I had gained in six years of groundwork among the Saigonese allowed me to select people who would not just be sympathetic to our goals, but who had prestige and broad associations themselves among the city's diverse groups and factions. When the incense, prayers, and feasting were over, we began our discussion on the theme of what was to be done. As I anticipated, the guests shared common convictions about the crisis facing the South, and they were sufficiently alarmed about it to take action—at least now that they could see there would be mutual support. Given the general agreement and the sense of urgency, the group moved quickly to establish a committee, to be called (at my suggestion) the Movement for Self-Determination.

For its president the newly minted movement chose Nguyen Long, a lawyer, for vice president engineer Ho Gia Ly, an upper level official in the Transportation Ministry. Three others were picked to round out the leadership: Nguyen Ba Nghe, a factory owner; Tran Huu Khue, a teacher; and myself. All of those named enjoyed high social positions and were well known in the city. Except for Long, none of the other four was politically inclined, nor (as far as they knew) was I.

The fact that such dignified and essentially conservative individuals, with no political ambitions and little detectable tendency toward activism, could be marshaled in this manner was tremendously encouraging. In effect, I had only provided the setting and some muted guidance. Given this impetus, the *gio* guests had moved with an alacrity that confirmed our reading of the city's mood. Now it remained to act.

The first order of business was to write and publicize a manifesto. The others were happy enough to accept the draft that I had prepared, and they also approved the wording I had devised for a leaflet. Both of these documents denounced American intervention and demanded the right to self-determination. I ran them off on the copying machines at my office. "The Self-Determination Movement," headlined the leaflet:

AMERICA FOR AMERICANS. SOUTH VIETNAM FOR SOUTH VIETNAMESE. WE DEMAND THAT THE NLF AND THE GOVERNMENT NEGOTIATE PEACE BETWEEN THE TWO BROTHERS.* SOUTH VIETNAM MUST HAVE THE RIGHT TO DETERMINE ITS OWN FUTURE.

But even as we began publicizing our message, the Front was growing increasingly nervous about American movements. Pressure in Washington had been mounting steadily since Lodge's resignation. During July, our weekly analysis of American strategy suggested that Johnson had already made the decision to intervene and was now seeking a pretext. Our belief was that the American president would do everything he could to avoid recognizing the NLF as a legitimate

* That is, the Saigon regime and the NLF.

entity. Any such recognition would signal the failure of American containment policy in Southeast Asia, of which South Vietnam was the keystone. He would therefore attempt to compel the North Vietnamese to end their support for the Front, hoping that, left to its own resources, the NLF would slowly wither away. We could then expect that in the very near future the United States would strike out against the North in some sort of sustained fashion in order to gain the necessary leverage.

We didn't have long to wait. The American strategy of applying force to North Vietnam began in early August with the first bombing raids—ostensibly triggered by the Gulf of Tonkin incident, but in reality part of a long-term plan to force Hanoi to sever her ties with the Southern revolutionaries. Even as it began, though, this strategy was bound to fail. Although the Americans might have believed there were no other options, this particular approach simply didn't take realistic account of our situation. The Saigon government was a brittle reed that might break at any moment under the political and military pressures it was experiencing. With the fate of the Khanh regime hanging by so frail a thread, we could not be induced to draw back from the attack or abandon any of our programs or policies. Despite our acknowledged difficulties, Saigon's instability put us in a position of strength that we saw no reason to give up on bended knee at the negotiating table. At this point the United States was thinking in terms of long-range military pressure. But as the United States moved to escalate the military conflict, we addressed our energies to the political front, knowing that a decisive political victory would gain all our objectives and obviate whatever effort the Americans could make.

But for this there was not much time. American policymakers, after all, were reading the same cards we were. Before too long they would realize that military pressure against Hanoi would be unavailing, at least in the short run. At that point they would be forced to move to shore up the Southern government. And this they could only do by taking on a fighting role in the South Vietnamese countryside. In this way they might buy enough time for the Saigon leadership, such as it was, to work out its problems and assert effective control. With the past decade as prologue, this hope may well have appeared fanciful to some. But Washington was clearly not yet prepared to give up on the issue. Direct intervention might also create sufficient time for Hanoi to feel the screws tightening. We therefore had only a brief period (it turned out to be seven months—the time between Tonkin and the marine landing at Danang) to push the Saigon government into negotiations.

In December of 1964, I received instructions from Phat to sharpen the political struggle further by creating a campaign that would make direct popular overtures to the government for a negotiated end to the civil war and that would attract worldwide as well as domestic attention.

Accordingly, through the Self-Determination Movement, I organized a meeting of ten or twelve forceful Saigonese personalities whose voices, I felt sure, would draw an immediate response from the regime. Our first gatherings were held at my house late in the month, just at the moment Albert Thao returned so unexpectedly from the United States. With Thao hiding in the bedroom, we went about planning our moves. Drawing on the resources of the Self-Determination Movement, we would undertake a petition campaign in Saigon and the province capitals, demanding immediate negotiations with the NLF. We would then present the petition to the government in the full glare of international publicity.

After these preliminary sessions, the Committee to Defend the Peace was formally constituted in the Vo Tanh Street offices of the Self-Determination Movement during the first days of 1965. Its leading figure was Dr. Pham Van Huyen, who had been Diem's commissioner of refugees in 1954. Huyen was a Northerner himself, who had fled from the Communists after the Geneva Accords were signed. His daughter, Mme. Ngo Ba Thanh, was also a member. This outspoken and conspicuously educated woman held law degrees from the universities of Paris and Barcelona and from Columbia University and had taught comparative law at the University of Strasbourg. During the post-Geneva period, she had served as Diem's chief judicial adviser. Among the committee's other members were the artist Dang Van Ky, an influential journalist named Cao Minh Chiem, and Ton That Duong Ky, professor of history at Saigon University and a member of Vietnam's hereditary nobility.

These people lost no time. Leaflets were circulated throughout Saigon and the provinces, urging people to join the petition campaign. The petition itself was printed and taken door to door by groups of enthusiastic student volunteers, who had been organized by the Self-Determination Movement. It denounced American attacks on the North and called on the government to achieve national concord through negotiations "between the two enemy brothers."

As thousands of signatures were gathered, the Peace Committee called a press conference for the evening of February 1, 1965, to be held in a restaurant in the center of Saigon. By this time the regime had realized that a serious affair could be brewing—and they struck, arresting Dr. Huyen, who had been acting as the primary spokesman.

But the press conference went off on schedule anyway, with the artist Ky substituting for Dr. Huyen on the speaker's platform. The restaurant was crowded with foreign as well as Vietnamese reporters as Ky read the petition—Madame Thanh translating into English. Thanh then took the microphone herself to issue a fiery denunciation of her father's arrest.

In the middle of this, the police arrived, anxious to terminate the affair before it got out of hand. But with all the foreign reporters looking on, they hesitated, unsure about what to do. Meanwhile, the committee handed out statements in Vietnamese, French, and English, and Madame Thanh announced a march on the government. By this time, the police had had enough and stopped the proceedings, declaring that the meeting was over and everyone should return home.

Madame Thanh and the others, however, were not the kind of people to be easily put off. Outside the restaurant, the committee and its followers divided into two groups. One marched off toward the Gia Long Palace to present the petition to Pham Khac Suu, the nominal head of state under Khanh, the other to the International

Control Commission office to request that they convey the petition to the Front.

A few days after this tumultuous press conference, I got into work a little later than usual to find two well-dressed visitors waiting for me. When I asked them into my private office, one of them told me that there was "an urgent problem," then introduced himself as a National Police officer. With this he handed me a letter from Pham Van Lieu, director of the National Police, inviting me to meet with him personally. Though my two visitors were as polite as could be, this was clearly the sort of invitation that couldn't be refused. I asked them to wait a bit so that I could give directions to some of the department heads; then, after letting people know that I might be gone for a while, I walked out the door with them.

Once outside, they asked me to ride in their car, but I said, "No thanks, I'll have my own chauffeur take me if you don't mind." Before I knew it, the agents had climbed into the back seat of the company's Ford Falcon, one on either side of me, signaling their own driver to follow behind. When we got to police headquarters, they told my chauffeur that there would be no point in waiting around, that he might as well go back to the sugar company.

Inside, the two led me, not to Pham Van Lieu's office, but to a large interrogation room full of arrested people, who milled around the reception area or sat in front of the twenty or so desks, talking with plainclothes police agents. As I was taking all this in, I started picking out people that I knew, until I recognized almost all of my colleagues from the Self-Determination Movement, as well as the top figures from the Peace Committee. Other well-known people were here also, arguing noisily with the tired-looking interrogators. Apparently the police had made a clean sweep of everyone in Saigon society who had either helped promulgate the petition or had simply signed it.

Nothing about this scene surprised me. Dr. Huyen, arrested just before the press conference, had been followed into jail a day later by lawyer Long, president of the Self-Determination Movement. Since then I had been expecting the government to move strongly against both organizations before the commotion they were generating had a chance to reach a critical mass. My own arrest, I knew, was just a matter of time.

As I sat there awaiting my turn with an interrogator, new people were constantly being led in through the doors: students, workers, businessmen, intellectuals. Among this stream of our supporters, each minute some well-known face would appear. It was as if the city's elite had somehow mistaken the address of an upper-crust social gathering.

When my turn at the desks finally came, I sat down opposite a worn-out, middle-aged police functionary, whose enthusiasm for the day's work was already waning quickly. In a mechanical voice he began asking me about my connections with the Front, making assertions that I courteously denied—with a hint of disdain that he could even suggest such a notion. I knew he would find it hard to believe that someone in my position might be associated with the NLF, any more than he could believe it of the scores of other businessmen, government officials, doctors, and lawyers crowding into the room. If all these people were Vietcong, the only ones left would be the police and the army. Both of us understood that this line of questioning was no more than a formality, and he didn't even react visibly when I declared that, if aspiring to peace was a crime, then I was proud to admit that I was guilty. He looked as if he had heard it before.

After ten minutes or so of this, my interrogator had had enough and motioned to a guard to take me away. "Away" turned out to be not back to the street, but to the jail wing of the police headquarters, where I was escorted into a large cell. It already housed about thirty of my collaborators from the Self-Determination Movement and the Peace Committee. As I walked in, I was greeted by applause and cheers from the cell's inhabitants, as if I were the guest of honor at a surprise party. Each new arrival—and they kept appearing at brief intervals—received the same welcome. The guards seemed almost deferential, looking a bit awed at the collection of luminaries they were being called on to restrain.

I was in this cell for a week when Prime Minister Phan Huy Quat announced that Dr. Huyen, Professor Ky, and the journalist Chiem would be expelled to North Vietnam. These three had been singled out because they were the leaders of the Peace Committee, which had made itself especially obnoxious with its petition and foreign publicity. Their fate was meant as a warning to the rest of us who might be considering further protests. The police complained to me that the Self-Determination Movement had allowed these Peace Committee people to use our offices for meeting space. We had thus aligned ourselves with those who were undermining the nation's government. Such activities, I was informed, were intolerable.

Many of the signatories of the petition were asked to sign a statement declaring that they had been seduced into putting their names on the appeal and that they would sign no similar statement in the future. The leaders of the two organizations, however, were not to get off so lightly. (A Diem period law gave the military jurisdiction over anybody charged with subversive activities.) Lawyer Long, Madame Thanh, artist Ky, teacher Khue, engineer Ly, and myself, together with quite a few of the others, were to be bound over to the Chi Hoa Central Prison, pending a hearing before the Military Tribunal.

At Chi Hoa we quickly found out that life for some of the prisoners could be quite bearable. At least it was for us. Only the entranceway to our cellblock was kept locked, so that we could move around freely. The guards who looked after us were friendly and relaxed. They had no compunctions about going to my wife for gifts of sugar, a custom they knew they could continue after my release. (They did.) We were allowed long periods outdoors and free access to books, newspapers, and almost anything else we might need. Incarceration gave us the opportunity to organize a common life, to cook and eat together, and to discuss exhaustively the issues that preoccupied us. In effect, the police had given us free room, board, and meeting place, allowing us to develop and strengthen our friendships and make plans for the future. In our cells, members of some of Saigon's best families started to feel a sense of solidarity and brotherhood, the kind of emotions that attend on fighting and suffering for a cause. They began to feel like revolutionaries. For a number of them, this was the beginning of careers of political activism that the government would later have cause to regret.

The day following my interrogation, while I was still being held at the police headquarters, my wife came to visit me, bringing fresh clothes and a basket of food. After my transfer to Chi Hoa, she was allowed one visit a week, each time replenishing my little larder and exchanging clean laundry for dirty. Neither of us was particularly concerned about the situation. The family was getting along fine. And I doubted that the government would take further severe action after the deportation of Huyen, Chiem, and Ky. My Front identity, I was certain, was absolutely secure. My wife even felt comfortable enough on this score that on one of her visits she delivered a note congratulating me on "your brave action for the cause of peace and your nation," signed by "Tam Chi," the code name of Huynh Tan Phat.

None of my fellow prisoners felt any more anxiety than I did. We were, after all, the privileged. Even if we were to be dismissed from our jobs, we could always find new ones. There were few highly trained technocrats in Vietnam, and our skills were simply too valuable to sacrifice. Besides this, we knew we could rely on our many family ties, friends, and professional associates for help. In the closely interwoven world of Vietnam, these reciprocal relationships and mutual obligations were the essence of survival, providing a web of security in which everyone participated both by ingrained reflex and vested interest. Among other visitors during my stay at Chi Hoa, was my chief, undersecretary Tuan, who came by to express his support and friendship. The gesture meant a great deal to me. But it was not at all atypical in a society where personal loyalties are characteristically more highly valued than institutional relationships.

Just as we were settling into life at Chi Hoa, the prison opened its doors to another wave of detainees. Albert Thao's coup had come to its inconclusive end several days earlier, and all those arrested now flooded into the cells on the level above ours. During our daily walks and periods outside the cells, the two groups (among the guards we were identified respectively as the "peace group" and the "coup group"), mixed and talked, exchanging news and information and reinforcing each other. Of course none of the military or political leaders connected with Thao's coup suspected—any more than did the peace petitioners—that their efforts had been orchestrated by agents of the Front. Nevertheless, among them they had participated in the NLF's last desperate battle to ward off American military intervention. Two weeks later, on March 8, 1965, American marines landed on the beach at Danang.

It wasn't until August 8 that the Military Tribunal finally convened, charging the Self-Determination Movement leaders with "threatening state security and engaging in subversive activities." A number of other individuals were brought to trial at the same time as part of a general government crackdown against peace activists of every description. Among these was the popular poetess Nguyen Ngoc Suong, charged with undermining the morale of the troops through her poems in praise of peace. She was, said the tribunal president, as dangerous as the legendary Chinese general Truong Luong, who had sapped the will of the enemy by playing sweetly to them on his flute before battle.

The tribunal sentenced Suong to five years in jail for her demoralizing poetry. Her husband, who was a member of the Peace Committee, was given ten years with five years of internal exile. The same sentence was handed down to lawyer Long and teacher Khue. The rest of us were sentenced to prison terms of varying lengths, sentences to be suspended. I received only two years, the result of a $5,000 bribe my wife paid to the tribunal president, a man who was later to become special adviser for security under Thieu.

In front of the tribunal I made a brief statement to the effect that "For the cause of peace I will struggle whenever I find it necessary to do so." Then I went home. I had been in jail for more than six months.

Prison
Once More

As a parting shot, meant to remind me of my continued vulnerability, the tribunal had also seen fit to suspend me from my job for an additional six months. This was a more severe punishment than they may have realized. Vietnam was a country where the French love of titles and place had been superimposed on a native tradition of deference to the mandarinate. The result was a society almost painfully sensitive to the nuances of status. In this world, my position was essential to the credibility I needed to continue my proselytizing and organization work. So, shortly after I got home late in the summer of 1965, I began casting around in earnest for ways to recapture my lapsed prestige.

One step was to petition the government for reconsideration. To Undersecretary Tuan and others in the administration I argued that I had been completely within my rights to work for self-determination as I had. I had committed no crime. Furthermore, by law I could only be removed from my position for incompetence, and no one had ever voiced any questions on that score. Slowly my case made its way to the desk of Prime Minister Phan Huy Quat, where it languished without any hint of a decision.

Meanwhile, I tried another approach. Together with a few of my business friends, I began to develop plans to establish a private bank. We made all the necessary legal and financial arrangements, and started working to acquire the necessary government certification. It was while this red-tap-strewn process was under way that I received an invitation from Undersecretary Tuan to come and see him at his office. He was now ready, he said, to take me back at the sugar monopoly, not as director general this time, but as chief comptroller.

With my job situation finally resolved, I turned again to the work of proselytizing Saigon's upper stratum of bureaucrats and professionals. This sort of political activity, which I had now been carrying on for many years, was still significant in terms of undermining the regime's strength. There was no question, though, that the massive infusion of American troops that had taken place during the past year was forcing us to shift our weight into the military arena. As we had anticipated, intervention had changed the character of the war, requiring a movement away from the focus on political activity that had marked the first part of the struggle.

The military buildup, by which we were striving to meet our enemy's dramatically enhanced strength, was changing the makeup of the revolutionary forces as well as the development of strategy, as more and more Northern troops moved South and Northern cadres began to dominate the political apparatus of the NLF army. In the midst of these momentous changes, I received word through a liaison agent that Tran Bach Dang would shortly want to meet with me to discuss the Front's new urban strategy.

Tran Bach Dang was the permanent Party secretary for the Saigon/Cholon/Giadinh region and was in overall charge of mobilizing the urban intelligentsia. He himself was an extraordinarily effective proselytizer, who had brought numbers of highly placed individuals into the Front's secret network, including not a few industrialists, bankers, and some of Vietnam's best-known writers. He was also chairman of the Youth Liberation Association, a countrywide organization of dedicated younger revolutionaries that some thought of as the Party's Red Guard.

During the second week of June, Dang and I met at the house of one of our friends, the deputy director of a large textile company, to go over the policy decisions that the Front had formulated in what was known as the 1966 Resolution. Generally speaking, this document reflected the recent shift in policy, while striving at the same time to maintain a balance between the political and military dimensions of the conflict. It outlined a governing strategy for the next two years that emphasized both the armed struggle in the countryside and political struggle in the cities. In Saigon the focus was now to be on mobilizing revolutionary activity among young people.

Specifically, we would be looking for new ways to use the city's volatile and often militant youth to heighten the political confrontation between the regime and the urban population. The tone of our thinking on this issue is well expressed by a letter addressed to the Saigon Party Committee in the spring of 1966 by "Comrade Ba" (Le Duan):

> We must use all means and methods to motivate and rally the youth and the women because they represent the principle forces in the political and military struggles in the cities.
>
> In order to rally and organize a large mass of people, we must develop a great number of transitional organizations, operating overtly or semiovertly under many disguised forms. These are designed to induce the masses to respond to our struggle slogans in an easy way and at the same time to cover our core elements, which will be able to operate successfully.
>
> There are many forms to these disguised organizations. We must not be rigid about their forms of organization, their names, their regulations and leadership, provided that they are able to rally the masses and that we are able to transform them step by step according to the direction of the revolution, maintain and develop the ranks of the masses, uphold the revolutionary spirit of the masses through various forms of struggle from low to higher levels. The important thing is to maintain within the core of these organizations elements that are Party members or loyal and reliable youths and women.*

The American troop landings, when they finally happened, had deprived us of the overwhelming sense of urgency that was widely felt by a people frightened of the consequences of intervention. It

* Indochina Archives document, "Letter from Comrade Ba to Saigon Regional Party Committee," p. 27.

would now be necessary to be more careful in orchestrating movement toward the general uprising that was still our objective. Emotional and fearless, the youth groups could be used to catalyze other factions and movements, and to provide cadres who could direct the street revolution when it came.

There was nothing actually new in this focus. The leadership had always recognized the potential of youthful elements to function as the prime motivator in bringing about revolutionary crises. The Vanguard Youth had been the principle "motor" in precipitating the insurrection during the August Revolution of 1945. In 1965 we had resurrected the name for what was envisioned as a militant organization of young people recruited from the high schools, universities, and factories by Dang's Liberation Youth cadres. This effort, however, had failed to generate much enthusiasm and had been allowed to lapse.

In preparing for a fresh crescendo of protests, Dang now asked me to mobilize a citywide youth movement that would gather all the various youth organizations not yet associated with us—the Buddhist youth, Catholic youth, high school and university student associations, working-class youth, and others—to provide the core of our renewed effort to bring about the general uprising. This was not to be done directly. Instead the aim would be to create an umbrella organization that we would control surreptitiously, bringing forceful antigovernment leadership into play only when conditions had sufficiently matured. Once again I would have to go public.

In the preliminary planning sessions I held with Ta Ba Tong, the Front's adjunct chief for mobilizing the masses, I was introduced to several support personnel. One of these was Ba Tra ("Number Three Tea") who would be my liaison agent. Ba Tra was a Vietminh resistance veteran, the brother-in-law of Dr. Cung, one of my original NLF colleagues. He seemed to be an energetic and determined cadre, although his speech was larded with revolutionary phraseology— something that made me a bit nervous in light of the open nature of the activities we were planning.

Calling on the reputation as a dissident I had acquired through my work with the Self-Determination and peace groups and by my imprisonment, I sent out word to the different youth leaders that we should organize a meeting. We could dramatically increase the youth bloc leverage, I told them, if all the groups could find a way to act in concert. The response was enthusiastic, and I set up a meeting for June 30 at a house in the suburb Thu Duc. Here I actively took the lead, proposing that we create a comprehensive organization that could coordinate political activity. My suggestions were welcomed and generated a good deal of discussion, the result of which was the establishment of the Young People's Association of South Vietnam. I was named the first president—though at age forty-three, I wasn't quite sure that I qualified.

During the meetings and discussions that followed this initial gathering, Ba Tra took more of an active role than I would have wished, talking at length about the spirit of sacrifice that must imbue everyone and of the need to struggle ceaselessly with no thoughts of giving in. No particular harm came of it. But his lack of discretion was disconcerting, especially considering that his position as liaison agent demanded extremes of caution.

But though Ba Tra's strident manner concerned me, he was proving to be an effective administrator, who completed his sometimes detailed and complex tasks promptly and well. By this time my own life had entered high gear, and efficiency in those who were assisting me had become an especially precious commodity. I was now attempting to juggle three roles at once. With my new comptroller's job as a front, I continued to cultivate the Saigon intellectuals and managerial class, working now toward the development of a Third Force of independent nationalists, which was not destined to materialize formally (though I could not have guessed it then) for another three years. While this proselytizing activity was covert, pursued in an underplayed fashion calculated to avoid detection by the police or suspicion by contacts who proved unresponsive, my youth work was a different story.

Here I was a public figure. In my role as president of the Young People's Association, I was in frequent contact with the leaders of Saigon's many youth clubs and organizations, holding meetings, dinners, parties, doing my utmost to bring them in—offering leadership posts in my movement, doing favors, utilizing whatever blandishments suggested themselves. I held regular monthly meetings of all the leaders, those who had joined and those who were still prospective. I organized general get-togethers of young people, where we would discuss the heavy responsibility of youth during this difficult period in our country's history, putting forward the example of the morally committed young people in more developed countries (France, the only Western nation I knew well, was my favorite model).

All of this was watched with polite interest by the police. Though on occasion I would gingerly approach political ground, it was never too near and always with a patriotic flourish. We did nothing to oppose the government outwardly, never expressing any sympathy with the Front or discussing revolution directly. I was indeed not organizing for an immediate revolutionary objective, but to create ties and sympathy, to seek and exploit common feelings, and to raise a spirit of ardent nationalism—which could later be tapped. I was working toward an apparatus of control, a network ready for the manipulation that would come in time.

The police regarded me as an irritating, untrustworthy, and certainly eccentric individual, but not as someone out to damage the regime. To further the image I was seeking to project as an unstable though essentially harmless political idealist, I began to mold my private life on the pattern of Saigon's fun-loving and frivolous upper classes. I continued to function competently at the comptroller's job, but without hinting at any excessive zeal for work. Weekends I would spend with my wife and daughter at our beach house on Cap St. Jacques or in the mountain resort of Dalat, socializing, playing tennis, and swimming. Weeknights I joined my friends at nightclubs and restaurants, or helped arrange the surprise parties and "four color card game" evenings that were essential fare on the social menu. My salary, almost three times that of a cabinet minister, barely covered expenses. But I was confident that the watchers had classified my Young People's Association activities as nothing more than the political do-goodism with which Saigon's wealthy occasionally entertained themselves. In this whirlwind of effort and pretense, the year passed quickly.

At a quarter after twelve on June 16, 1967, I was driving home from work to have lunch with my wife. Suddenly a car cut in front of me and jammed to a halt, forcing me into the curb. Before I was aware of what was happening, two men had jumped out, wrenched open the front doors, and knocked me away from the wheel into the middle of the seat. I knew immediately that these were security people, but I managed to yell at them, "What do you think you're doing? What are you, gangsters?" As we drove off, they showed me their security IDs and said that General Loan had "invited me to come in for a talk." Nguyen Ngoc Loan was South Vietnam's secret police chief, who would later, during the Tet offensive, catch the whole world's attention when a cameraman snapped his summary execution of a Vietcong captive by firing a shot into his head in the middle of the street. Even earlier Loan was not known for the gentleness of his methods, and this "invitation" was certainly a good deal rougher and more unnerving than my previous arrest had been. As we drove toward Cholon, Saigon's Chinatown, I began to protest that this was not the way to security police headquarters. The only answer I got was a hard shove back into the seat. Catching my breath, I noticed the Hoa Binh marketplace pass by outside the window, with its bustle of vendors and housewives. After a few more blocks, we pulled up in front of a villa that I recognized as the old Binh Xuyen headquarters, a place the sect had used as a casino and center for its drug empire. As we got out of the car, I saw next to it what looked like an abandoned sawmill, or lumberyard, surrounded by barbed wire.

Inside, my captors pushed me into what must have been the receiving room, where they ripped my belt out of my pants and took my shoes off. They also confiscated my papers. Then they walked me down a corridor into the office of the chief of this place. The door swung open, and I found myself face to face with a burly, uniformed man, whose slit eyes and brutal expression were fixed on me with a concentrated hatred. I thought to myself immediately, Here is a butcher! (I was shortly to learn that he was in fact a professional torturer and had personally done in many people. At the moment I didn't know that, but everything about him bespoke sadism and ferocity.) My mind raced for a strategy, some plan to deal with him. They couldn't possibly know about my Front identity. They must have gotten fed up with my agitation finally, that's all, and brought me here to teach me a lesson. Of course they'd probe for a connection, but (I thought) if I deny everything, what can they do? Put up a resolute facade, play the role of the aggrieved citizen to the hilt, and ultimately I'd come out of this safely.

While these thoughts flashed through my head, the butcher roared out at me, "You are Vietcong! I arrest you!" Before I could open my mouth to answer, he screamed, *"Do you want to see your comrade?"*

Then he turned his slit eyes toward a guard standing next to the door and bellowed, "Bring in that bastard Ba Tra!"

All my strength seemed to drain from my body. Ba Tra! My throat suddenly constricted, making it hard to breathe. It was as if an immense fatigue had sprung on me out of nowhere, leaving me with neither energy nor willpower. There was no point now in denying anything, I told myself. My frantic efforts to think out a strategy shut down as if someone had thrown a switch, and I was overcome by utter helplessness.

After a pause to let his revelation sink in, the butcher started talking again, more softly now, but with a snarling edge to his voice.

"You know, I have the right to beat you to death. You and all the other Vietcong they bring in here. There aren't any laws here to protect you. In this place you are mine."

Somehow I found the voice to answer, saying something about loving the country and following my conscience. The words came directly from my heart, though they couldn't have meant a thing under the circumstances. This man, I knew, was only telling me the truth. Communists (and all Vietcong were considered Communists) were specifically excluded from the protection of the law by Article 4 of South Vietnam's constitution.

At this point the guard returned, shoving Ba Tra in front of him.

The former zealot stared at the floor, unable to look me in the face. He had inside his head the entire secret network involved in organizing Saigon's upper classes. I knew in a moment that, if he had betrayed me, he had betrayed us all.*

I said nothing. There was nothing to say.

With a jerk of his thumb, the butcher motioned the guards to take me out. Grabbing me under the arms, they manhandled me out the door and around a corner leading into another corridor. The scene that presented itself in this hallway struck me with horror and a fright so terrible that I felt I had lost my soul. Sprawled out on the floor the whole length of the corridor were people chained together by the ankles. Many of their faces were bloody and swollen; here and there, limbs jutted out at unnatural angles. Some writhed in agony, others just lay and stared dully. From the tangle of bodies came groans and the sound of weeping, and the air was filled with a low, continuous wail. My heart began to race. On one side of the hallway were doors that apparently led to the interrogation rooms. From behind these came curses and spasmodic screams of pain.

About two-thirds of the way down the hall, I was prodded into one of the rooms. It was small, about ten feet square, with a desk and chair near the far wall. An interrogator sat behind the desk, but at first I did not look closely at him. On the floor to one side of the desk lay a woman—unconscious, her face as white as a corpse.† At the back of the room and to the left was an alcove that had once been a bathroom. A board covered the toilet bowl, and on the board lay another woman, also motionless. As I was taking this in with a kind of numbed disbelief, I was shoved into the chair in front of the desk opposite the interrogator. I was next.

* In fact, Ba Tra had been arrested a week or ten days earlier than I, and under interrogation had denounced all the secret cadres with whom his job as liaison agent put him in contact. He had broken down under the threat of torture, it was learned, without actually having been maltreated. Later on, the Front condemned him to death for treason, and he was assassinated during the Tet offensive of 1968.

† The woman on the floor, though I only got to know her later, was the wife of Tran Bach Dang. She had been given repeated electric shocks and had passed out. Several years afterward, she was to become a member of the PRG delegation to the Paris peace talks.

This officer, whose face I cannot seem to remember, pushed some paper and a pencil across to me and told me to write out a full description of my activities. Then he got up from the chair and went out, leaving me and the two unconscious women alone. I wrote, for what I think must have been several hours, describing my part in the Self-Determination Movement and the Peace Committee, and my work with the Saigon youth groups—everything I thought Ba Tra might have disclosed, taking care to mention nobody he was not in a position to compromise. During this entire time, the women lay there without either moving or uttering a sound. Nobody came in to check them, to see if they were alive or dead.

Sometime after I had finished writing, the officer came back, looked over the papers, then took them away. It was only then that the woman on the floor began to stir. Slowly she half-opened her eyes and looked cautiously around. Not seeing the interrogator, she stared at me and whispered hoarsely, "You don't know who I am, but I know you. Ba Tra has given them everything. Only tell them what he knows." I nodded, trying to get across that I had done exactly that.

A bit later a guard came in with a bowl of rice and a little dried fish for me. Only now did I realize how ravenously hungry I was. I gulped it down, wondering when the interrogator would return. But no one else came into the room. Madame Tran and the other woman continued to lie there, moaning from time to time. I sat in the chair, unable to gather my thoughts, my mind a vacuum.

It must have been close to midnight before another guard came in to take me back to the chief's office. This time the butcher didn't scream, but his face still seemed bloated with rage. "You," he said, "are a Communist Party member."

I denied it. "I admit I'm in the Front, but I'm not in the Party. I've never been a Communist." This seemed to irritate him.

"Look, don't you understand. Ba Tra has told us everything, about you and about all your friends. We know you are a Communist."

"No, you're wrong," I answered. "I've never been a Communist. Ba Tra doesn't know anything about that."

"You must be a very stupid person. Don't you know what happens to you here if you don't admit it? Do I have to spell it out for you? We have measures here for people like you—heavy measures."

I looked at his eyes and told him again that I was not a Party member, trying to will him to believe that I was telling the truth. For a moment he stared at me, then turned to the guard and said, "Take him out."

Holding my arm, the guard led me to a nearby room that looked like a medieval torture chamber. Iron hooks and ropes hung from the ceiling, as did chains with ankle and wrist rings. These latter devices were well known among the activists and Front prisoners, who called them the Airplane. In one corner was a dynamo. Several tables and benches stood in the middle of the floor or were pushed up against the walls.

They pushed me down onto one of these low benches, on my back with my head hanging over the end. Then they handcuffed my hands under the bench, and shackled my legs to the other end. Pressing a compress over my eyes and nose, they wrenched my mouth open and began pouring soapy water down my throat. I tried to twist my head away but couldn't. I gagged, unable to gasp in any air. I was suffocating—then I lost consciousness.

When I came to, one of the guards was pressing heavily on my stomach, forcing me to vomit. Everything came gushing out, the water, whatever else had been in me, and the horrible bitter taste of gastric juices—a taste that filled my mouth for days and which I still vividly remember. (Although I didn't know it then, the soapy water kills all intestinal flora, leaving a permanently damaged digestive system.) I jerked my head around, struggling to avoid drowning in the flow of my own vomit.

When I had finished choking up the soapy water, the guards unchained me and dragged me down the hall to the cell that was now to be my home. It was a bare cubicle about six feet by four. There was no furniture of any sort, no bed or even a wooden plank, no toilet or bucket, not even a hole in the ground. I collapsed onto the cold cement floor, staring into the darkness. A thin light filtered in from the corridor through the barred upper half of the wooden door.

I lay there for what might have been two days, perhaps three. It was impossible to judge time in that perpetual grayness. From the depths of the hallway came the intermittent cries of those being tortured. I only sensed the guards as they appeared at the door to leave a bowl of rice on the floor. Once or twice I summoned the energy to knock for someone to take me to the bathroom. The rest of the time it was as if I were paralyzed. Except for the alarming swelling and constant pain in my abdomen, I felt nothing.

After several days in this state of collapse, I was taken back to the butcher. I knew he would insist again that I admit I was a Communist, but I was still intent on holding out. It was part of the regime's ideology that anyone who opposed them must be a Communist. They could not accept the fact that there might be people who hated them for the travesty they had made of the country's life, for their intolerance and corruption and cold indifference to the lot of their countrymen. Any opposition, as far as they were concerned, had to have an insidious external source, and they were going to label it for what it was and stamp it out. I was determined that as far as I could help it, they would not get any satisfaction from me.

This time around, the butcher took what he no doubt considered a more humane approach.

"OK," he told me, "now you know the kind of thing that can happen to you here. It can get worse, much worse. But none of this is necessary. You know what I want from you. Once I have your admission, we can forget all about the rest of it."

I didn't answer, but kept staring in front of me, avoiding his attempt to engage my eyes.

"No one," he went on, "can stand up to me. No one is tough enough. I'm telling you this honestly. There's no use in even trying. Admit it now; don't put yourself through what's going to happen to you when you'll only end up admitting everything anyway."

I answered him with a bravery that I certainly did not feel. "I am not a Communist," I said. "No matter what you think I am. I can't tell you what you want to hear. There's nothing I can do about it, no matter what happens."

The butcher just shrugged, dismissing me back to the cell for two more days to think about it some more. By this time I felt a little better and was starting to eat the bowl of rice and scraps of dried fish that was handed into the cell twice a day. Then one night I was shaken awake and led back to the office for another round of brow-beating. This time, though, the guards didn't return me to my cell after the brief interrogation, but instead herded me down the hall to the torture chamber.

Inside, they tore my shirt off, attached electrodes to my nipples, and began to crank the dynamo. As they turned the handle, brightly colored stars began to dance and sparkle in front of me. Then a sudden explosion of pain ripped through my body, and I had just enough time to feel my eyes pop out of their sockets before I blacked out.

The next thing I knew I was lying on a floor somewhere. I was surprised that I could make out people lying around me. Obviously the electric shock had not blinded me, even though the pain in my eyes had been excruciating. I tried to sit up, but found I couldn't. Then I saw that I was in the hallway outside the interrogation rooms, the place that had frightened me so when I had first arrived five or six days earlier. Other prisoners were sprawled to the right and left, all of us chained together by the ankles. One of them was massaging my temples. The same low wail filled my ears; it was coming from all around me.

I didn't stay in the hallway long. One of the guards noticed that I had come to, and he stooped to unlock my ankles. Then he dragged me off and dumped me on the floor of my cell. I lived there lost in a haze, in a kind of semicomatose state between wakefulness and sleep. I remember being taken to the butcher's office a number of times, but I can't recall what happened there. I lay in the dark on the hard cement without eating or sleeping, listening to the screaming night after night and day after day. Time passed, punctuated only by the rice bowl that appeared regularly on the floor next to me. I was conscious only that I was deep into a spiritual and mental crisis from which I might never emerge. At some point, I realized that I wanted to die, that not only had I no fear of death, I welcomed it. I willed it.

The next occurrence I distinctly recall was being led back to the office to find my wife standing there next to the butcher. She was crying. Suddenly I found myself weeping too. The butcher strode out, and we were alone. As my wife unpacked a basket crammed with food and clothes, she began to tell me about the family, our daughter, and my parents. We both cried silently as we spoke. I could hardly force the words from my mouth. I had been taken, she said, almost a month ago. She had searched all over, trying desperately to uncover some clue to my whereabouts; finally she had bribed a high National Police official for the information.

"You should tell them," she said, "that you are a Communist. What difference does it make? It'll keep them from torturing you. I'll try to find a way to get you transferred to the National Police prison. Here they can kill you, and nobody will ever know. It might be better at the National Police. I'll find somebody, somebody who can arrange it. Just stay alive until I get it done. . . ."

With this, the butcher came back and told my wife it was time for her to go. When she had, he said to me, "Now I'll give you some time to think over what your wife told you." At the time it puzzled me that he knew what had passed between us. But subsequently my wife told me that she had only been allowed to visit on condition that she try to persuade me to sign an admission.

In any event, her words had made their impression. Back in my cell I couldn't think of anything else. By the time they brought me to the office again, I was ready.

"You know," I told the butcher, "I am not a Communist. I never have been. But if you want me to say I am, I'm prepared to do that. What do you want exactly?"

With this, he motioned me to sit down and gave me a pencil and paper. "Just write that you are an active member of the Party," he said.

I wrote it. Then I had to rewrite my previous description to include the "fact" that I was a Communist, even assigning myself a date on which I had supposedly joined.

When I left the butcher's office, I was not shoved back into my dark hole. Instead, the guards took me to a collective cell, a garagelike place with only a cement floor to sleep on but with thirty or forty other prisoners to share the days and nights. I felt as if I had climbed out of hell and had reentered the world of the living.

About ten days later, I was bundled into a car and driven to the National Police headquarters. My wife had indeed found someone else to bribe. I found out later it was the butcher himself. His price had been $6,000.

Tet and
a Secret
Exchange

Had she known about conditions at the headquarters prison, it isn't likely that my wife would have paid anything to anyone. As soon as I arrived, I was put into solitary confinement. My new cell was slightly larger than the one at the secret police jail, about six by six, and it boasted a cement bench on one side, so there was no need to lie on the floor. In the far corner was a hole that served as a toilet. The door was solid steel, with a small port that could be opened only from the outside. Through this port my food was handed in twice a day. Inside, the cell was pitch dark. There was no window and no bulb. Whenever the guard opened the port to stick in my rice bowl or say something to me, a square of light from the corridor would shine into my eyes. Other than that it was perpetual night. I was like an animal in a cave.

In this place I was to exist for the next six months. There were no exercise periods, no interrogations, nothing. I was simply thrown in and forgotten. Psychologists might term what I was experiencing "sensory deprivation." I thought of the cell as my coffin. And in this coffin I just lay, feeling an immense fatigue the entire time, as if I were physically and mentally debilitated. I have read accounts by others who have gone through similar experiences. I am sure that everyone in such a situation reacts differently. In my own struggle to remain sane, my body and mind seemed almost to short-circuit—

leaving me in a condition of reduced functioning, where all the vital activities simply wound down. It was like being in a state of suspended animation, which, as far as I knew, might last forever. I was aware that the food port would open twice a day, that I would pass out my empty rice bowl and be handed a full one. Once a week I would be led, stumbling and blinking, down the hall to take a shower.

What saved me from lapsing into permanent catatonia, I think, was the prison grapevine, which came alive each night. Putting my mouth right up next to the crack in the food port, I could talk softly to my neighbors on either side. Gluing my ear to the same crack, I could hear their return whispers, telling me about themselves and about their neighbors next to them, and so on down the corridor of isolation cells.

My immediate neighbors turned out to be two NLF cadres, whom I had met briefly in the common cell at the secret police jail. They too had been tortured before their transfer here, a good deal more severely than I had been. Both were high-ranking Party organizers who worked (as I did) under Tran Bach Dang and had also been arrested in the Ba Tra debacle. One, Tran Van Kieu, was chief of the Saigon/Cholon/Giadinh Workers' Committee, while the other, Mme. Le Thi Rieng, headed the Committee for Women.

Kieu and Rieng had been part of the Proselytizing Committee, which ordinarily met once a month at various safe houses in Saigon— including at times my own. Unaware of Ba Tra's disclosures, the two cadres had been caught at one of these meetings. Whereas the secret police had had no reason to truly believe that I was a Communist, Kieu and Rieng were in fact bona fide Party members. As such they had been subjected to what the butcher called heavy measures, and both were suffering a great deal of pain from infected wounds, which were of course going unattended.

With our ears pressed up against the doors, straining to catch each other's words, as well as any sound of guards coming into the hall, we talked about how we might be able to get antibiotics smuggled in and messages carried out. We shared deep fears for people in our networks, whose fates we were unaware of. I was especially nervous, since any ill-advised meeting at my home would endanger my wife, who—though she stood firmly behind me—was entirely nonpolitical in her own right. She had been extremely uncomfortable with my activities ever since I revealed my Front association to her during my first prison stay.

Besides these guarded and hurried whispers, there was at first no other diversion from the interior world in which I existed. After a time, though, another lifeline opened up—the visits my wife was now permitted to make once a month, for which I would be brought down to the reception room, almost blind and very nearly mute. These visits were not happy occasions, particularly for my wife, who watched with horror her husband's deterioration visit by visit. But for me they were something else to hold on to, something to keep me connected to the world outside my coffin.

But these brief and fragile links to the outside only retarded my progress into an interior universe. Gradually I paid less and less attention to the occasional intrusions into the blackness. By the middle of November, I had been in the cell for four months. I no longer hoped to survive.

I would have taken heart had I known that Tran Bach Dang had made contact with the American embassy in an attempt to set up a prisoner exchange. Many of Dang's chief Saigon cadres—including his wife, the woman on the interrogation-room floor—had been rounded up after Ba Tra's arrest, and the Front was now offering its highest-ranking American prisoners in an attempt to recover some of its losses.

The Americans were interested and began meeting with Dang's deputy, a cadre named Sau Ha. Both sides strove mightily to keep these negotiations secret from other parties. Somewhere along the line, though, Air Marshal Ky and his partner, Nguyen Van Thieu (they were now vice president and president respectively), had become aware that talks were going on and had made an attempt to disrupt them. Unhappy with the idea of the Americans and NLF negotiating behind their backs, they had Sau Ha tracked from one of the meetings and had arrested him.

It was at this point that I learned something was up. Shortly before Christmas, Kieu and Rieng were taken away, and Madame Dang was moved into the cell next to mine. The night she arrived, she whispered through the door that she had heard a trade of some sort was being discussed. A few days later, she too was taken away. No one on the corridor had any information about what had happened to her. But we assumed that the rumors were true and that an exchange had in fact taken place.

What had really happened was somewhat more complicated. When the Americans found out about negotiator Sau's arrest, they were enraged. Tran Bach Dang had bitterly denounced their failure to insure the negotiator's safety, and fearing for the lives of their officers being held by the Front, the Americans had now brought heavy pressure to bear for Sau Ha's release. Then, as a gesture of goodwill, they forced the government to free Madame Dang as well.

But the hard-line faction within the regime and its police had still not given up their attempt to compromise the Americans. From Sau Ha, the police had confiscated the list of those people the Front wanted returned. Looking for a way to convince the Front of American bad faith, someone ordered the execution of the top two people on this list—my former neighbors Kieu and Madame Rieng. Of course, none of us on isolation row were aware of the background of these events, but a bizarre chance later allowed us to learn of the murders of our colleagues.

At the end of January Kieu and Rieng had been taken out of their cells and loaded into a prison transfer van. Ostensibly on their way to some other jail, they had been gunned down by their guards inside the van. The story of this incident became known only because a third prisoner in the van had also been shot but had awkwardly survived her execution. After the shootings, the prison guards had driven to Cho Quan Hospital to unload the bodies, telling the orderlies that these were Vietcong who had been killed in street fighting. But on examination it turned out that one of the corpses was still alive.

The third person was an ethnic Chinese labor leader who worked at Vinatexo, the country's largest textile plant. She had been organizing

Mme. Le Thi Rieng, head of the Committee for Women and my neighbor in the isolation row at the National Police Prison. She was murdered by the police in 1967.

the many other women of Chinese descent who worked in the plant and was suspected by the government of being a Chinese agent. After she had sufficiently recovered from her wounds, this woman was returned to the prison, and before long her story was the chief item of news on the prison grapevine. All of this—Madame Dang's disappearance and then the murders of Kieu and Rieng—created waves of excitement in the isolation cells, for whose inhabitants any news at all was a valuable distraction.

In fact, my own isolation had been ended a week or so prior to the circulation of the murder story. One day the door of my cell had opened unexpectedly, and another prisoner was pushed in. If I was astonished to have company, I was even more overjoyed to find that my new cellmate was Dinh Xang, president of the Chamber of Industry and a longtime friend. Though not an NLF member, Xang had supported the Front in various ways. Occasionally, we had used his house for meetings, and it was through this connection that Xang had come into contact with Ba Tra. Subsequently, he too had been grabbed in the mid-June roundup. Xang's presence did wonders for my state of mind. Whereas before I had simply lain on the cement bench staring into the blackness, now companionship and discourse reentered my world, challenging the disorientation into which I was rapidly sinking.

One night, perhaps a week after Xang had joined me, our talk was interrupted by the distant sound of exploding firecrackers. Tet Mau Than, the Lunar New Year, was announcing itself in its customary fashion. It was January 31, 1968. (We didn't know that the government had banned all fireworks and firecrackers that year and the sounds we were hearing had a different origin.) But as the popping noises got louder and nearer, we realized that we were listening to small-arms fire. Then the heavy thud of larger guns joined in.

All of a sudden the prison came alive with shouting and the sound of guards running through the halls. A coup was under way! Xang and I guessed it immediately. But who could be behind it? As we speculated about the firing, we began to make out the distinctive crack of Chinese-made AK47s. Outside in the hallways the commotion grew. The guards seemed to be in a frenzy—rushing all over, screaming orders and curses at each other, and slamming doors with great resounding clangs. One yanked open our food port and yelled, "If they get in, we'll shoot everybody! Understand?" The unimaginable was happening—Vietcong were in the city, obviously in force. Now we could hear helicopters hovering near the prison and bullhorns blaring at people not to go out in the street.

As we listened, our ears pressed up against the door, the battle seemed to flare around us. There was no doubt now that the police headquarters itself was under attack. In the confusion and staccato sounds of firing, I found myself thinking that this must be the general uprising and military offensive that the 1966 resolution had directed us to prepare for. My entire being was focused on the fighting outside and the shouts of the guards, trying to judge what was happening. I prayed the attackers would break in and free us. I was obsessed by the thought of freedom.

For the next day or so the fighting continued, becoming more and

more sporadic and distant, then finally dying out altogether. Whatever
had happened outside, the temporary exhilaration within the cells
quickly evaporated, giving way again to the daily battle against tedium
and darkness, made worse now by the deflation of hopes. Once again
our bowls of rice and dried fish started appearing twice a day at the
food port. During the battle, the guards had simply forgotten to
feed us.

Sometime toward the end of February, three weeks or so after
Tet, a jailer appeared at my door and said briskly, "Prisoner Truong,
bring everything with you and follow me." These were ominous
words. My first thought was that now they were going to shoot me.
You were only told to bring everything with you if you were going
to be either transferred somewhere or eliminated. And there was no
reason to transfer me anywhere. Kieu and Madame Rieng had been
executed. Now, I thought, it's my turn. Curiously, the prospect didn't
frighten me. For eight months, in the secret police jail and now here,
I had been living in darkness, for most of that time without a soul to
talk to. It had been for me a period of practically unrelieved despair,
when I had often questioned whether I was still sane. I had already
discovered that death held no particular horrors.

The guard led me down the stairs, walking slowly as I shuffled
along next to him, then into the office of the prison director. Here
were several more policemen and two women, both of whom I
recognized. One was Sau No, the one whom I had seen lying across
the toilet in the secret police interrogation room. The other was
Duy Lien, a clandestine agent for the Front in the Saigon/Cholon/
Giadinh area. Sau No's left arm hung limply at her side, a result (it
turned out) of electric shocks administered by the secret police./

I exchanged glances with the women, to give them a sign that we
were going to be killed. Their expressions registered the same exhausted resignation that I suppose was in my face. Then we took our
little bundles and marched outside to a transfer van waiting in the
courtyard, just as Kieu and Rieng had done. Although I had not been
outside for so long, I didn't even notice the sun or the air. I considered myself dead already.

As the van drove off, our guards sat opposite us, staring impassively ahead. I caught myself watching them closely, wondering when they would unlimber their guns and start shooting. After about ten minutes, the van stopped, and we were forced to get out. We had pulled up at a place I recognized, not far from the Gia Long High School. Parked in front of the van was an American army Red Cross truck and several American military cars.

The three of us were led to the truck and helped in through the back doors. Inside, two Americans dressed in civilian clothes sat on benches along one side. They gestured for us to sit down, greeting us in impeccable Vietnamese. One asked, *"Coso khong?"* ("Are you afraid?") To which Duy Lien answered, "There's nothing to be afraid of. Why, were you afraid during Tet?"

"Me?" said the American. *"Suc may!"* ("Hardly!")

As the truck moved off, a few scraps of conversation went back and forth, mostly between Lien and one of the Americans. I heard the words dimly, trying to focus on what this strange turn of events might mean.

After a while the truck stopped, and we climbed out, finding ourselves in a residential neighborhood in the vicinity of the Tan Son Nhut airport. Here we were taken into a house where several other Americans—military people this time—were waiting for us. At first I found it difficult to concentrate on anything except the luxury of the place, the comfortable furniture and the air-conditioning. The fabric covering the sofa I sat down on seemed to have a luscious, velvety texture. I am sure there was nothing special about it or about the house either. But to my raveled senses it might as well have been the Taj Mahal.

Almost immediately an American major appeared and sat down across from us. One of the others brought in Coke and a plate of cookies and put them on the coffee table in front of our sofa. As the major spoke, the talkative American from the Red Cross truck translated into Vietnamese. We had been brought here as part of a prisoner exchange. Soon we would be handed over to our own people. Meanwhile we would stay in this house and rest. I could hardly believe what I was hearing.

I was still taking it in when one of the soldiers asked us to come with him upstairs. Here he showed me my room, then took the women to another bedroom down the hall. I looked around at a bed with clean white sheets on it, a set of terry-cloth towels laid out on the spread. Next door was a bathroom with a hot-water shower. The whole thing seemed like a four-star hotel. But all of these dazzling luxuries were lost in the overwhelming thought of joining our comrades in the Maquis.*

We stayed in this "hotel" (probably a CIA safe house) for two days, waiting for the Front to make contact. For all three of us the excitement and anticipation generated feelings of vigor and renewed life. I began to lose the sense that I was living in a fog, in which other people and things had only a vague and shadowy existence. I felt as if I was emerging from a sort of semideath.

On the second day, a Front representative arrived at the house and introduced himself to us. Both Madame Lien and Sau No recognized him at once as a liaison officer they had often worked with. The liaison talked for a while with the major, then left, telling us to be ready to travel the following day.

The next morning over breakfast, the major handed us several presents: a small booklet, a radio, and a packet of Vietnamese money. When we refused to accept them, he insisted, saying that the booklet contained an urgent communication that had to be delivered to the highest NLF authorities. After talking it over among ourselves, we decided to take the booklet, but refuse the money and radio. We didn't need the money, and the radio, we thought, might contain some sort of electronic homing device.

As soon as the liaison arrived, the five of us got into one of the

---

* I have been using the French word *Maquis* ("resistance movement") because it is the equivalent of the Vietnamese "Bung," which is what the guerrillas in the South generally called themselves. "Bung" translates literally as "marsh" or "swampland," the common terrain of the Mekong Delta. "Rung," the word for "jungle," would often be shortened to a simple *r* when it referred to the jungle strongholds.

cars parked in front of the house, the major driving, the liaison next to him, and the three of us in back. An American MP jeep preceded us, another followed as we moved off in the direction of the airport. Entering Tan Son Nhut, we drove across the tarmac to a waiting helicopter, feeling as if we had vanquished fate.

Once we were seated, the helicopter took off immediately, South Vietnam's countryside unfolding under us in what appeared to my starved eyes as a profusion of beauty. We flew for about half an hour before setting down on a soccer field in what I was pretty sure was the Trang Bang district, about fifty miles northwest of Saigon. On the field a Southern army captain—chief of security for the area—was waiting for us. The American major exchanged a few words with the captain, telling him to make sure security for this trip was tight. Then a Lambretta three-wheeler drove up, and we all piled in, except for the major. There were no handshakes and no good-byes.

The Lambretta took us ten or twelve miles down a bumpy country lane, stopping finally at a little roadside coffee shop. Here we had something to drink while the liaison checked to make sure we hadn't been followed. When he was satisfied, he sent the captain and the Lambretta back, and ushered us onto another three-wheeler. After driving twenty minutes or so we pulled to a halt at a spot where a jungle path crossed the road. Here we got off and began to walk into the bush.

About two kilometers down this path, we stopped, expecting to see the guerrilla unit that, according to the liaison, was supposed to meet us here. But nobody was waiting, and when after another ten minutes they still hadn't appeared, we decided to keep moving, afraid of going back and half-suspecting that we were being tracked. In our weakened condition, the three of us could only walk slowly, and we found we needed to stop and rest frequently. Perhaps an hour later we were surprised by a group of guerrillas moving down the trail in the direction we were coming from.

By incredible chance, the leader of this group was Duy Lien's husband. They hadn't seen each other for almost a year and could not believe that they had met in the middle of the jungle under such circumstances. Lien's husband had heard nothing about a prisoner exchange and was not there looking for us. His armed propaganda unit was on an entirely different mission, as part of the second round of the offensive that had been initiated at Tet. While Lien and her husband went off to spend a few minutes alone, the rest of us sat down to talk, eagerly gathering in the guerrillas' news of events since our arrest. Before long, though, the Liens were back; the unit was on a tight schedule that even such a remarkable encounter couldn't be allowed to disrupt. Before moving off, Lien detailed four of his men to escort us back to their headquarters. Then he left, looking over his shoulder toward his wife, who gazed at him until the unit had disappeared among the trees. It was the last she was to see of him. A month later we heard he had been killed when the propaganda unit was caught in a B-52 attack on its way home from the mission.*

On the back seats of our new escorts' bicycles, we made better progress, arriving before too long at the headquarters that had been established to direct the 1968 offensives. Here we met Mai Chi Tho, the brother of Le Duc Tho who would later become Henry Kissinger's adversary in Paris. Mai Chi Tho was second in charge of the Saigon/Cholon/Giadinh Party apparatus, a man who, though he looked and sounded almost exactly like his brother, was as jovial and expansive as Le Duc Tho was taciturn and cold. He embraced us warmly and listened as we reported what had happened since we left the prison. We gave him the major's booklet and laughed about the radio, speculating on what kind of deviousness the Americans might have been up to. Meanwhile, Tho had a message sent to COSVN (Central Office South Vietnam), informing them of our arrival and asking instructions. The reply came immediately: We were to report as soon as possible, using whatever routes were safest.

But whatever the route, the trip to COSVN would be a difficult and dangerous one, and none of us was healthy. To try to regather a bit of strength before undertaking this trek, we decided to rest. It was a week before we felt we could even attempt it.

* During the French war Lien's husband had served as private secretary to Le Duan, at that time the Party's chief representative in the South.

The entire distance was about a hundred miles along a military trail through the jungle. Under constant threat of attack or bombardment, we traveled only at night, sometimes by bicycle, sometimes on foot. From one control point to the next, we slowly made our way, all of us shocked at how much our stamina had been sapped by the months of isolation.

We were on the trail over two weeks before we reached COSVN, the famous Central Office of South Vietnam, which the Americans spent so much energy attempting to locate and erase. The first sign of it was a wooden gate across the trail and a control point manned by about ten guards. Here our escorts waited until soldiers from inside the gate rode up on bicycles to take us to a small guest cottage, much like a peasant's house. After we had rested a bit, another group of escorts carried us along a circuitous route largely hidden from the sky by the jungle canopy. Occasionally we would pass another little cottage, until at last we stopped at one of them, which turned out to be the headquarters building. From a distance it was a simple peasant hut; up close you could see the system of tunnels and bunkers that jutted off from it.

Waiting for us inside this complex was General Tran Nam Trung (code names "Hai Hau" and "Nam Nga"*), commander-in-chief of the NLF armed forces and one of COSVN's second secretaries. At this time General Trung was the permanent member of COSVN, directing the headquarters staff. As was true at most times, the various other members were elsewhere, engaged on the particular missions for which they were responsible.

COSVN was, and had always been, people rather than a place. It was a leadership group made up of delegates from the Central Committee of the Workers' Party (Lao Dong), several of whom became members of the NLF Central Committee as well. COSVN executed the directives of the North Vietnamese Politburo and coordinated the action of the Party and the National Liberation Front.

* "Nga" was Trung's wife's name. It was common for the high cadres to take either their wives' or children's names in order to confuse the Saigon intelligence community.

When circumstances required it, the various members would be called together by the permanent staff, occasionally at different locations, but commonly at the headquarters area, which we had finally reached after such an exhausting journey. This complex, so elusive to the American and regime hunters, was located on the Mimot rubber plantation, straddling the Vietnam/Cambodia border in the Fishhook area (see map on p. 169).

Among General Trung's more important colleagues in COSVN were Pham Hung (code name "Bay Hong"), Politburo member and first party secretary; Pham Van Dang (code name "Hai Van"), who was the chief of organization; Nguyen Van Linh (code name "Muoi Cuc"), in charge of propaganda and training; Vo Van Kiet (code name "Sau Dan"), head of the Saigon/Cholon/Giadinh zone and Mai Chi Tho's boss; and General Hoang Van Thai, commander-in-chief of Northern forces in the South and ultimately responsible for all military affairs.

We spent some time with General Trung, briefing him on our experiences, then retired for a rest that we needed badly after the arduous journey. Shortly afterward, he sent the three of us on to the NLF hospital for high cadres located on the Cambodian side of the Vam Co River, a trip of several days from COSVN. Here I was to remain for the next month, gradually regaining strength and receiving treatments for the stomach problems that had tormented me since my stay with the secret police.

12

The Alliance, South Vietnam's Third Force

During my stay in this lovely, secluded hospital, away from worries about B-52 bombings or sudden helicopter assaults, I was under the care of a most unusual doctor. Though in her forties, Thuy Ba had about her the cheerfulness and perpetual optimism of a college student—despite the fact that she had served as a nurse in the jungle throughout the French war, prior to regrouping North after Geneva. In Hanoi she had completed her medical studies, graduating as an M.D. in 1960. At that point she had decided to return South, traversing the rudimentary Ho Chi Minh Trail of that time in a trek that lasted six months. She was the first woman to accomplish this murderous journey, which in the early days claimed the lives of almost half of those who attempted it.

While I was in the hospital, I received a letter from Huynh Tan Phat, congratulating me on my release and asking me to come to the NLF headquarters as soon as I felt able to travel. Phat wrote that the Front was in the process of establishing the Alliance of National, Democratic, and Peace Forces and that he hoped I would be able to participate in the planning.

The Alliance of National, Democratic, and Peace Forces was an organization that had become necessary as a result of the American intervention that began in 1965. (I had been working toward the establishment of the Alliance as early as 1966.) One of the consequences of this cataclysm was that the NLF had been forced to rely to an ever-greater extent on its Northern ally. In order to confront the massive American presence, troops, war matériel, organizational expertise, and propaganda support were required on a scale that dwarfed the Front's capacities. Over a period of time, North Vietnam had committed more and more of its resources to the war, until it had become, as Party leaders liked to phrase it, "a giant rear area" supporting the front lines. As a result, the NLF had found itself ever more obviously dominated by the Party and by the Northern government.

It was now past time for a strong effort to reestablish the image of the South's revolution as a broad-based movement that included Southern nationalists of every stripe. As one wag in the hospital put it, the blue half of the NLF flag had become too red. What was required was an organization structured along governmental lines, made up of the strongest nationalist figures in the South who had not joined the Front (and who consequently were not tainted, in the popular mind, by communist sympathies), an organization that could credibly maintain an aura of autonomy and independence. The fact that the Alliance would inevitably be branded by its enemies as a puppet of the NLF was not considered an overwhelming obstacle. At the very least the Alliance would add a substantial new counterweight to the Communist overbalance, and among the uncommitted it would help restore the NLF's eclipsed coalition-based orientation.

Originally, the plan had been to set up the Alliance aboveground prior to Tet at the latest, so that had the offensive succeeded, a more widely acceptable movement would be in place either to establish or participate in the formation of a new government. But the Ba Tra episode had shredded the Front's organizing strength in Saigon, effectively precluding a major effort of this sort. Compounding this disaster, shortly after Ba Tra's arrest, a key cadre in the Saigon/Cholon/Giadinh finance division had also been picked up. Under torture, he had revealed the principal figures in that vital network, precipitating another wave of arrests. By mid-1967 the Saigon organization was reeling from these two blows, forcing a substantial delay in its time-table. Consequently, it wasn't until March of 1968 that renewed plans for the Alliance began to harden. For me, this meant leaving the hospital for a trek along the Vam Co River to NLF headquarters, hidden in the jungles of Tay Ninh between Parrot's Beak and the Fishhook, about forty miles southwest of the COSVN complex.

When I arrived, the scene at NLF headquarters was like a family reunion. In addition to my colleagues from the Front, I was surprised to see many other old friends from Saigon, many of whom had always been somewhat wary of the NLF, but who had now agreed to participate in the Alliance. Among them were individuals I had spent many hours with as part of my proselytizing activities going back to 1958. To my great pleasure, Dr. Duong Quynh Hoa

Dr. Duong Quynh Hoa.

was in the group. She had been a childhood playmate, and we had remained close companions during our school years. Growing up to be an ebullient woman of sparkling intelligence and great moral courage, Hoa had gone to Paris to study medicine, returning to Vietnam in 1958 to open a private practice. Since her return she had been openly sympathetic to the Front, an orientation that kept her under constant surveillance by the secret police, making it impossible for her to engage in any political activity. Now, after Tet, she had finally decided that everything possible must be done to get the Americans out of the country, and she had joined the Alliance, moving to the jungle in order to do so.

Another friend, Lam Van Tet, was also there. Tet was an engineer who had served on the civilian council (the National Supreme Council), which had been set up by the generals after Diem's overthrow ostensibly to govern the country. Tet too had been persuaded by the New Year's offensive to go into opposition, and Tran Bach Dang's intellectual mobilization people had moved him to accept the idea of joining the Alliance. Thanh Nghi, a writer famous for his definitive French-Vietnamese dictionary, had come out into the jungle as well, as had two other widely known individuals, Professor Nguyen Van Kiet and engineer Cao Van Bon.

Among those I was especially happy to see was Lucien Pham Ngoc Hung, one of Albert Thao's elder brothers. Lucien had been arrested after Albert's coup against Nguyen Khanh in February of 1965 and had remained in jail for over a year. He was a wealthy businessman, who had had a somewhat checkered history of resistance activities. As a journalism student in Paris, he had worked with the Vietminh press delegation at the Fontainebleau Conference; then in 1954 he had assisted in the same capacity at Geneva. By 1955 he was back in Saigon, where he went into the paint industry along with partners Cao Van Bon and Nguyen Huu Khuong, and built up a large manufacturing business. This inseparable triumvirate of Lucien, Bon, and Khuong had been arrested together in the Thao coup, and now all three of them had joined the Alliance.

Although these people (and the others who had arrived for the founding of the Alliance) had for years been in sympathy with many of the Front's goals, most had stopped short of associating themselves formally—for a variety of reasons. Foremost among these was ideology. By and large these were Western-educated individuals with generally liberal and democratic (in the Western sense of the term) political principles. They tended to be sensitive to economic inequities and social injustices, but not in a way that would move them to political action. They were decidedly not dogmatic people, and they had an instinctive distaste for those who were. On the other hand, their political open-mindedness was overlaid by a powerful sense of Vietnamese nationalism. As a consequence, their attitude toward the NLF was characteristically ambivalent. The Front's strong stand for independence and rejection of foreign domination appealed to them, but they were put off by the organization's deference to the Party and by the Communist ideologues who were playing key roles.

But as the conflict deepened, these people, along with the rest of the politically literate Southern population, were less and less able to maintain their preferred attitude of detachment. By 1968 the entire country was embroiled in a vicious all-out war, which had already ripped apart much of the fabric of society. A Northern army was operating in the countryside, the cities had swollen with homeless refugees, the Americans were subjecting their enemies (and anyone else who got in the way) to state-of-the-art methods of extermination. South Vietnam had been turned into a crucible of suffering—a nation that was finding out, in its flesh, what it means to be a pawn in a world of great powers. It was a situation that cried out for involvement.

For many of those who were to make up the Alliance, Tet had been a turning point on their road to a decision. The offensive had pointed toward a future of even greater and more pervasive violence. It had left the Southern resistance bloodied, but as single-mindedly intent on victory as ever. And it had demonstrated the vulnerability of the Americans. Psychologically, it was a critical period, one in which people felt called on to make decisions, and every decision carried with it unpredictable and potentially disastrous consequences.

Within this context, people like Lam Van Tet, Than Nghi, and the others were moved at last to throw their weight, openly and heavily, into the battle against the Americans. It was a decision they regarded largely in terms of national salvation. But once they had made it, they were also human enough to look for good and substantial reasons for playing down their suspicions of the NLF and their dislike of the Party's dominance over it.

Such reasons were easy enough to come by. In the first place, they had heard for years the solemnly proclaimed avowals of the DRV that the South was "a special and unique situation, very different from the North." "The South," said Le Duan, Party secretary general, "needs its own policy." "Construct Socialism in the North," rang the slogan. "Develop the National Democratic Revolution in the South." "No one," as Pham Van Dong (DRV prime minister) liked to declare to his Western visitors, "has this stupid and criminal idea of annexing the South." Over the years, such statements, persistently and fervently reiterated in broadcasts, manifestos, and even in internal Party documents, had had their effect.

The Alliance people were hardly satisfied by such disclaimers. It would be neither fair nor accurate to make such a claim. But the DRV's sworn objectives did provide a reassuring background. What counted much more significantly in the process of accommodating themselves to partnership with the Communists were personal relationships, which tied together Alliance members and members of the Front. Although Vietnamese are often suspicious and inconstant in their feelings toward organizations and institutions, they place great value on personal loyalties and trust. Between the intellectual, upperclass nationalists outside the Front and those within (both Communist and independent), associations ran deep. In the stratified world of Vietnam, many families in the traditionally monied and governing classes had known each other for generations. They had gone to school together, raised children alongside each other, and intermarried. They had incurred toward each other debts and obligations of every imaginable sort. They were fish living in the same water. Dr. Hoa and I had spent our childhoods together. I had often hidden Lucien Pham Ngoc Hung's brother Albert from government police intent on murdering him. While he was a hunted fugitive, Albert had managed to visit my mother to reassure her about my own safety. Multiply such situations and incidents over an entire social stratum and extend it for generations, and you have some idea of the personal bonds that existed between the people who joined together to form the Alliance and those in their parent organization, the NLF. Under these circumstances, a world of tradition and cultural expectations militated against the likelihood of personal betrayal.

Indeed, the war was replete with instances of friends and relatives protecting each other, even though they were fighting on opposite sides. To mention just two, General Tran Van Trung, Thieu's chief of psychological warfare, hid in his own house a sister-in-law who was the Vietcong cadre in charge of the Hue People's Uprising Committee. Similarly, Cao Van Vien, at one point commander-in-chief of the Southern army, protected two of his wife's nephews, the sons of a Communist cadre. Neither of these men had any particular love for their enemies, but family loyalty they considered sacrosanct.

One contributing factor to this Vietnamese propensity to place trust in persons comes from the culture's ingrained Confucianism. Of the basic ethical principles in this philosophical tradition, the fifth is *tin* ("faithfulness"). Forgoing *tin,* a person becomes devoid of honor, of face. He loses his essential humanity. Among the very deepest feelings of one raised in a Confucian society is the inhibition against betraying those with whom one enjoys a relationship of trust.

This is the point conveyed by perhaps the most ubiquitous of the moral tales that abound in Vietnamese life, the legend of the Three Kingdoms. According to the legend, a thousand years ago there was a king in China named Tao Thao. Among his other kindnesses, this king had given shelter and refuge to a wanderer by the name of Quang Cong. In the course of time, China had split into three warring parts, and now Quang Cong was the chief general of one of Tao Thao's enemies. The moment came when Quang Cong and Tao Thao were to meet in single combat.

Before the combat, Quang Cong's king spoke to him, saying that he was afraid Quang Cong would feel unable to kill Tao Thao because of Thao's previous kindnesses. But Cong swore to his king that he would indeed kill Thao if he had the chance. In the battle, Cong subdued Tao Thao. But when Thao reminded him of their past relationship, Cong could not bring himself to harm his former benefactor. "It would be better," thought Quang Cong, "to kill myself rather than break faith with this man and be disdained by all." ("Rather die than lose face" runs a popular Vietnamese proverb.)

So Quang Cong came to his king and said, "Kill me. I have broken my word to you. I cannot harm Tao Thao." But hearing this, the king did not become angry, as Quang Cong had expected. Instead he said, "If I kill you, I would lose my best general. Moreover, and more important, had you killed Tao Thao I would have lost all my respect for you. You would have been dust in my eyes. Now I know that you are the Quang Cong I thought you to be."

So quintessential is the story of Quang Cong that his cult has an unsurpassed popularity in the Vietnamese countryside to this day. In most peasant cottages there will be a space set aside for incense and a likeness of this archetype of personal loyalty.

This inbred Vietnamese psychology goes some way toward explaining why in the war's final stages, Nguyen Van Thieu did not believe Nixon and Kissinger would finally forsake him. Regardless of everything he knew about American domestic politics (and he was well-informed) and everything he had heard directly and explicitly from the American leaders, Thieu simply could not bring himself to believe that in his extremity the Americans would abandon him to fate. Their engagement had extended too long and had encompassed too much. Of course Thieu was also betting on the American geopolitical investment in South Vietnam. But in addition, a relationship of personal commitment had been created. Trapped in his Vietnamese habits of thought, Thieu imagined that this relationship must prevail, regardless of apparent political realities and logic.

In much the same fashion, once the members-to-be of the Alliance had made their decision to join, they substantially abandoned themselves to the trustworthiness of their new comrades. It is possible that Kissinger and Nixon did not fully comprehend their ally's expectations.

But the DRV Politburo and their representatives at COSVN and in the NLF were exquisitely attuned to the mental nuances of their Southern compatriots, and they played on these nuances with rare artistry. This, I think, is not a full explanation for the phenomenon of nationalist/communist concord. But once the nationalists had made their intuitive and perhaps romantic leap toward the NLF, such psychological furniture as this provided comforting reasons to ignore fear and suspicion.

The actual congress to establish the Alliance took place in early May. We prepared in advance its manifesto, program, and the various organizational details. In tone, the platform differed from that of the NLF by being somewhat more distinctively Southern and somewhat less revolutionary. "At present," it stated, "our country has in fact two different political systems in the South and in the North. National reunification cannot be achieved overnight. Therefore, the South and the North should hold talks on the basis of equality and respect for the characteristics of each zone."

Trinh Dinh Thao, to whom I had offered the NLF presidency nine years earlier, now accepted a call to lead the Alliance. Thao was a tiny, round-faced individual of almost seventy, who gave the impression of being someone's amiable and debonair grandfather. He combined a deep and sentimental patriotism with a profoundly pacifistic nature, characteristics that made his decision to become actively involved an especially difficult and painful one. Lam Van Tet, the ex-government official, was named vice president, together with a Buddhist leader, Thich Don Hau. For secretary general we chose Ton That Duong Ky, the aristocratic former professor who had worked on the Peace Committee and had been expelled to the North from our common cell in Chi Hoa. I became a permanent member and vice president of the Alliance Committee for Saigon/Cholon/Giadinh.

As soon as it was established, the Alliance sent agents to many of the South's major centers to form clandestine regional committees. These immediately began to mobilize support from nonaligned elements for negotiations with the Front. Meanwhile, President Thieu took cognizance of this new opponent by having the Alliance leaders sentenced to death in absentia and confiscating their property. A number of the condemned had their families quietly removed from Saigon and brought out into the jungle. The expectations most of them had had of staying only briefly with the NLF now evaporated, and the whole group began to gird up for an extended sojourn. Perhaps not even the most pessimistic, though, would have guessed that their return home would be delayed seven years.

During this same period, Nguyen Van Thieu was in the process of consolidating his own hold on power, and Saigon was wearily suffering through another of the familiar rounds of repression. As always happened in such periods, numbers of moderates were pushed toward the Front, though now the Alliance provided a more congenial home for many of them. Among those who joined were Professor Le Van Giap, president of the Association for the Defense of

Trinh Dinh Thao, president
of the Alliance of
National, Democratic, and
Peace Forces.

Vietnamese Culture, and Ho Huu Nhut, then president of the Saigon University Student Union. Nhut and other new members had been agitating peacefully for free elections, only to find themselves arrested under Article 4 of the constitution, outlawing Communists or procommunist activity. Disgusted, Nhut went into real opposition, disappearing into the jungle to join first the Alliance and later the Provisional Revolutionary Government as vice minister for education and youth.

Setting up its own separate headquarters near the NLF complex, the Alliance now joined COSVN and the Front in coordinating strategy for the South. It was a period of frequent liaison meetings and open exchanges, symptomatic perhaps of the importance that Party leaders in Hanoi accorded the indigenous Southern resistance at this stage of the war. DRV attentiveness toward its allies was apparent in the receptivity COSVN showed toward proposals emanating from the Front and the Alliance, and by the general spirit of partnership that facilitated every sort of business.

Symbolic touches were not missing either. In the spring of 1969, President Thao led an Alliance delegation on a visit to Hanoi. On their arrival, Thao was somewhat surprised to find himself treated as a visiting head of state. The Northern government had pulled out all the stops; crowds had been mobilized to cheer on the official cavalcade, and receptions and banquets were the order of the day. The delegation was scheduled as well to visit Ho Chi Minh (who was then suffering his final illness and in fact died several months later), but in a characteristic gesture, Ho refused to allow them to come to his cottage on the grounds of the Presidential Palace. Instead, he sent a message to Thao saying that the representatives of the proud Southern people should not have to come to him; rather it would be his honor to go to them. Early that evening, well before he was expected, Ho arrived at the house where the Alliance delegation was staying. He was not accompanied by an entourage, and his presence was not announced. He simply walked in through the back door, as if he were an intimate friend or member of the family. The first person he stumbled across was Madame Thao, standing in front of a mirror

Trinh Dinh Thao and Madame Thao (*both seated at center*) in the jungle. This photograph was taken shortly before the Alliance's visit to Hanoi.

putting the final touches on her makeup. At first she didn't recognize him. But as soon as she realized who this frail old man was, she was overcome by emotion. With tears running down her face she called Thao and the others. All of them were moved beyond words by the honor Ho was paying them through this gesture of simple friendship.

It was a story that was repeated time and again by all of the Alliance delegates when they returned to the South. Ho's personal warmth thus touched not only Trin Dinh Thao and his wife, but the entire Southern leadership. As a demonstration of esteem, it had an unsurpassed effect, further highlighting the prevalent sense of North-South fellowship in this struggle. (A minor side note to this incident is that Madame Thao never used cosmetics again, so ashamed was she that Uncle Ho had seen her making up.)

As the Alliance leaders looked back on their first year of activity, they could see positive results. The moderate, noncommunist ele-

A meeting of the Alliance. The slogan reads, "Fatherland, Family, Peace, Happiness." Trinh Dinh Thao (*right, standing with back to the camera*) is addressing the group.

ments they infused into the struggle's leadership brought new energy to the ceaseless effort to mobilize antigovernment opposition. In broadening the revolution's base, they had given it new durability as well as renewed vigor. Vis-à-vis the Northern allies, they constituted a well-organized and wholly Southern faction, which would have a say in affairs whose control had fallen ever more securely into the hands of the DRV's Politburo and Military Management Committee.

It was also a year that had brought other events of great though mixed significance. Tet and the related series of offensives in the spring and summer of 1968 had resulted in unexpectedly high casualties for both the NLF guerrillas and the Northern main-force troops. But these actions had also awakened what appeared to be a critical and growing divisiveness in American public opinion. On March 31, two months after Tet and while the battle for Khe Sanh was still under way,

Trinh Dinh Thao addressing the Alliance.

Lyndon Johnson announced that he would not run for reelection. There was little doubt in our minds that the domestic pressure stimulated by our persistent military action was largely responsible. As the Western antiwar movement flared, we felt hope that Americans might now be forced into a negotiated settlement that would include NLF representation in the Southern government. Indeed, a month and a half after Johnson's personal withdrawal, formal negotiations opened up in Paris—the first several months of which were largely taken up with haggling over the right of the NLF to participate on an equal footing with the Saigon government.

But while our psychological and political strategies were opening paths, which in the long term would yield decisive results, another of 1968's major events was less encouraging. On November 7, Richard Nixon was elected president. As far as we were concerned, there was no question that Nixon would prove an obdurate opponent, who would bend every muscle to achieve a military resolution to the war. From this new president we could expect increased violence and, undoubtedly, new strategies to achieve the old ends.

13

The Provisional Revolutionary Government

The primary new strategy was not long in announcing itself. By early spring of 1969, Nixon began public discussion of the criteria for a withdrawal of American troops. This was clearly a subject the newly inaugurated administration had been considering for some time. During March and the months that followed, the outlines of the American plans slowly revealed themselves. Washington was going to make a gesture—perhaps more than a gesture—toward reducing its forces in Vietnam.

This move, we knew, would be presented as a signal of American willingness to compromise at the negotiating table. In reality, however, its purpose was to placate public opinion in the United States. Our analysis that antiwar sentiment was having an increased impact on American staying power was thus confirmed at the source. It was evident that we had succeeded in opening what we now began to refer to as our fourth front—the first three being political, military, and diplomatic—and we started monitoring domestic developments in the United States even more attentively.

In fact, there was nothing particularly original about the steps Nixon was taking to forestall a political crisis in his own front yard. The strategy American spokesmen were labeling "Vietnamization" was quite similar to the so-called *jaunissement* ("yellowing") that had been tried by the French commander De Lattre de Tassigny seventeen years before. It involved assigning more of the burden of fighting to South Vietnamese government troops—and consequently blurring the image of the United States as a primary combatant while reinforcing the image of the Thieu government as an independent entity.

But unlike the transparently phony French attempt to portray their war as a civil conflict, Nixon's Vietnamization policy had serious implications. In contrast to France, the United States had the capacity to maintain immense military pressure against strategic targets and supply routes as well as to provide effective close combat support—even if most of its ground troops were withdrawn. In short, all the corpses would henceforth be Vietnamese. This policy also stood a chance of accomplishing the dual goal of disarming opposition to the war, at home and abroad, while simultaneously sustaining the Thieu regime in Saigon. Thus the struggle might be prolonged indefinitely.

Vietnamization, as we saw it, was a political maneuver meant to strike at us by hamstringing opposition to the war in the international and domestic American arenas. We decided to respond by countering this threat on precisely the same battlefields. We had long been developing plans to set up formal NLF governmental structures at regional and lower levels; we now moved to create a central political entity that could treat with Saigon on the basis of formal, legal standing. Such a new governmental unit would bring many domestic advantages, of course, but, more important, resistance in the South would now acquire a new international stature.

We knew the creation of this government would be regarded by the Nixon administration as an exercise in propaganda. But this reaction was essentially irrelevant. Our goal was to influence public opinion: domestically, where a noncommunist government would give us added credibility with the South Vietnamese populace; internationally, where we would be able to compete with Saigon for formal recognition (and the potential support that would come with it); and in the United States, where we would enhance our claim of representing the Southern people, giving the peace movement additional ammunition. The administration's effort to portray the Saigon regime as an autonomous, legitimate government would now be answered by another Southern government fighting hard in every international forum to establish its own claim to legitimacy. From here on in we would be able to wage full-scale diplomatic warfare.

The organizing congress for this government—to be called the Provisional Revolutionary Government—was held on June 6, 7, and 8, 1969, off Route 22 in the Fishhook area, just on the Vietnamese side of the border. These dates were chosen so that we could upstage (to some extent at least) the Nixon-Thieu meeting scheduled for June 8 on Midway Island, at which "Vietnamization" would be formally inaugurated. For this congress, the NLF's 9th Division set up a tight, three-perimeter security system. In the center of the secured area, a kind of congress palace was constructed to house delegates from the NLF, the Alliance, the People's Revolutionary Party,* as well as from the usual assortment of mass organizations, ethnic groups, and geographical regions. Designed by Huynh Tan Phat†—exercising perhaps a nostalgia for his forsaken architectural career—the building featured wooden walls topped off by a roof of parachute silk and a large painting over the entrance depicting the forward momentum of the Southern fighters and people.

In keeping with its symbolic significance, the congress was organized with as great solemnity as we could muster, given the circumstances. Banners and flags decorated the walls. "Strengthen the Great United Solidarity" read one prominent slogan. "South Vietnam is Independent, Democratic, Peaceful, and Neutral" said another. Instead of the noisy milling around that usually marked the opening of our gatherings, this time the delegations marched ceremoniously into the hall, in strict hierarchic order. NLF President Nguyen Huu

* The PRP was established in 1962 as the southern branch of the Vietnamese Workers' Party (Lao Dong). However, it did not invariably espouse a communist line, but adapted itself to the requirements imposed by working in coalition with other factions.

† Phat had also conceived the halls used for the initial NLF meeting at Xom Giua and for the Phuoc plantation meeting of the Saigon Regional Committee.

Presidents Thieu and Nixon on Midway Island announcing the Vietnamization program, June 8, 1969. The PRG inaugural ceremonies were scheduled on the the same day to deflect attention.

Tho and Alliance President Trinh Dinh Thao led the presidium members in a slow and dignified step between two rows of honor guards. The strains of "Liberate the South" filled the hall, followed by the Alliance anthem, "The Voice of Mountains and Rivers."

Trinh Dinh Thao delivered the inaugural statement, which was followed by the now familiar order of business: the current political, military, and diplomatic analyses, then reports on activities from the

PROVISIONAL REVOLUTIONARY GOVERNMENT

various mass organizations and regional representatives—all of which took up two full days. On the third day, Huynh Tan Phat proposed a list of cabinet secretaries. Phat himself was nominated chairman, Dr. Hoa for minister of health, and the soon-to-be internationally known Nguyen Thi Binh, for foreign minister. I was named minister of justice. In addition, an advisory Council of Elders was established

The meeting hall designed by Huynh Tan Phat for the inaugural ceremonies of the PRG.

Procession of the members of the new PRG entering the hall between rows of honor guard.

consisting of Presidents Tho and Thao, Lam Van Tet, and other older members of the NLF and Alliance. Reflecting the ingrained Vietnamese respect for age, this council was part of the ongoing effort to reconcile tradition with revolution. In that sense it was good propaganda, but there was a strain of reality to it as well. All of us simply felt more comfortable with such an arrangement.

With the list of nominees confirmed, the grandfatherly Trin Dinh Thao presented the closing remarks. A final vote was then taken, and the PRG became a living entity. Videotapes and press releases describing the events were distributed throughout the world, and two days later television screens and newspapers everywhere were announcing the birth of the PRG.

In point of fact, the real business of putting the government together had taken place a month earlier in a series of working meetings between the NLF and the Alliance. The most pressing decisions then concerned who should be nominated to the various cabinet posts, with credibility and a moderate political image the primary (though not the sole) considerations.

The Presidium members at the inaugural ceremonies: Trinh Dinh Thao in tie at center; Nguyen Huu Tho in glasses to his right.

During these discussions I had initially been proposed as minister of the interior. My wide contacts and the fact that I had taken care not to create many enemies recommended me for the job, as did the low profile of my political views. Equally important, perhaps, was the fact that my five brothers were working on the other side: two in the air force (Hoang a major and Due a lieutenant); Quynh, director of the Saigon General Hospital; Bich, director of the Foreign Exchange Department of the National Bank; and Khue, deputy director of Shell Oil's South Vietnam operations.

With this array of immediate family as well as other more distant relatives scattered around Saigon's government, military, and private industry, I would make (so the feeling went) a reassuring figure at Interior. My views about the necessity for reconciliation were well known, and my presence at the head of the ministry that controlled the National Police would speak strongly for the PRG's postwar intentions. After several days of fitting together the pieces, however, I yielded this portfolio to Dr. Cung, in favor of the Finance post. The doctor possessed many of the same qualifications that I did for the

At the inaugural ceremonies. *From left to right:* Ung Ngoc Ky, vice minister to the chairman; Luu Huu Phuoc, minister of information and culture; I, as minister of justice; Cao Van Bon, minister of economy and finance. The slogan on the back wall reads, "Warmest welcome to the Provisional Government."

Interior post, but he did not have my background in economics.*

At that point we were anxious to save the Justice portfolio for Nguyen Long, the lawyer who had been president of the Self-Determination Movement. The same Military Tribunal that had sentenced

---

* Dr. Cung was erroneously believed by American intelligence sources to be an advocate of terror, "deeply feared by his associates." The reality was exactly the opposite. Cung had been a physician in the provinces before becoming the director of Saigon's Polyclinic. He was the kind of person who enjoyed the good life and was a dedicated player of the "four color" card game so popular in Saigon society. Cung naturally shrank from argument and seemed to have a need to reconcile people. He was known as a born conciliator. Most of us felt that left to himself he would never have become actively involved in revolution. His wife, however, was a domineering, militant individual, who had succeeded in inducing him to join the Front in its early days. Her brother was the infamous Ba Tra.

American intelligence errors in the biographical analysis of Cung indicate the effectiveness with which leading Front figures were shielded from scrutiny. There was little chance that even captured cadres would know much about these people that the enemy might find useful. At the same time, whatever information prisoners or turncoat VC chose to give would be exceptionally difficult to verify.

me to a two-year suspended term back in 1964 had given Long ten years to serve in jail. The old lawyer's failing health, however, had induced the regime to release him, and he was now living quietly at home. Unfortunately, he had been too weak to risk attending the PRG congress, and to appoint him while he was still in Saigon would have been to sign his death warrant.

Consequently, we decided at last that I could best serve in the Justice Ministry [my Paris law degree gave me the necessary formal qualifications]. In terms of influencing domestic opinion, this portfolio was, with Interior, a critical one. And indeed, the aftermath of Tet had left us with a special need to address fears among the Southern people that a revolutionary victory would bring with it a bloodbath or reign of terror.

Members of the new government being formally inaugurated. I am at the extreme left; Dr. Hoa, the new minister of health is at the extreme right.

The only city where the 1968 combined offensive and uprising had been successful in its own terms was Hue, the graceful old imperial capital in the center of the country. On January 31, NLF and Northern troops had taken the city and had held it for more than three weeks before being pushed out by American marines, with their over-whelming firepower and constant air support. This initial victory, however, had not turned out to be one of the revolution's prouder moments. After my exchange, I had hungrily gone through stacks of old Saigon newspapers, in an attempt to catch up with what had been going on during my eight months in isolation (in the jungle we received the Saigon papers daily for use by the leadership cadres). The accounts I read of Hue's experience with revolutionary rule, though no doubt exaggerated by the Saigon press corps, were unsettling, to say the least.

Large numbers of people had been executed, most of them either associated with the government or opponents of the revolution. But others had been killed as well, including some captured American soldiers and several other foreigners who were not combatants. I had questioned Huynh Tan Phat in private about these atrocities. He had expressed his sorrow and disappointment about what had happened, and explained that discipline in Hue had been seriously inadequate. Fanatic young soldiers had indiscriminately shot people, and angry local citizens who supported the revolution had on various occasions taken justice into their own hands. According to Phat there was absolutely no policy or directive from the Front to carry out any massacre. It had simply been one of those terrible spontaneous tragedies that inevitably accompany war.

I did not find this explanation particularly satisfying. But I must also admit that neither did I pursue the issue. In the context of a bloody and atrocious conflict, the events in Hue were not, for me at least, the kind of stunning blow that forces the reconsideration of basic assumptions. In addition, I believed that, among the less rigid and violence-prone people of the South,* there was substantially less

* Hue was in the central region.

likelihood of such things happening. Perhaps this was an excessively chauvinistic way of thinking, but I felt there was some validity to it regardless. I also considered that my Saigonese friends and I would be able to exert a good deal of control in our own home grounds. For a variety of reasons, then, I had let the events in Hue pass.

But of course they had not passed, just receded into the background, from where they now injected themselves into my thinking about the Justice Ministry. I was indeed anxious to make a strong public statement about the PRG's antipathy to "revolutionary justice." But I also felt that this post would leave me especially well placed to influence the course of events—at whatever point we might succeed in our drive toward a coalition government. With these thoughts in mind, I gladly accepted the portfolio.

Once the list of ministers had been determined, we sent a report of our conclusions on to Hanoi through the COSVN liaison. The Politburo's suggestions, returned through the same channel, were that we should include additional individuals from Central Vietnam, among them Nguyen Doa, Tran Nam Trung, and Hoang Bich Son. Trung was the general who had greeted my two companions and me at COSVN after our release from prison. Doa, an old man by this time, had been Pham Van Dong's elementary school teacher, while Son had been a student leader in Hue prior to joining the resistance (at this writing he is Vietnam's ambassador to the United Nations).

With these people incorporated into the government in appropriate positions, the PRG was complete—awaiting now only its formal confirmation by the organizing congress. A month later the birth notices, films, and pictures were sent out, just in time to share media attention with the Nixon-Thieu troop-withdrawal announcements. As the North Vietnamese embassies throughout the world opened a vast propaganda campaign, launching the PRG's quest for international recognition, I began the job of building a ministry in the jungle.

14

Life in
the Maquis

It was along the Vam Co River some miles below NLF headquarters that we chose sites for the various PRG ministries. This rugged and heavily forested area, flanking the Cambodian border and deep within the "Iron Triangle" of sanctuaries and bases, provided as good protection as we could get from the marauding B-52s and helicopter-borne assaults. Here we could have easy communication with COSVN on the Mimot plantation to our north and immediate access to the emergency escape routes across the frontier. As work on bunkers and shelters for the Justice Ministry progressed, I began to get accustomed to life in the jungle.

Before too long the urbanites of the PRG had settled into an existence that contrasted dramatically with their previous life-styles. Except for several interruptions for diplomatic missions, this jungle dweller's life was to be mine for the next six years. With some minor exceptions, it was a life shared by all the guerrillas, from PRG President Huynh Tan Phat down to the lowliest messenger boy. Those of us in the ministries had our supplies carried for us when we were on the move and our food cooked, but these perquisites did little to affect the sense of close fellowship that touched almost everyone.

If anything set the leadership apart, it was our access to information. Aside, of course, from the daily briefings, we had the Saigon newspapers and our personal radios, on which we could tune in to the

BBC or Voice of America as well as to the Vietnamese stations (North and South) and the Australian Vietnamese language broadcasts. (Those few fighting men who did have radios were strictly forbidden to monitor enemy stations.) These sturdy, Japanese-made transistors—a hundred of them—had been a gift to Ho Chi Minh from the Japanese Communist Party, symbols perhaps of the relentless spread of Japanese technology. (Later we would acquire large numbers of Honda motorbikes.) Ho apparently couldn't find any better use for them than to give them, as his own gifts, to the PRG and Alliance leadership.

But despite the radios, life's conspicuous features were the same for everyone. We lived like hunted animals, an existence that demanded constant physical and mental alertness. In the Iron Triangle,

My home in the jungle. The area in front was cleared so that poisonous snakes such as the *cham quap* would be visible.

wariness and tension were the companions of every waking moment, creating stresses that were to take an increasing toll on our equanimity as the American bombers closed in on the bases and sanctuaries in late 1969 and 1970.

Ready to move at any instant, we kept our personal encumbrances to a minimum. Two pairs of black pajamas, a couple of pairs of underpants, a mosquito net, and a few square yards of light nylon (handy as a raincoat or roof) were all that a guerrilla owned. The fighters, of course, carried weapons and ammunition in addition, as well as "elephant's intestines," our term for the long tubes of rolled cotton that could be filled with rice and slung across the back.

In addition to rice, each man's personal larder was rounded out by a small hunk of salt, a piece of monosodium glutamate, and perhaps a little dried fish or meat. The rice ration for both leaders and fighters was twenty kilos a month. Eaten twice a day, at about nine in the morning and four in the afternoon, the ration did not go far. But by and large it was our entire diet, a nutritional intake that left us all in a state of semistarvation.

Under these circumstances, food was a continual preoccupation; the lack of protein especially drove us to frenzied efforts at farming or hunting whenever it was feasible. Occasionally units would be stationed in one place long enough to raise chickens or even pigs. I will always remember one chicken feast, where we shared out a single bird among almost thirty of us, cutting it into the smallest possible bits and savoring each shred. I think I have never eaten anything quite so delicious.

Rarely, some sort of special shipment would come in from Cambodia, occasioning real celebrations. More often the guerrillas would go off on ad hoc hunting expeditions, returning at times with kills of every description. Elephants, tigers, wild dogs, monkeys—none of these were strangers to our cookpots. Still, even protein-starved as I was, I had a hard time choking down monkey meat or dog. Some people think of dog as a Vietnamese delicacy. But, in fact, it is only native to the Northern cuisine. Southerners tend to regard it with the same sort of distaste Westerners might. Elephant is another unap-

petizing item, a tasteless rubbery substance as tough as old shoes.
Dried, it was slightly more palatable.

Another dietary supplement which I eventually learned to eat—
if not with relish, then at least without gagging—was jungle moth.
Often, as we sat around our oil lanterns at night, talking or going over
plans, we would catch the big moths fluttering around the light. With
the wings off and barbecued quickly over a flame, it wasn't exactly a
tasty morsel, but it wasn't that bad either. All this was a far cry from
the carefully prepared dining my mandarin upbringing had taught me
to enjoy, a contrast that provided a bit of sardonic merriment for
those of us who had traded in Saigon's comforts for the uncertain
hospitality of the jungle. Sometime during the second or third year
after my release from prison, most of the exotic fare no longer
appeared on our jungle menu. By then the tigers, elephants, and
monkeys had all but vanished from the forest—into the stomachs of
the guerrillas.

In addition to our clothing and rations, each of us received pay of
either sixty or seventy-five piasters a month—the leadership cadres
getting the extra fifteen. (Sixty piasters at that time equaled about two
dollars.) With it we could buy sugar, tobacco, salt, soap, toothbrushes,
or some other domestic item by placing an order with the unit's
supply cadre. This much-courted individual would travel each month
along with the finance cadre to NLF headquarters to pick up the rice
allotment and payroll. Once these were distributed, they would hike
to Cambodia for the more esoteric purchases requested by their units.
When I first arrived, their habit was simply to go to any of the border-
area towns for their marketing. But later, Cambodian businessmen
set up special, more convenient trade outlets, a kind of Vietcong
jungle PX.

Although the Cambodian markets were favored for the security
they afforded, the Vietnamese villages in the vicinity occasionally
provided supplies unavailable elsewhere—especially after 1970. Up
till then our usual means of transportation was bicycle or foot. But in
the winter of 1969–1970 the whole country was inundated by an
invasion of Japanese motorbikes. In one way or another, these bikes

made their way out from the cities and into the hands of even the most remote country people, who would then smuggle them to the guerrillas. Quite often the peasants would get their bikes from the local Saigon army forces—in our case the ARVN's 5th and 18th Divisions. Eventually, our Finance Department was able to set up regular supply channels directly between these divisions and the Front, forgoing the peasant middlemen.

From that point on we had a regular supply, not just of Hondas, but of typewriters, radios, cigarettes, and a variety of other goods. Before long there was a thriving business between senior officers of these ARVN divisions and the Front in weapons and ammunition as well. Among the most popular items were grenades and Claymore antipersonnel mines. More than a few American soldiers were killed with these mines bought from their ARVN comrades. American walkie-talkies were in high demand too, though our troops were used to the Chinese AK47 rifles and never developed much of a taste for the American M-16.

But neither these supply sources nor the matériel flowing down from the North along the Ho Chi Minh Trail alleviated the chronic malnutrition or the tropical diseases that battened on the weakened men. In the jungle the prime enemy was not the Americans or the *nguy* ("puppets," our term for the Saigon government and its troops) but malaria. Very few escaped, and its recurrent attacks ravaged the guerrillas, who called it their jungle tax. For each of my years in the jungle, I spent approximately two months in the hospital, battling the high fevers and general debility of the disease. What with the protracted nutritional deficiencies and the malaria, almost all the jungle dwellers were marked by a jaundiced and sickly pallor. On more than one infiltrating mission this gave them away. Any knowledgeable and semiobservant person could spot a full-time guerrilla at a glance.

Malaria was such a problem that in 1971 Dr. Pham Ngoc Thach, North Vietnam's minister of health, made a study tour of the guerrilla areas as part of an attempt to devise some preventive measures. It was an indication of our medical inadequacies that Dr. Pham himself fell victim to the disease during this tour and died in the jungle. No

Medical personnel inside
the ministry's infirmary.

The pharmacy.

statistics were ever kept that I know about, but it is certain that we lost more people to malaria than we did to the enemy.

Snakebite was another plague, although antidotes had become widespread by the time I arrived in the jungle. In the tropical swamps and forests, a wide variety of poisonous snakes flourish, and the guerrillas' minimal footwear (mainly rubber thongs) made them especially vulnerable. The most deadly was the *cham quap,* a small brown krait closely resembling a stick and indistinguishable from dry branches in the undergrowth. Its venom took effect almost instantaneously and had to be counteracted by immediately swallowing one snakebite capsule and macerating another to apply to the wound. For years these creatures and others only slightly less toxic had taken

The chief cook and his supply staff.

Preparing food.

The kitchen for the Ministry of Justice, and our "General Hoang Cam" stove.

a steady toll of lives, and they continued to be a dangerous and painful hazard.

When neither sick nor fighting, the guerrillas spent their time building bunkers, raising vegetables, and training, constant training. It was a life of hiding and preparation: hiding from attacks, preparing to meet attacks, or training to carry out their own missions. If there was a half-day break in some movement, either away from or toward an engagement, they would dig trenches and bunkers. Food preparation, both in the headquarters complex and on the move, utilized what we called the "cuisine of General Hoang Cam" after a Vietcong general who had devised a system of smokeless cooking. We would build our fires in trenches or depressions, into the dirt sides of which we would dig a horizontal chimney. Almost all the fire's smoke would go into this chimney and be absorbed by the earth, very little of it emerging from the hole at the far end to mark our positions. Over thirty years and more of jungle warfare, the guerrillas had developed many tricks of this sort to shield them from their enemies—tricks that had by this time become second nature.

Training for the NLF fighters included hefty doses of class time, featuring sessions on current news, political and military issues, and the history of the revolution—all intended to strengthen their determination. As a general rule there was no political indoctrination; Marxist subjects, for example, were never touched on. Instead, instructors would devote their attention to elaborating Uncle Ho's great nationalistic slogans: "Nothing Is More Precious Than Independence and Liberty"; "Unity, Unity, Great Unity! Victory, Victory, Great Victory!" and the others. These would be used as homiletic texts, around which would be woven the themes of patriotism and the sacred duty of expelling the Americans.

Among the Northern troops the curriculum differed considerably. Having grown to manhood in the austere Marxist climate of the DRV, they were used to taking their ideology straight, and their political cadres and instructors kept up a steady infusion of Marxist precepts and class analysis. Had we attempted similar indoctrination of the Southern peasant guerrillas, they would have considered it worse

The NLF artistic company visiting the ministry on an entertainment tour in the jungle.

Madame Thao (*center*), Dr. Hoa (*behind her*), and myself (*extreme right*) posing with members of the artistic company.

torture than the regime could possibly devise for them.*

The harshness of this life amidst the septic jungle, with its continual training and constant watchfulness, was occasionally broken by a visit from an entertainment unit, running movies or staging a show. For the most part, their plays and songs were on standard subjects: guerrilla warfare, revolutionary heroes, ethnic folkways, and the like. But they were always welcomed enthusiastically for the relief they provided from a rigorous and danger-filled routine.

Even more welcome were the leaves of absence that the guerrillas were periodically granted. Those who came from the countryside could make their own arrangements to get back home and visit their families. But for the city dwellers, the logistics were more difficult.

* After the war, one American writer declared that the average guerrilla couldn't have told dialectical materialism from a rice bowl. By and large, this was true. As far as most of the Vietcong were concerned, they were fighting to achieve a better life for themselves and their families, and to rid the country of foreign domination— simple motives that were uncolored by ideological considerations.

Infiltrating into areas under secure government control to see wives and children who had often been marked as Vietcong dependents was a chancy business. To get around this, from time to time we would be able to bring families out to the jungle, something that was done for soldiers as well as cadres. But such meetings were necessarily brief and dangerous themselves. (Vo Van Kiet's wife and children were killed on their way to one such rendezvous, when they were caught in a B-52 raid.) More often than not these men went for extended periods without any contact at all with their families.

But for all the privations and hardships, nothing the guerrillas had to endure compared with the stark terrorization of the B-52 bombardments. During its involvement, the United States dropped on Vietnam more than three times the tonnage of explosives that were dropped during all of World War II in military theaters that spanned the world.* Much of it came from the high altitude B-52s, bombs of all sizes and types being disgorged by these invisible predators. The statistics convey some sense of the concentrated fire-power that was unleashed at America's enemies in both North and South. From the perspective of those enemies, these figures translated into an experience of undiluted psychological terror, into which we were plunged, day in, day out for years on end.

From a kilometer away, the sonic roar of the B-52 explosions tore eardrums, leaving many of the jungle dwellers permanently deaf. From a kilometer, the shock waves knocked their victims senseless. Any hit within a half kilometer would collapse the walls of an un-reinforced bunker, burying alive the people cowering inside. Seen up close, the bomb craters were gigantic—thirty feet across and nearly as deep. In the rainy seasons they would fill up with water and often saw service as duck or fishponds, playing their role in the guerrillas' never-ending quest to broaden their diet. But they were treacherous then too. For as the swamps and lowland areas flooded under half a foot of standing water, the craters would become invisible. Not infrequently some surprised guerrilla, wading along what

* Source: Carl Berger, ed., *The U.S. Airforce in South East Asia*, U.S. Government Printing Office, 1981.

he had taken to be a familiar route, was suddenly swallowed up.

It was something of a miracle that from 1968 through 1970 the attacks, though they caused significant casualties generally, did not kill a single one of the military or civilian leaders in the headquarters complexes. This luck, though, had a lot to do with accurate advance warning of the raids, which allowed us to move out of the way or take refuge in our bunkers before the bombs began to rain down. B-52s flying out of Okinawa and Guam would be picked up by Soviet intelligence trawlers plying the South China Sea. The planes' headings and air speed would be computed and relayed to COSVN headquarters, which would then order NLF or Northern elements in the anticipated target zones to move away perpendicularly to the attack trajectory. Flights originating from the Thai bases were monitored both on radar and visually by our intelligence nets there and the information similarly relayed.

Often the warnings would give us time to grab some rice and escape by foot or bike down one of the emergency routes. Hours later we would return to find, as happened on several occasions, that there was nothing left. It was as if an enormous scythe had swept through the jungle, felling the giant teak and go trees like grass in its way, shredding them into billions of scattered splinters. On these occasions—when the B-52s had found their mark—the complex would be utterly destroyed: food, clothes, supplies, documents, everything. It was not just that things were destroyed; in some awesome way they had ceased to exist. You would come back to where your lean-to and bunker had been, your home, and there would simply be nothing there, just an unrecognizable landscape gouged by immense craters.

Equally often, however, we were not so fortunate and had time only to take cover as best we could. The first few times I experienced a B-52 attack it seemed, as I strained to press myself into the bunker floor, that I had been caught in the Apocalypse. The terror was complete. One lost control of bodily functions as the mind screamed incomprehensible orders to get out. On one occasion a Soviet delegation was visiting our ministry when a particularly short-notice warn-

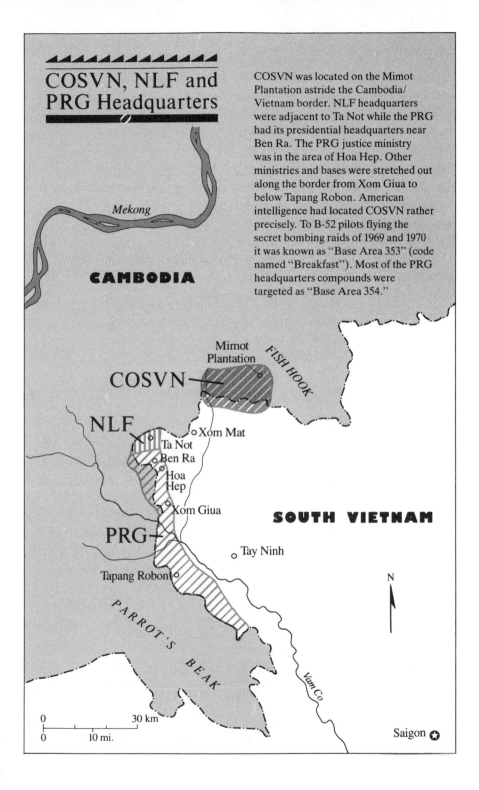

COSVN, NLF and PRG Headquarters

COSVN was located on the Mimot Plantation astride the Cambodia/Vietnam border. NLF headquarters were adjacent to Ta Not while the PRG had its presidential headquarters near Ben Ra. The PRG justice ministry was in the area of Hoa Hep. Other ministries and bases were stretched out along the border from Xom Giua to below Tapang Robon. American intelligence had located COSVN rather precisely. To B-52 pilots flying the secret bombing raids of 1969 and 1970 it was known as "Base Area 353" (code named "Breakfast"). Most of the PRG headquarters compounds were targeted as "Base Area 354."

Mekong

CAMBODIA

COSVN

Mimot Plantation

FISH HOOK

NLF

Xom Mat

Ta Not

Ben Ra

Hoa Hep

Xom Giua

SOUTH VIETNAM

PRG

Tay Ninh

Tapang Robon

N

PARROT'S BEAK

Vam Co

0   30 km

0   10 mi.

Saigon ✪

ing came through. When it was over, no one had been hurt, but the entire delegation had sustained considerable damage to its dignity —uncontrollable trembling and wet pants the all-too-obvious outward signs of inner convulsions. The visitors could have spared themselves their feelings of embarrassment; each of their hosts was a veteran of the same symptoms.

It was a tribute to the Soviet surveillance techniques that we were caught aboveground so infrequently during the years of the deluge. One of these occasions, though, almost put an end to all our endeavors. Taken by surprise by the sudden earthshaking shocks, I began running along a trench toward my bunker opening when a huge concussion lifted me off the ground and propelled me through the doorway toward which I was heading. Some of my Alliance colleagues were knocked off their feet and rolled around the ground like rag dolls. One old friend, Truong Cao Phuoc, who was working in the foreign relations division, had jumped into a shelter that collapsed on him, somehow leaving him alive with his head protruding from the ground. We extricated him, shoveling the dirt out handful by handful, carefully removing the supporting timbers that were crisscrossed in the earth around him. Truong had been trapped in one of the old U-shaped shelters, which became graves for so many. Later we learned to reinforce these dugouts with an A-frame of timbers that kept the walls from falling in. Reinforced in this manner, they could withstand B-52 bomb blasts as close as a hundred meters.

Sooner or later, though, the shock of the bombardments wore off, giving way to a sense of abject fatalism. The veterans would no longer scrabble at the bunker floors convulsed with fear. Instead people just resigned themselves—fully prepared to "go and sit in the ancestors' corner." The B-52s somehow put life in order. Many of those who survived the attacks found that afterward they were capable of viewing life from a more serene and philosophical perspective. It was a lesson that remained with me, as it did with many others, and helped me compose myself for death on more than one future occasion.

But even the most philosophical of fatalists were worn to the breaking point after several years of dodging and burrowing away from the rain of high explosives. During the most intense periods we came under attack every day for weeks running. At these times we would cook our rice as soon as we got out of our hammocks, kneading it into glutinous balls and ducking into the bunkers to be ready for what we knew was coming. Occasionally, we would be on the move for days at a time, stopping only to prepare food, eating as we walked. At night we would sling our hammocks between two trees wherever we found ourselves, collapsing into an exhausted but restless sleep, still half-awake to the inevitable explosions.

Pursued relentlessly by such demons, some of the guerrillas suffered nervous breakdowns and were packed off for hospital stays; others had to be sent home. There were cases too of fighters rallying to the Saigon government, unable to cope with the demands of life in the jungle. Times came when nobody was able to manage, and units would seek a hopeful refuge across the border in Cambodia.

In the middle of this, my assistant, Le Van Tha, and I went about establishing the PRG's Ministry of Justice. For this effort we had with us in the jungle about fifty officials and a security force of thirty or so guerrillas. In the most general terms, our job was to prepare ourselves for participation in a coalition government. Within this framework we divided the task up into two parts. The major preoccupation was to devise plans for transforming the legal system in effect under the Saigon regime into one that would be appropriate for a mixed government. Along these lines, we went about modifying the laws concerning workers' rights in order to incorporate such principles as strict regulation of working hours and health and safety conditions, guaranteed minimum wages, and protection from layoffs. The more incendiary issues we avoided, saying as little as possible about such vexed subjects as land reform or civil freedoms. Our rule of thumb for navigating such treacherous waters was *Them ban, bot thu* ("More friends, fewer foes"). Formal pronouncements on land ownership were gratuitous, bound to alienate either those landowners who supported us or the peasants for whom this was the chief issue. Attempts to clarify basic rights would have been even more volatile, exacerbating latent conflicts between the Western-style liberals and Marxist ideolo-

Group of PRG and Alliance peopl
in the jungle. Cao Van Bon, min
ister of economy and finance, is a
left, Lucien Pham Ngoc Hun
(Albert Thao's brother) is in th
dark shirt at the rear

Le Van Tha, my deputy in
the Ministry of Justice.

gues within our own ranks. So we busied ourselves addressing the safer, though still significant, issues that we considered part of our brief.

We also received regular reports documenting the activities of the Saigon government's courts and other legal machinery. These we would study carefully, tracking the different developments and classifying personnel. On the basis of various types of information, we divided the Saigon legal community up into three parts: those who covertly supported us; those who were sympathetic but non-committal; and those who were opposed. Our purpose here was to understand clearly whom we might be able to work with in the event of a coalition. Through our people in the city, we tried assiduously to convert sympathy into active support and irreconcilability into open-mindedness.

By this time the shattered Saigon networks had been rebuilt, and we had been successful in inserting people into the Thieu administration at all levels and into the Southern army as well. The Justice

Department had its complement, though none of our ministry's operatives achieved the status of some other NLF agents of the period.
Even so, our information was thorough, and I was satisfied that our
proselytizing work was progressing satisfactorily.

In the liberated areas there was little to do. The military justice
section had jurisdiction over all incidents relating to the fighting, and
quarrels or disputes among people were most often mediated by the
local political cadres, though the cadres would often come to us for
advice on more difficult cases. Our guiding principles in such situations
were those of traditional Vietnamese justice, which depends on the
authority and wisdom of the elders to conciliate disputants and
educate them to the ethics of the culture.

Internal problems among the fighters were handled by political
commissars, who accompanied the troops and were versed in the
techniques of criticism and self-criticism. On the whole, however,
controversies were few. Although the guerrillas were short of food
and often sick, they maintained the kind of esprit and comradeship

An ad hoc meeting at the PRG headquarters.

that animates people who are fighting for a common purpose in which they believe with all their hearts. They got on, under horrendous conditions, through mutual support and a rough but genuine love for each other. Ironically, when faced with the disillusioning realities of postwar life, many of the former guerrillas looked back on the common life they shared in the Maquis as an idyllic period, a time to be especially treasured because it would not come again. Their leader, General Tran Van Tra, put it this way:

> Each achievement of each human being
> Is the achievement of all.
> If you have accomplished something
> It is due to the help of others.
> We eat the fruit. But we must honor
> Those who planted the tree.
> When you return to the city in victory.
> Never forget your life in the jungle.
> Thanks to your comrades
> You have succeeded.
> Now in success,
> Forget not their friendship.

Tra's poem was printed in his history of the war, of which only one volume appeared, though five were projected.* It was sentiments like these, extolling loyalty and apotheosizing the wartime sacrifices of the Southern people (and implicitly contrasting them with post-war realities) that resulted in the confiscation of this volume and Tra's disappearance from public view.

---

* *Vietnam: History of the Bulwark B2 Theatre,* Vol. 5, Ho Chi Minh City, 1982, title page. This poem does not appear in the English translation prepared by the Foreign Broadcast Information Service (JPRS Document 82733).

Race
Against Death

The first months of 1970 were a precarious time. Even before the new year began, intelligence sources in Phnom Penh informed us that Cambodia's Prince Sihanouk was coming under increased American pressure to allow stepped-up bombing of our Cambodian sanctuaries. Through the years of war, Sihanouk had bravely and ingeniously maintained Cambodia's neutrality, in part by turning a blind eye toward happenings in the border region. Indications that the Americans were looking for a more formal acquiescence to their strikes against our bases and supply routes were ominous indeed. Coupled with this information, Soviet and Chinese sources inside the Cambodian government were now sharing with us intimations they had been receiving of a possible anti-Sihanouk coup.

In preparation for whatever might eventuate, all our headquarters units began fine-tuning their contingency plans. The escape routes we would use if necessary led west across the Vam Co River and into Cambodia's Prey Veng Province, then north toward Kratie. Depending on circumstances, we could take up positions there, on the west bank (the far side) of the Mekong, or continue north up the Ho Chi Minh Trail toward Laos. Strong elements of the NLF's 5th, 7th, and 9th Divisions were brought into the area to provide security for any movements we might be forced to make.

RACE AGAINST DEATH

Then, on March 18, 1970, while Sihanouk was vacationing in France, his opponents struck, deposing him as head of the Cambodian government. Sihanouk's removal was for us a cause of instant anxiety, as we now looked over our shoulders at Cambodia, not as a refuge but as a potential danger. With Sihanouk's less-than-farsighted minister Lon Nol in power, Phnom Penh immediately began to stare in our direction with undisguised hostility. Sensing the possibility of entrapment between a Saigon/American offensive from the east and Royal Cambodian Army pressure from the west, COSVN did not wait to monitor developments in the Cambodian capital. On March 19 the permanent staff moved out toward positions that had been readied deep inside Kratie. By the time troops from the American 25th Division struck the headquarters area during the American/Cambodian incursion, the COSVN command staff had been gone almost two months.

With these portentous events as background, the NLF, PRG, and Alliance complexes readied themselves for emergency withdrawal. As we reviewed defensive measures and logistical planning, the B-52 raids reached a peak of frequency. Each day massive explosions rumbled in the distance, shaking the ground under us as the bombers incessantly probed the surrounding jungle. Then on March 27 at four in the morning, we were awakened by the familiar thunder—nearer now than it had been in recent days. All the officials and guards made for the shelters, listening intently. The concussive *whump-whump-whump* came closer and closer, moving in a direct line toward our positions. Then as the cataclysm walked in on us, everyone hugged the earth—some screaming quietly, others struggling to suppress attacks of violent, involuntary trembling. Around us the ground began to heave spasmodically, and we were engulfed in a monstrous roar. Then, abruptly, it stopped, leaving behind it nearly a hundred dazed Maquis, shaking their heads in an attempt to clear the pressure from their ears. The last of the bomb craters had opened up less than a kilometer away. Again, miraculously, no one had been hurt. But we knew that the time had come. Following advance groups, which had already crossed the Vam Co, the main body—all the ministries and command units spread out over a fifty- or sixty-kilo-meter arc—began the trek into Cambodia.

By March 30 the Justice Ministry was already established in one of the sanctuary complexes, working and sleeping inside bunkers. Early that morning, three days after the near miss by the B-52s, I was thrown out of my cot onto the bunker floor by a series of explosions rocking the area. Glancing quickly out through the bunker opening, my guards and I saw helicopters hovering just above the trees, maneuvering in to land. I could make out the faces of ARVN soldiers and gun barrels protruding from the open doorways. By this time, fire was stuttering out from the dugouts and shelters as our security people began loosing a fusillade of small-arms and machine gun fire at the attackers. Over the radio, voices crackled through with news that the other ministries were also under attack.

Hour followed hour as the firing surged, died down, then flared up again. All day long I hunkered down in the shelter, my two body-guards watching the fighting closely, occasionally letting off a volley from their AK47s through the embrasures. Squirming around on my stomach, I gathered together the most important papers, knowing that, whatever the cost, we would have to break through the encirclement when night came. It was a matter of desperation; none of us had any question that we would be captured the following day if we were still in the complex.

With darkness, pressure from the Saigon troops eased off. They undoubtedly knew that our main force units were in the area, and they were afraid of being trapped themselves. At the signal, my guards and I slipped out of the bunker under the dying glow of a flare. There was no firing as we headed westward into the jungle along one of the prearranged escape routes toward the security corridor the 7th Division was setting up. I ran as far as I was able, then slowed into a kind of shuffling trot, gasping for breath. Some of the ministry officials were on the trail in front of me. I could hear other people hurrying behind. From the bunker complex the firing was picking up, filling the night with the staccato bursts of AK47s and M-16s.

Behind us the security teams fanned out, screening our flight and deflecting pursuit. Half-running, half-walking between my guards, I made my way along the trail, unable to see a thing in the blackness of the jungle. All night we slogged along, unsure of what was happening in back of us but determined to keep moving. As the initial rush of adrenalin wore off, my legs began to feel leaden, and my throat ached with thirst. When word was finally passed that we could stop, I slumped to the ground where I was, stupefied with exhaustion. Just before I passed out, I managed to scoop up a few handfuls of water from a stagnant pool next to the trail.

When I awoke it was 6 A.M. The first thing I noticed was that the swampy puddle from which I had drunk the previous night was the repository of several large piles of buffalo excrement. But I hardly had time to reflect on this unpleasant surprise before we heard the shriek of approaching jets. We dived into the jungle just as several American planes shot by, machine-gunning the trail. Under sporadic bombing and strafing attacks, we moved ahead all morning, an entire column by this time made up of the NLF, PRG, and Alliance ministries and support personnel. Though it was impossible to get firm information, it seemed as if we had not incurred any serious losses in the maelstrom of the previous day's assault.

As we walked, our troop strength was more and more in evidence. General Hoang Van Thai had deployed his defense forces to create a secure corridor from the rendezvous point (the place we had stopped for a few hours of sleep) and the Cambodian province of Kratie, our destination to the north. Though as we trudged along, the situation was unclear, there was no doubt at all that Thai's arrangements were undergoing a serious test. We knew that the Saigon troops had launched a thrust against us from the east while Lon Nol's Royal Cambodian forces were moving in from the west along Route 7, a road that intersected the corridor. Knowing that we were in great danger, we walked as fast as we could all day, our only food the cold rice balls we ate as we marched. Meanwhile, the 9th Division threw up a screen against the ARVN drive, while the 5th moved to block the Cambodians on our left. Along the corridor between them the headquarters and government personnel fled. closely shielded by units from the 7th.

Toward the end of the next day, April 2, a motorcycle driver picked me out of the line of march. He had been sent by PRG President Phat to take me to the 7th Division's headquarters farther to the north, where the rest of the NLF, PRG, and Alliance leadership was already assembled, including Mme. Nguyen Thi Dinh, deputy commander of the NLF armed forces. Early the following morning, we all moved out toward Route 7 only a few miles to our north, aware now that the highway was already under attack.

Fighting to break through the PLAF blocking forces, the ARVN and Cambodian vanguards were struggling to gain control of the highway before we could get there, which would cut off our escape and seal us into southern Cambodia, where we could be surrounded and cut apart. We were not sure whether the forces trying to head us off were aware of exactly who or what they were after, and to this day I do not know whether American and Saigon government military analysts realized how close they were to annihilating or capturing the core of the Southern resistance—elite units of our frontline fighters along with the civilian and much of the military leadership. But as we hurried through the corridor, *we* at least were quite clear about the stakes involved in breaking out. Our efforts were thus tinged not only with the desperation of men fleeing the grasp of a merciless foe, but with anxiety for the very existence of our struggle.

It was at this point that Dr. Hoa, seven months pregnant and supported on one side by her husband, on the other by a bodyguard, went into labor. It had been expected that she would require a cesarean section, so a surgical team had accompanied her on the move into Cambodia. But as it turned out, whether because of the constant walking or for some other reason, the birth came normally— and precipitously. On a square of nylon laid out on the jungle floor, the minister of health gave birth to a baby boy, noisy and apparently well, despite his ill-timed appearance and the confusion into which he had been born.* Carrying this new addition to the revolutionary forces, we neared Route 7, listening intently for incoming artillery rounds amidst the sounds of battle to our right and left.

Just before we got to the highway, word passed down the column that our line blocking the Cambodians was holding—at least for the moment—and that the 9th Division had counterattacked Saigon forces at Krek, about ten kilometers to the east.† Buoyed by this news we crossed 7 and pushed northward in the first of what would become a series of forced marches.

Before long our relief at having avoided entrapment was submerged in an exhaustion beyond description. As day, then night, then day again passed with constant harassment, little sleep, and cold dinners eaten for the most part on the trail, the middle-aged and elderly ministers, with their middle-aged civilian staffs, all of them weakened by disease and half-famished, began to break down physically. As we walked, the rains, typical for that time of year, poured down continuously, turning the red Cambodian earth to a sticky clay that sucked at our rubber sandals, until the last of them had been lost or discarded. Barefoot, pants rolled up above our knees, we shuffled ahead in the ankle-deep mud, each step an energy-draining struggle. Those who had bicycles abandoned them beside the muck of the trail. Like robots, we made our way through the downpour, each man grasping the shirt of the man in front of him for support and direction.

For five days it rained without letup. By this time I could barely stand, let alone walk. I moved along in a slow-motion daze, conscious only of the man in front of me—whose shirt I continued to clutch—and the mortar rounds and artillery shells that crashed sporadically into the jungle alongside our column, from time to time sending us sprawling face first into the mud. At night we slung our

* Our happiness at this event turned to sorrow seven months later when the premature infant succumbed to malaria.

† During the ARVN push into Cambodia in the winter of 1971, Route 7 would again become the scene of vicious fighting. At that time, Saigon forces suffered severe local defeats at Chhlong near the great Chup rubber plantation and at Dampierre, where the PLAF 5th Division screen was now holding against the Lon Nol army.

hammocks from the rubber trees, propping our nylon squares over us in a useless attempt to keep off the torrents of water. When morning came, it was difficult for any of us to tell if we had slept or had simply lapsed, temporarily comatose.

But as we continued northward, we all sensed that there was less urgency to our movement. At some unidentifiable point we realized that no more shells were exploding dully in the sodden trees. At last, in the jungles outside Kratie, 150 kilometers or so north of Route 7, we were able to stop and rest. For several days we did little other than sleep and enjoy the luxuries of hot tea and prepared food, items we hadn't seen for a week and a half. With an opportunity to relax and begin recuperating from this ordeal, spirits started to revive. COSVN's Pham Hung and General Trung joked that "Even though we ran like hell, still we'll win," sentiments that Henry Kissinger anticipated in his 1968 *Foreign Affairs* article: "Guerrillas win if they don't lose. A standard army loses if it does not win."

In taking stock of the situation, we had not in fact lost a great deal. In terms of casualties, our luck had continued to hold. Despite the close escape and the rigors of the march, all of the leadership had manged to arrive at Kratie unharmed. Here we linked up with the COSVN staff, which had previously been evacuated to the region, also without loss. In the expanses of Cambodia's northern provinces, we were less vulnerable to the B-52s and relatively immune to assault, since our forces had de facto control over the region (and had had for some time).

The ARVN attacks that we had so narrowly survived were a precursor to the large-scale American incursion into Cambodia that jumped off a month later. The wider war that resulted from these actions was an almost immediate benefit to us. The American/ARVN attack indeed caused damage and disrupted supply lines. But our antagonists had no staying power in Cambodia. The United States at this point was already in the process of a staged unilateral withdrawal, which could not be truly compensated for by increased air activity. The Saigon forces by themselves were hard-pressed to meet the military challenge they faced in South Vietnam, without adding

Cambodia to their burden, while Lon Nol's army was quite simply unprepared for the kind of warfare it now had to face.

Nixon and Kissinger had gambled that a limited foray into our base areas and supply routes would have a telling effect. But they had seriously exaggerated their own ability to inflict damage relative to their opponents' elasticity and durability. Unwisely, they had traded a few immediate and short-term military gains for the unpredictable consequences of intruding into an already volatile Cambodia and for severe, long-term political debits at home. To our analysts, monitoring the American domestic scene, it seemed that the Cambodian invasion had stimulated a divisiveness equaled only perhaps by the Tet Offensive two years earlier. We had indeed, as Pham Hung said, run away, but Nixon had paid dearly for our temporary discomfiture by sustaining major political losses. Kissinger's argument that the invasion had gained a year may be true. But to our way of looking at it—from a political and diplomatic perspective as well as militarily—the United States action had resulted in a resounding victory for the Front.

Nevertheless, the whole affair had given us a bad fright, not to mention a period of acute physical hardship. Outside Kratie, though, we had a chance to catch our breath before moving on to the western bank of the Mekong. There, behind the natural defensive barrier of the river, we built our new headquarters.

Once we were established here, our first task was to gain the goodwill and support of the local population, a particularly delicate problem given the historical anxieties Cambodians have felt about Vietnamese. In this effort we were immeasurably helped by Sihanouk's proclaimed support for our struggle. On April 24, a week before we took up residence on the Mekong, the anti-American Indochinese leaders, now including the prince, held a minisummit in Canton. Called by Pham Van Dong [DRV Premier], the meeting included Pathet Lao leader Souphanouvong, and NLF President Tho, as well as Sihanouk. At its conclusion the prince issued a statement denouncing the United States and giving the NLF and North Vietnamese formal permission to use Cambodian territory.

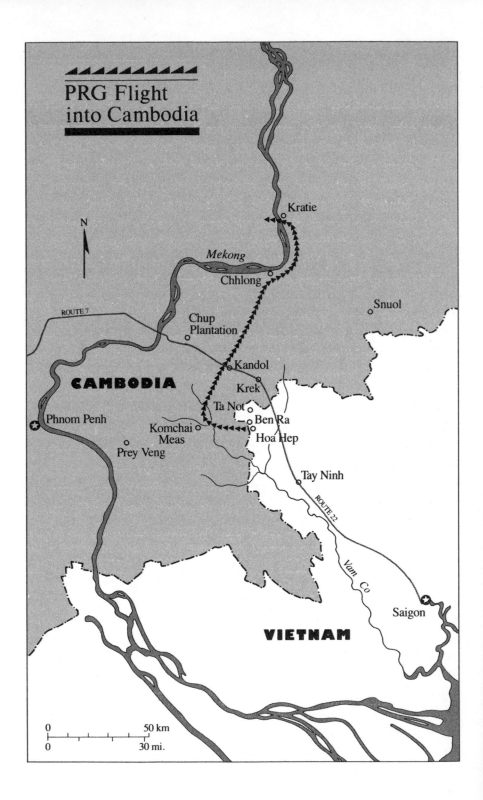

▲▲▲▲▲▲▲▲▲
PRG Flight
into Cambodia

N

Mekong

Kratie

Chhlong

Snuol

ROUTE 7

Chup
Plantation

Kandol

CAMBODIA

Krek

Ta Not

Ben Ra

Komchai
Meas

Hoa Hep

Phnom Penh

Prey Veng

Tay Ninh

ROUTE 22

Vam Co

Saigon

VIETNAM

0   50 km

0   30 mi.

Among the local Cambodians, Sihanouk was revered not just as a political leader, but as a semidivinity. To them, his overthrow was traumatic, an action that combined the abominations of lèse-majesté and sacrilege. Now we were operating with the prince's blessing, giving us a legitimacy in their eyes that we would not otherwise have enjoyed. To reinforce this advantage, we saw to it that our personnel maintained the strictest propriety toward their hosts. Troops were under strict discipline; in individual instances of theft or other infractions, the violators were immediately shot and their punishment announced publicly. The continuing B-52 strikes were another ally in the effort. To the Cambodian villagers, these bombings brought an incomprehensible terror, precipitating the more militant into the ranks of the Khmer Rouge and leaving the rest increasingly sympathetic toward the Americans' enemies.

Although (or perhaps because) our bases were now more dispersed and harder to pinpoint, the high-level raids became more and more frequent, eventually building to a crescendo of eighty-one attacks per day—a good deal more than we had endured even in the weeks just prior to our evacuation from Vietnam. In the middle of this renewed deluge, I suffered an acute malarial seizure and was trundled off to our cadre hospital deep in the jungle. But even here, safety was an unattainable commodity. While I was under care in one of the hospital's bunkers, a B-52 attack struck nearby, shaking the room and sending some tabletop medical cabinets flying around. My bodyguard threw himself on top of me, but fortunately neither of us was struck by the caroming furniture. After this, I was transferred to an even more remote hospital, where I spent the next two months convalescing.

It wasn't until the end of June that I was fully recovered from the general anemia these relapses always brought. When I finally returned to the headquarters complex, I quickly found that not all had been well there either.

16

First Troubles
with the North

As soon as I arrived, I sensed a change in the mood. My usually convivial and enthusiastic friends were sullen and at first oddly uncommunicative, as if in my absence a barrier had been erected between us. Once they opened up, their talk was laced with anger and recrimination. There was a problem, they let me know, and the root of the problem was one Ba Cap, the new administrative and liaison chief for the Alliance.

This Ba Cap was a vociferous and abrasive individual, easily angered and not shy about venting his anger, even toward those he was supposed to be serving. A Northerner of unyielding Marxist principles, he might have been especially chosen to gall the heterodox Southern nationalists who populated the Alliance. For some unknown reason, he had been brought in to replace the well-liked Chin Chien ("Fighter Number Nine"), who had traveled to Hanoi with a group of elderly Alliance, PRG, and NLF members who were being evacuated and afterward had remained in the North. Being liaison chief was a centrally important function, which involved Ba Cap and his staff in the closest daily contact with all the Alliance and PRG leadership. And once emplaced, he had lost no time in demonstrating the many differences between himself and his cheerful predecessor.

My old friend Nguyen Van Kiet, the former French professor

and Saigon education official, found an early opportunity to take me aside. He was livid.

"What's going on here?" he began reproachfully. "I joined the Front. I made that decision. We all did. You know what it's cost us." He was starting to tremble. "Now these Northerners are treating us like uninvited guests. This Ba Cap is the most irritating son of a bitch I've ever come across. He can't keep his mouth shut about this petitbourgeois business; it's like a propaganda broadcast you can't shut off. He criticizes us every chance he gets. Everybody is sore as hell about it."

As I heard more, it became clear to me that this was hardly just a matter of personal bad temper. Ba Cap had informed his subordinates (also Party functionaries from the North) that he wanted all of the PRG and Alliance leaders to understand that they were being served, not because of any merit of their own, but only because they were representatives of the proletariat and the Party. Ba Cap's cadres had carried out his instructions faithfully and had managed to alienate the entire group. This was a new attitude and an unsettling one—in striking contrast to the careful solicitude the Lao Dong had always shown to the non-Party Southern leadership. Whatever was going on, Ba Cap would never have initiated a switch like this himself, however irascible his nature.

The reaction of Kiet and the rest, myself included now, was especially resentful. Many of us were from well-to-do families and had been used to the good life before we enlisted in the revolution. Our reasons for joining were perhaps varied, but we all regarded ourselves as people who had already sacrificed a great deal for the nation and were quite ready to sacrifice everything. Many of us had struggled in one way or another against the French, and in moving to the jungle all of us were decisively committed against the Americans. Whatever comforts we might previously have enjoyed were part of history. We were not touched by guilt about our class background, and we felt that our motives were every bit as pure as those of our ideologically minded colleagues. The idea that some of the cadres regarded our previous, citified life-styles as a subject for mockery and contempt was

Ba Cap (*left, in white*), the Northern administrative chief for the Alliance, and Chin Chien (*right*), his more amiable predecessor.

insupportable. After the prisons, B-52s, diseases, and malnutrition, it was outrageous to suggest that we were somehow second-class revolutionaries. There was no mourning when, in the early fall of 1970, Ba Cap fell victim to a B-52 raid.

But even after his exceptionally unpleasant personality was gone from the scene, the general attitude of the cadres persisted. Apparently, revolutionary comradeship was not the universal bond it had appeared. As my colleagues and I looked back over the past several years, a pattern seemed to emerge. We began to see that the importance of our role at any given time could be measured by the level of treatment we were receiving. In 1968, as the Party's control over the revolution became increasingly obvious, it had been necessary to broaden the struggle's nationalist base. In 1969, Nixon's Vietnamization policy called for an international (as well as domestic) legitimation of our activities. To meet these requirements, the Alliance and Provisional Revolutionary Government had been brought to life in a flourish of deference to Southern goals. Conversely, 1970 was a year for military developments; the war had spread throughout Cambodia and Laos, and the American ground forces were embarked on what appeared an irreversible withdrawal. It was a year of fierce fighting that brought both reverses and victories. But with the Americans on their way out, for the first time we could hope that the balance of military forces might eventually turn in our favor. With some of the Party's leaders glimpsing a vision of armed triumph, the political front suffered a loss of stature. And as the Alliance and PRG roles became less central, we began to hear more and more about our class deficiencies.

At a PRG cabinet meeting held not too long after my return from the hospital, I approached PRG President Phat directly about what was happening. To what, I asked him, could we attribute the behavior of the cadres? And what was his opinion of the situation? I knew that Phat's response would tell me a great deal about the depth of the problem. However discreetly he might try to phrase the answer, he would have no choice but to reveal the Party's true attitude.

Both what Phat said and how he said it were disconcerting. "In all likelihood," he told me, "Ba Cap's class orientation is quite correct. On the other hand, his zeal in terms of revolutionary tactics and strategy is in error. . . . We'll look into it and see what can be done." Phat's tone—formal, awkward, vaguely apologetic—conveyed his discomfort about facing me. Translated, it all meant that, a year after Ho Chi Minh's death, the ideologues were firmly in control, and they were not inclined to waste effort on their junior partners, whatever they might be broadcasting to the rest of the world.

Despite Phat's glib phrases, it was apparent that nothing at all could be done. Among ourselves discussions were animated by growing feelings of resentment and anxiety. A sense of estrangement from our allies inserted itself, where before there had been harmony and cooperation. We knew that we were involved in an unpalatable double game, though it was still unclear where the game might lead. Certainly the notions many of us held about brotherhood in struggle were eroding quickly.

With hindsight it is easy to look back on that period as one that might have been—perhaps should have been—decisive, a golden opportunity to understand our true relationship to the Northern-controlled Party and to do something about it. Had clarity and logic prevailed, that indeed is what might have happened, and numbers of Alliance and PRG people might have moved away from the revolution, or at least strongly factionalized it. But to try to see the situation as the Southern nationalists did in mid-1970, one cannot look at it through the eyes of logic alone.

In the first place, none of us had chosen our paths lightly. None of us had embraced revolution in a half-hearted fashion or without the deepest soul-searching. Problems or not, by 1970 the time for considering other roads to Vietnamese independence was long past. For myself, the decisive moment had come when I returned from France in 1955. Many of the others too had watched Diem carefully in his first years, before making a choice they knew would determine much about how their lives would be spent. The year 1968, after Tet Mau Than, was another such crux, a turning point for some who had been contemplating their country's future for a decade and a half.

For still others, liberation had always been tied to the Party—not necessarily because they were ardent Communists, but because as far back as 1920, the only ally Vietnamese nationalism had even known was the Communist International. Ho Chi Minh had grasped this support with the fervor of a drowning man, and he had woven the fabric of independence out of the twin fibers of nationalism and communism. But even as Ho immersed himself in the Comintern doctrine of expansive revolution, he had stayed open to other op-portunities. His unique political vision, darting ahead through decades, had always retained a sensitivity to options and potential allies. And the opportunities had come, in 1944 and 1945 when he conducted a low-level courtship with Americans, in 1946 at Fontainebleau when he thought the French could be won to partnership, even in 1954 when the war with France ended and the United States was faced with its own decision.

But no other allies had ever materialized for Ho, and as we reflected on our relationship with the Workers' Party in the summer of 1970, no other allies presented themselves to us either. We were locked in. France and the West had helped shape much of our political thinking, but it was a bitter paradox that France and the West had given us nothing to go along with it, no hope and no help toward adapting their own values to our society. To all appearances, it had never occurred to Western leaders to try to accommodate Vietnamese aspirations for independence, decent government, and economic progress within their policies. On the contrary, the French had given up control only inch by bloody inch. And the Americans regarded the country as a pawn of strategy, turning a blind and ignorant eye to the motivations of its people, infusing strength into dictators, and nurturing the former officers of French colonialism. Neither domestically nor internationally was there anywhere else to turn for the required support, even as the scales began to drop from our eyes.

These things were so evident to us, so much a part of our history and makeup, that to describe the situation in terms of "weighing facts" and "making a choice" is in itself a falsification. But this or something like it was the context of my thinking in the summer of 1970, as the Party's own manipulative heart began to reveal itself. The revelation, it's true, did create something of a dilemma, but not much of one, not considering the nonexistent alternatives.

Beyond this, there were good reasons for believing that we could still emerge from this struggle in a position of some strength. Although General Giap was now talking about a "regular war" (as opposed to a guerrilla and political war) and military victory, in fact few people were sanguine about such predictions. As long as American strength supported the Saigon government, the idea of total victory seemed wistful and vague, a Vietnamese equivalent to "the light at the end of the tunnel" metaphor that American politicians were growing fond of during the same period. The Front's armed forces had suffered agonizing and irreplaceable losses during the frontal assaults of Tet. What might happen to the Northern main-force divisions in the meat grinder of American air power was anyone's guess. Certainly Khe Sanh was not an encouraging precedent.*

Perhaps some psychological residue from our firsthand experience of the B-52 deluge was helping to form our views on this subject. We knew the effects of these attacks when they were directed at our hidden and bunkered headquarters compounds. It took no great imagination to predict how troops massed for conventional battles in a "regular war" would fare. Everyone also vividly recalled that prior to mid-1967, DRV General Nguyen Chi Thanh had conducted a strategy in South Vietnam of direct confrontation against ARVN and American forces, and that the horrendous casualty rates that resulted had forced a reversion to tactics of attrition and political struggle.

All this suggested strongly that some kind of negotiated settlement was at least as likely an outcome as a decisive military resolution. And if events moved in that direction—and we could only act adroitly enough—the significance of the Alliance and the PRG would be substantially reenhanced, in reality as well as for show. Any political compromise would create an opportunity for the Southern nationalists to carve out a distinct role for themselves, as a swing or third force operating between the Party and the American–Thieu forces.

This was especially so, since in our judgment the publically announced PRG and Alliance positions truly reflected the desires of a great majority of the Southern people. The South Vietnamese found themselves trapped between their loathing of the Thieu dictatorship and their fears of communism. Given these political realities, there was nowhere for most people to turn, so they paid outward allegiance to whoever held the whip hand. But had a negotiated settlement given political viability to a middle way, we were convinced that substantial popular support would surface. That had been both the conviction

---

* Khe Sanh was the American fire base in Central Vietnam that had been surrounded by North Vietnamese forces early in January of 1968. For almost three months, the attackers were exposed to continuous air strikes by B-52s and low-level aircraft, suffering fearsome casualties. Eventually the siege was abandoned.

and the hope that sustained many of the Front and Alliance people from the beginning. And none of us who understood things that way saw any reason to change our assessment.

As it was, the course of the war had put us in an uncomfortable position, progressively decreasing our real power while at the same time emphasizing our propaganda function. And recently the discomfort had become acute. But if our analysis of popular feelings was anywhere near correct, there was a large base of support— political and regional—that could be organized, *if* the objective circumstances allowed for it. And those objective circumstances could be brought about by a coalition government.

I asked myself then if such thinking was naive, considering the Front's subordinate military role and the organizational control exerted by such Party members as President Phat. I thought not. If a coalition was to result from the bloodletting and mutual exhaustion that were likely to follow the American withdrawal, political power would inevitably gravitate toward the middle. The incentive for both sides would be to control the center, and those who were at the center would find themselves with leverage to use against either side. There seemed to be good practical reasons, then, to ride the current. Moreover, though our idealism might be suffering an aggravated assault at the moment, it was hardly dead. When all was said and done, these problems with the gentlemen from the North were still (we thought) an argument between brothers.

But brothers or not, tension persisted. In the PRG ministries we continued the work of preparing for a postwar coalition, much as we had been doing before the move to Cambodia. But from month to month we worked in greater isolation. Contacts with COSVN were less frequent and more strained. The flow of information between ourselves and those who were directing the war diminished substantially. We were less aware of the whole picture than we had previously been—less well briefed and rarely consulted. News of the ARVN defeats in Laos and in Cambodia, at Chup and Dampierre came, places familiar to us from our flight to Kratie a year before. There was no question that these clashes were a rehearsal for the "regular war" scenario being shaped by the Politburo Military Committee—North Vietnamese Army divisions facing Saigon troops operating with American air support, but without the benefit of American assistance on the ground. As the summer of 1971 passed, we know that preparations were under way for major offensive operations in early 1972, which would fully test this new alignment of forces.

Meanwhile, in Paris, Le Duc Tho was treating Henry Kissinger to a brilliant display of "talking and fighting," using the negotiations to cover as long as possible the next real move in the war, the upcoming dry-season campaign in the South. One of his important tactics was the "anyone but Thieu" proposal, a variation on the time-honored theme of isolating the principal enemy. To Kissinger, Tho insisted that the removal of Thieu, either through elections or in some other way, was the prerequisite to a negotiated solution. I do not know the extent to which the American government took this ploy seriously. But judging from Kissinger's memoirs, this and the other North Vietnamese talking points absorbed a great deal of his attention during the summer of 1971. In Kratie we awaited the more substantial developments we knew were coming, understanding that in this stage the war had moved into spheres far removed from our orbit of influence.

Whatever developments we might have expected, none of us guessed that our next battle would be a set piece war of words, with the Party idealogues arrayed on one side and the NLF/PRG/ Alliance political leadership on the other. It began when, in the fall of 1971, the Party decided we could afford to spend three months studying the fine points of Marxism-Leninism. Perhaps it was a dramatization of the nadir our fortunes had reached. Or perhaps it was simply an indication of how seriously our ideological recalcitrance was viewed. Whichever the case, at almost the same time that Xuan Thuy (Le Duc Tho's nominal superior) was entertaining George McGovern with chimerical peace proposals in Paris, other party experts on the west bank of the Mekong were preparing to educate South Vietnam's revolutionary bourgeoisie to the truths of dialectical materialism.

Invitations to these seminars, which were to last three months, were handled in the friendliest fashion. Everyone was aware that unfortunate conflicts had developed, and we were now being asked to come and participate in discussions that would help clarify the roles of the various revolutionary factions in our common struggle for independence. Sessions would be led by specialists from the Nguyen Ai Quoc* Institute for Higher Cadres, many of whom had been trained in Moscow and were working on the COSVN staff. For a brief moment I thought that maybe this was a belated consequence of President Phat's promise to "look into the situation," and that we might have a frank exchange of views and ultimately some sort of mutual acknowledgment of the nature of our alliance.

Any ideas I might have had along these lines were set straight at our initial meeting. The first major subject on the agenda had nothing to do with clarification of roles, with future strategy, or with anything else pertinent to the war. Instead we found ourselves presented with the Marxist proposition that "matter is of primary nature" and that the material universe exists independently of and prior to thought and spirit. This thesis had very hard going with a group of Asian intellectuals who, French-trained though they were, had imbibed Buddhist and Confucian spirituality with their mothers' milk. The argument heated up quickly, the Marxists striving to assert their axioms and demonstrate the inevitable historical corollaries, while their opponents responded with stubborn sarcasm and expressions of disbelief. As the debate reached into the stratosphere of inconsequentiality, I began to feel disoriented. The war that was to decide the future of the homeland was raging on, and here we were in the middle of the Cambodian wilderness, debating doctrines of essence and existence. The whole thing had a surreal quality to it.

It was with a sense of relief that I watched the discussions on

* Nguyen Ai Quoc ("Nguyen the Patriot") had been one of Ho Chi Minh's best-known pseudonyms.

these abstract issues wind to a discordant close and the second set of questions take their place. What, we were asked, is the proper relationship between patriotism and communism, nationalism and internationalism? If those who had organized these seminars envisioned a series of authoritative lectures, punctuated by well-mannered questions from the audience, they must have been profoundly disappointed. Almost at once the air grew thick with invective and acrimony. Those who spoke for the primacy of nationalism also espoused democratic freedoms and national independence. The party cadres flung back the tenets of international class struggle and the dictatorship of the proletariat. National independence or the class struggle, which was it to be? Which had historically motivated the Vietnamese people in their fight against colonialism and imperialist aggression?

It is self-evident, my colleagues and I argued, that the desire for national independence has provided the circumstances for the struggle for land and democratic freedoms. It is the nationalistic uprising that has created the conditions for a proletarian revolution as well. Consequently, national liberation is the primary mover; there is no *necessary* connection between Marxism-Leninism and independence, let alone a causal relationship. The cadres shouted back the lessons they had learned about the interdependence of the class struggle and the war against imperialism, but they were finding it rough going against the Western-trained intellectuals, who had sharpened their debating skills in the French schools.

To sustain their arguments the intellectuals made free use of quotations from Uncle Ho. *"Nothing,"* they recited, "is more precious than independence and liberty"—with the emphasis on "nothing." "It is dogmatism [citing Ho again] to ignore uniqueness and to prefer to draw profit from the experience of others"—the "others" being Communist revolutions elsewhere. Finding Ho Chi Minh in the lists against them seemed particularly upsetting to the cadres, as they floundered around for a strategy to counteract such specious malice.

By the time the third major subject reached the floor, whatever amity existed between the groups had long since expired under this constant verbal bludgeoning. The cadres had suffered more bourgeois obstinacy than they had ever dreamed of bearing. The nationalists were infuriated at the cadres' narrow-minded bigotry and by the thought that these sessions were set up to occupy them while the war was being carried on by others. Even without this rancorous prologue, the last subject—the role of the intelligentsia in the national revolution (as interpreted by the Party)—would have been enough all by itself, to induce apoplexy in the argumentative Southerners.

Now it was the cadres' turn to quote scripture: from Minister of defense Vo Nguyen Giap on the need for the various classes to accept the Party's leadership in order to "achieve national union . . . to neutralize all forces that can be neutralized and divide all [opposing] forces susceptible of division"; from Secretary General Le Duan on the role of social class:

> In our days capitalism has become anachronistic and has revealed to the light its hideous reactionary visage. . . . In the face of the powerful revolutionary movement . . . the intellectuals come forth from the national bourgeoisie and separate themselves from it, and especially do their children do this. And taking cognizance of historical evolution, little by little they change their views to join in a fundamental way the camp of the workers and peasants.

Infused with the authority of their sources, the cadres apparently considered the point made beyond any sane objection. We were to "come forth," to capitulate and renounce our "class of origin," rallying wholeheartedly to the proletarian revolution.

At this, Huynh Van Nghi, the husband of Dr. Hoa (who had given birth on the jungle floor), stood up and with great dignity declared, "If we accept the political direction of the Vietnamese Workers' Party, it is because we have perceived that up until now the Party has followed the correct path to national independence. And if we have joined the resistance, it is because our hearts, our consciences, our patriotic feelings have drawn us to respond to the appeal of the Fatherland—not to the appeal of the proletarian revolution! We see no reason for capitulation to anyone, or for denying what you are pleased to call our 'class of origin.' "

Nghi had hardly sat down before he was treated to a tearful

harangue from President Phat's wife, Bui Thi Nga. "We owe an un-repayable debt of gratitude to the Party," she said, pausing to choke down a sob. "The Party has saved our souls from the mud of capitalism and has revealed to us the shining road to the proletarian revolution." For an instant I thought that the ordinarily humorless Madame Phat, daughter of Northern bourgeois parents, was attempting sarcasm. Then I brought myself back to reality. She was, like the rest, just a fanatic. Had Phat himself been there, he would have cringed at her ingenuousness. But his wife, at any rate, had indisputably "come forth." From that point on, Madame Phat was known in NLF circles as the Guardian of the Pagoda.

Eventually the debates reached such a pitch of ardor that several of the most prestigious COSVN leaders began to participate, spreading oil on what were by now very troubled waters. Nguyen Van Linh, chief of propaganda, came in to take a conciliatory role, as did Tran Nam Trung, military chief, and Phan Van Dang, Party second secretary. They worked skillfully, moderating the tone of discussion, checking personal recriminations, and expressing muted sympathy for the views of the embattled nationalists. Clearly, they were anxious to avoid any permanent rupture, conveying tactfully to the NLF/Alliance/PRG people a subtle message of solidarity. As the seminars moved through their final days, my colleagues and I found ourselves relieved to know that the class-struggle ideologues did not represent the thinking of the Party's upper level. Our anger began to drain away. After the crudeness of the cadres' assault, we were gratified to find that among our Northern compatriots who counted, there was continued respect for our positions and our integrity. Obviously, there were several factions within the Party, and the younger Soviet-trained officials were a potential danger. But the heart of the alliance was undeniably sound—we assured ourselves of that.

It wasn't until five years later, months after the Great Spring Victory of 1975 had brought the Party to power, that I was able to appreciate fully the brilliant choreography that had swirled around us during that rainy season in Kratie. Whipsawed into anger and tears by the cadres' frontal assault on our principles, our dignity,

A group of PRG people. I am at extreme left; Dr. Hoa's husband, Huynh Van Nghi, is at extreme right.

and our sense of self-worth, we had been well prepared to embrace the reassurances extended to us by the COSVN leadership. None of us had recognized the classic interrogation technique for what it was: the brutal softening up followed by the kindly offer of friendship and accord. The Party had staged a dazzling performance.

17

1972:
The Watershed

Our foray into theoretical and practical Marxism gave way at the end of 1971 to more pressing concerns. As if to reinforce the positive denouement of the seminars, we now found ourselves closely involved with the many problems brought by the newly emerging phase of the war. That summer and fall had seen a lull in military activities, screened by the diplomatic pas de deux in Paris. But now both sides were focused on the imminent dry-season offensive, the results of which promised to shape the war's future and determine the nature of an eventual settlement.

At the PRG cabinet meeting held during the first week of January 1972, all of us were aware that the struggle was nearing a watershed. Although in the long view, the upcoming battles might only represent one stage in a conflict already well into its third decade, there was no question that the previous year and a half had brought potentially decisive changes. In Beijing and Moscow our allies were now responding to the overtures of American diplomacy, a development whose eventual ramifications were hard to predict but could not be positive. On the other hand, in Cambodia and Laos, the balance of forces was now clearly in our favor. Furthermore, Nixon would soon be running hard for reelection in a country that (if we could believe the American editorialists) had grown sick to death of the war. Most important of all, over 400,000 American troops had already been withdrawn from Vietnam, leaving behind an untried South Vietnamese army that was about to face a savage baptism.

Responding to the mood of expectancy and tension brought on by the approaching crunch, President Phat's political, military, and diplomatic report was more detailed and wide-ranging than usual. Instead of the standard cabinet briefing, Phat launched into a full review of recent events, followed by an outline of strategy for the coming year. According to Phat, 1970 and 1971 had been characterized by our effort to frustrate the designs of the Saigon troops and their American supporters. A high point had been the destruction of the South Vietnamese attack on the supply lines along Route 9 in southern Laos and in eastern Cambodia. We had also succeeded in enlarging the liberated areas in these countries. Together with the Khmer Rouge, we were putting insistent pressure on the Lon Nol regime, turning a dangerous threat—Sihanouk's overthrow—to our advantage and creating for the Americans a further dimension of intractable confrontation. For the future, the most conservative estimates indicated that we could look forward to maintaining a stabilized situation in the Cambodian and Laotian regions essential to the war effort.

Another important area of activity had been the war in the villages, particularly the effort to counteract the Phoenix program. This program, by synchronizing Saigon and American intelligence activities, attempted to identify and "neutralize" Front personnel operating in the hamlets and villages. "Neutralize" in the jargon of the program meant to capture, kill, or "turn" those who were identified. In many places the program was carried out in a lackadaisical or ham-handed fashion. Often Phoenix existed primarily in name, though at times it flowered into indiscriminate terror, as ordinary villagers were arrested, along with Front operatives, and tortured or arbitrarily executed. In some locations, though, Phoenix was dangerously effective. In Hau Nghia Province, for example, not far from our old base area, the Front infrastructure was virtually eliminated. Nevertheless, Phoenix had not been without cost for the other side. The abuse and extortion that accompanied the program inevitably generated additional sympathy for the Front. And terror, of course, was regularly answered by terror, so that, with the implicit modus vivendi that existed in many places broken, casualties mounted on both sides.

Phat also reviewed the rebuilding of our mass strength in the cities since Tet and the serious urban unrest facing the regime. In 1970 Thieu had decreed a militarization of the educational system, closing high schools and universities and forcing students to attend military lectures and training exercises. This aroused tremendous resistance, and student groups had carried out a protracted series of violent demonstrations, resulting in arrests, trials, and a surge of support for the Front—including the recruitment of a number of the top student leaders. Among these was Huynh Tan Mam, the president of the Saigon University Student Union, whose trial for subversion had become something of a cause célèbre.

At the same time, the regime had intensified the draft and increased payroll taxes, bringing on widespread labor unrest. Strikes and demonstrations fed on themselves. Organizations of disabled veterans were marching for their rights, while the Buddhists redoubled their opposition to government policies, rallying to the Front call for reconciliation and concord under the slogan "peace and neutrality." The most vehement protests of all were aimed at the foreign troops still in the country, particularly the Koreans, whose special brutality had led to a large number of civilian deaths in the central provinces. Building on local anger, our agents had organized mass demonstrations around the Korean camps in an effort to focus international (and especially American) public attention on the situation.

Phat then commented on the discord among Saigonese politicians created by the October presidential elections. Initially both Vice President Nguyen Cao Ky and former Diem coup conspirator "Big" Minh had intended to run. But Thieu was able to engineer Ky's disqualification from the race, and "Big" Minh, sensing the inevitable, backed away from a head-on clash. As might have been expected, Thieu's brazen manipulation of the election stimulated the cynicism of his opponents within the National Assembly and in the press, sharpening the divisiveness which the regime had to cope with.

Several American commentators have concluded that Le Duc Tho (negotiating with Kissinger at the time) would have agreed to a cease-fire in exchange for an open and fair presidential election. But in fact we had absolutely no illusions about these elections. In our opinion Nixon would never have gotten rid of Thieu under any circumstances. We knew that Ambassador Ellsworth Bunker was manipulating behind the scenes to arrange the appearance of a real election—one rumor was that "Big" Minh had been offered a very substantial amount of money to run. But whatever the appearance, the results of this race were a foregone conclusion.

To capitalize on the situation, we gave directions to our agents within Minh's entourage to dissuade him from running. Even while the Americans were struggling to demonstrate Thieu's commitment to democracy (despite Thieu's own lack of cooperation), we wanted to highlight his dictatorial maneuvering. Ours was the easier task. The elections gave us the opportunity to increase Thieu's domestic isolation and to aggravate the people's anger at him. At the same time, the DRV developed an active propaganda campaign (aimed as always at the Western mass media and antiwar movements) to hold Nixon responsible for the phony Saigon presidential contest. Speculations that Le Duc Tho would have been willing to arrange a cease-fire in return for a genuine election were (and remain to this day) a coup for North Vietnamese psychological warfare strategists.

More important, Phat pointed out, was the economic breakdown engendered by the American withdrawal. With the river of dollars drying up, the South's false economic boom had begun to deflate, bringing with it unemployment and precipitous price rises. Even soldiers' families had barely enough to live on, and they too were out on the streets protesting. As the regime's economic situation worsened, so did the endemic venality of Saigon's political, business, and military leaders. For the first time corruption had become so extraordinarily blatant that it began to spawn mass protests. Progressive economic dislocation boded especially well for the Front's ongoing efforts to organize the urban workers. Meanwhile, our own economic picture remained secure. Despite the diplomatic maneuvering going on among the United States, China, and the Soviets, supplies from our allies flowed in at an ever-increasing rate. Indeed, since October, when the Soviet Union and the DRV had signed a new military assistance agreement, these supplies had included unprecedented amounts of the most sophisticated Soviet weaponry.

Phat's conclusions were optimistic. The past two years had seen us move from a retrenchment, following the internal losses of Tet, to a position of increasing strength on the military and political fronts. We had capitalized on the defensive operations that protected our threatened sanctuaries and supply lines, and we had measurably improved our base of operations in the towns and cities. In spite of the inevitable setbacks and difficulties, especially in the countryside, we were at the moment better placed than we had ever been to exploit the weaknesses of Thieu and the Americans. In particular, Saigon's military weakness made the Americans vulnerable on the diplomatic front.

The political, military, and diplomatic report was followed by an analysis of the Paris negotiations, given by an official from the Ministry of Foreign Affairs. To close the meeting, Nguyen Van Linh (the COSVN secretary who had helped cool passions raised by the Marxism seminars) presented projections for the coming year. "It is imperative," he said, "to concentrate all our energy on the three fronts, to modify the balance of power even further and put us in a position of strength in the negotiations. To do this we must ruin the credibility of Nixon and his protégé Thieu, just as we did for Johnson in 1968. We intend to drive the Americans into a corner and force concessions from them before the presidential elections. If possible we mean to destroy Nixon's chances for reelection."

There was no secret about how all this was to be done. The only mystery about the spring offensive was when it would be launched.

In Vietnam the dry season begins in November. As the weeks, then months passed, the tension thickened. By March you could almost touch it. A brief flurry of notes from Le Duc Tho to Kissinger, ostensibly meant to rekindle the American enthusiasm for talking, in reality indicated that all forces were poised. On March 30 they struck, first in the northern provinces below the demilitarized zone, then in the Central region around Kontum, finally in Binh Long on the Cambodian border. Dong Ha fell, then Quang Tri on the coast. On May 21 the NLF flag was raised over Loc Ninh. An Loc, a provincial capital sixty miles from Saigon, was cut off. In battle zone after battle zone the South Vietnamese army, fighting now without American ground support, was running or deteriorating. The ARVN 3d Division had ceased to exist; so had most of the 22nd, as it attempted to defend the highlands. The 5th, our old trading partner from pre-1970 days, was at the point of collapse. In his memoirs, Nixon sketches the gloom at the White House. "It is conceivable," he said to himself, "that all South Vietnam would fall." At PRG headquarters on the banks of the Mekong, we thought so too, and as deep as Nixon's despair was at that moment, just so high was our euphoria.

The initial successes, though, began to slow appreciably as American air power made itself felt and as the better Saigon units dug in. B-52 strikes multiplied daily, making a shambles of logistics and causing appalling casualties among troops massed for conventional assaults. For the first time since 1967, North Vietnam itself was targeted for high-altitude attacks. By April 16, American bombing runs reached Hanoi and Haiphong, where the oil depots were struck. On May 8 in a major televised address, Nixon announced that the Northern ports would be mined while naval air strikes now would reach unprecedented levels. He was going to react, as he phrased it, "to the maximum extent." The showdown had reached its crisis. It seemed that this moment must hold the future hostage.

It didn't. The fact of the matter was that by the time Nixon gave his speech, the United States and South Vietnam had already lost the war (to the extent that such a thing can be predicted), and so, if we had only known it, had the Vietcong. Sometime between May 2, when Kissinger and Le Duc Tho met briefly and acrimoniously in Paris, and May 8, the date of Nixon's speech, the American leadership made the crucial decision. The trail of its consequences would end almost three years later on the roof of the United States embassy, as the last helicopter lifted off, and on the lawn of Saigon's Independence Palace, as the first North Vietnamese tanks broke through the gate.

These humiliations have been preserved in pictures. No photograph has yet been published of the Rex Dance Hall on July 18, 1975, the scene of the Southern revolution's final humiliation. But that too should hold its place in the iconography of the war's vanquished, and that too was in part due to choices made in Washington a month into the 1972 spring offensive. The decision itself came about through the Americans' arrogant reliance on power, combined with a fatal misunderstanding of the nature of their enemy and his strategy. It happened, or so it seems to me, something like this.

The last apparently serious diplomatic interchange between Kissinger and Le Duc Tho had taken place back in July of 1971. In October Le Duc Tho had gone home, claiming illness. In fact, preparations for the upcoming offensive were simply too advanced either to be further ignored by the Americans or hidden by the Vietnamese. At that point, Le Duc Tho had on the table his nine-point proposal, complemented by PRG Foreign Minister Madame Binh's seven points (presented at the plenary negotiations that were going on simultaneously with Tho and Kissinger's secret sessions). Briefly, both positions demanded an early deadline for complete American troop withdrawal. For his part, Kissinger was no longer insisting on a simultaneous withdrawal of North Vietnamese forces. But neither had he acquiesced in a continued Northern presence *after* the United States had terminated its involvement. Instead, the American position envisioned a gradual withering away of DRV strength in the South through an agreement prohibiting reinforcement or any "further infiltration of outside forces." Then, in April, as the spring offensive blossomed, Kissinger had angrily demanded the withdrawal of all Northern troops that had moved south during the offensive. Now, on May 8, a very different note was sounded.

From the White House that night Nixon's speech was ambiguous —hard-hitting in its denunciation of the North ("international outlaws"), but also holding the door open to a settlement. The United States, he said, would remove all military personnel within four months in return for a prisoner exchange and cease-fire. About the Northern divisions that had flooded southward for the offensive, or that had been stationed there prior to it, there was no mention of any kind. At a press conference the next day, Kissinger confirmed (albeit in the language of diplomacy) the president's offer: "We are saying that if our prisoners are returned and if there is an end to the fighting, we will withdraw all our forces. . . ."

> REPORTER. Would the North Vietnamese have to withdraw to North Vietnam?

> KISSINGER. We will be delighted to spell out our proposal as soon as serious negotiation starts, but . . . we would approach negotiations in a generous spirit and with the attitude of bringing about a rapid end to the war.

For all the verbiage that has been spent on these events, what had happened was actually very simple. Practically the entire North Vietnamese army was now inside South Vietnam—to stay. And stay it would, after the Americans pulled out and after the Saigon forces were defeated too. In early May, their concern mounting about South Vietnam's ability to hold, Nixon and Kissinger had decided that though there still might be a chance of staving off an immediate military catastrophe, they would have no choice but to accept, formally and explicitly, the fait accompli of a full Northern military presence in the South.

Their decision was of course induced by powerful factors. The American press was already screaming its rage about the renewed bombing of the North. Nor was there anything subtle about the reaction in Congress, which, as Kissinger has noted, was well on its way toward legislating the United States out of the war. Nixon and his security adviser could (and obviously did) anticipate a torrent of fury in response to the announced mining and stepped-up air strikes. In this expectation they could not have been disappointed.

Our assessment of all of this was that, regardless of whatever volcanic rhetoric we might hear, the American leaders judged that their domestic strength could not sustain the effort needed to win any significant military concessions. Perhaps too they wanted to show their new Soviet and Chinese friends that they were truly making a constructive effort. Finally, with their own presidential elections fast approaching, a negotiated settlement would help them gather in a rich political harvest. Under such circumstances, the best they could hope for (we felt) was a military stalemate that would acknowledge our gains, followed by renewed talks with a serious potential for success. To achieve this, we could expect the Americans to pursue the highest level of violence on the battlefield, even while standing ready to make concessions at the bargaining table.

It soon became clear that the Americans were straining every fiber to bring events to a conclusion along just these lines. They had moved in large-scale reinforcements for their fleet operations. In the sky new squadrons of B-52s and fighter bombers had made their appearance and were keeping up unceasing assaults over the Southern battlegrounds and Northern strategic targets. Public pronouncements by administration spokesmen expressed a conviction that the decisive battle was now under way. That sense of things is confirmed by both Nixon's and Kissinger's accounts of the period in their memoirs. Kissinger called the offensive a showdown. Meeting with Soviet Ambassador Dobrynin, he declared that the United States would now "bring the war to a decisive military conclusion." "To put it in the bluntest terms," he told Ellsworth Bunker, "we are not interested in half measures."

Nixon was even more consumed by the "showdown" mentality. "I cannot emphasize too strongly," he wrote in a long memo to Kissinger, "that I have determined that we should go for broke. What we have got to get across to the enemy is the impression that we are doing exactly that. . . . I intend to stop at nothing to bring the enemy to his knees. . . . He has gone over the brink *and so have we*. We have the capacity to destroy his warmaking capacity. The only question is whether we have the *will* to use that power. What distinguishes me from Johnson is that I have the *will* in spades."*

The American leaders were out to stop the offensive and "punish" (Nixon's term) their antagonists by demonstrating a capacity for massive and sustained violence. Combining these actions with a willingness to leave the North Vietnam/NLF army with the fruits of their victory, they hoped to create the conditions for an eventual agreement. At the same time they no doubt meant to signal their readiness to respond with an equally high level of violence to any future aggressiveness of the spring-offensive variety, brandishing their *will power* as a prominent factor in the agreement they so desired.

In looking back at this period and at the negotiations that flowed out of it, some writers have taken pains to denigrate Henry Kissinger's abilities. If the purpose of observing history is to learn from it, such exercises are not only nonsensical but dangerously misleading. The flaw in Kissinger's thinking was in fact hardly personal. In considering the problem of Vietnam, he had inherited a conceptual framework from his American and French predecessors that he either could not or would not break out of. And it was this conceptual framework that led him to disaster. Along with their political forebears, both Nixon and Kissinger suffered from a fundamental inability to enter into the mental world of their enemy and so to formulate policies that would effectively frustrate the strategies arrayed against them, the strategies of a people's war.

As they had in earlier years of crisis (in 1965 for example and 1968), American leaders in 1972 focused on the military dimension of their problem. To the extent that their actions and memoirs reflect their understanding, the spring offensive was to them primarily a battlefield exercise, amenable to the disciplined and effective use of force. It was the enemy's "last throw of the dice," a "go for broke" final battle. If countered properly, it could lead to final negotiations, whose agreements in turn could be guaranteed by the American will

---

* *The Memoirs of Richard Nixon,* Vol. 2, New York: Warner Books, 1979, p. 86.

and ability to inflict punishment. For all the subtlety and imagination with which Kissinger capitalized on the negotiating assets at his disposal, the psychological framework through which he exercised his intellect was that of a conventional warrior.

It was not a framework that equipped him adequately to deal with the problems at hand. Against the American military objectives of bracing the Saigon army, inflicting maximum tactical and strategic damage, and demonstrating determination, we were pursuing a mix of political and military objectives. Militarily, the ability of the Saigon army to withstand a major, protracted assault would be tested. At best, the offensive would cause the disintegration of enemy forces. More conservatively, we could hope to take and hold territory where adequate logistical support was available. In addition, we could establish effective small-unit operations in government-held areas, where regular army units were drawn off to reinforce the main battlefields. These were the military objectives. Far more important, though, were the political goals. The overriding aim was to get the United States out of Vietnam on the best basis possible, and keep her out—thus isolating the Thieu regime. To do this it was necessary to weaken still further Nixon's and Kissinger's ability to make war, by bringing domestic opposition to their policies to a head. We now judged that the conclusive isolation of the American government from its internal support was within reach, and this goal was one we were willing to make large sacrifices for.

This stage of the war, the stage of *danh va dam* ("fighting and talking"), was one in which our strategy was (as one COSVN leader had defined it) "aimed at stimulating and developing the enemy's internal contradictions and thereby making him more isolated, in order to deprive him of his propaganda weapons"—that is, to deprive him of his ability to sustain himself by communicating his position effectively to his supporters and potential supporters. Whether we achieved this aim in 1972 can most accurately be judged by those who were then observing the American domestic scene firsthand. Strong indications, however, came through in American media commentary. "President Nixon," wrote *The New York Times* editorialist after the May 8 speech, "is taking a desperate gamble . . . that risks the fundamental security and deepest interests of the United States for dubious and tenuous gains and that runs counter both to congressional mandate and to the will and conscience of a large segment of the American people. . . . Mr. Nixon is pushing the country very near to a Constitutional crisis; Congress can yet save the president from himself and the nation from disaster." Said *The Washington Post*, "The only relief in this grim scene is that Mr. Nixon is coming to the end of his term." For its part, the U.S. Congress had already prohibited funds for American operations in Cambodia and Laos, and the Senate would soon pass the Hatfield amendment, requiring the withdrawal of all troops in return for the release of POWs. The idea that continued American intervention was immoral was gaining widespread credence in the United States, according to our intelligence analyses, not only among the militant antiwar groups, but in the population generally. These were the signs that told us the offensive was a success, and at this stage of the war we received them with as much satisfaction as we received news of any military victory.

Indeed, in strictly military terms it was increasingly evident that American arms were again scoring victories, just as they had during Tet, in Cambodia, and in so many of the pitched battles in which they confronted Vietcong and North Vietnamese main forces. As the summer wore on, our losses had become prodigious, and we began to see that many of the territorial advances could not be sustained. In the final accounting, we had traded gains in strategic position for very high casualties. The paradox was that despite this, the spring offensive was for us a decisive triumph. "You know," said an American negotiator to his North Vietnamese counterpart three years later in Hanoi, "you never defeated us on the battlefield." "That may be so," came the answer, "but it is also irrelevant."*

It was irrelevant because the military battlefield upon which the Americans lavished their attention and resources was only one part

---

* Reported by Colonel Harry Summers in his book *On Strategy*, New York: Presidio, 1982, p. 1.

of the whole board of confrontation. And it was not on this front that the primary struggle was being played out. The conceptual framework of *danh va dam* dominated our strategy throughout the Paris talks, and its watchwords were "separate" and "isolate," its motto "Stimulate the enemy's internal contradictions." There were, as all political cadre learned by heart, three currents of revolution (*ba giong thac Cach mang*) in every people's war. The first two currents are the ever-growing international socialist camp and the armed liberation movement within the country in question. The third is the progressive movement within the colonial or neocolonial power. Until the balance of military power decisively favored the revolution, it was this third current that had to draw the most energy. In this case it was American public opinion—the minds and hearts of the American people—that had to be motivated and exploited. Here were the internal contradictions that we sought to stimulate first of all, as we moved step by step toward our goal of isolating the Thieu government from its allies.

At each stage in this steady movement, our antagonists consoled themselves with short-term triumphs: disrupted supply lines, bombed-out base areas, and high body counts. But inexorably, even as these apparent successes multiplied, they were sustaining irremediable long-term damage to their capacity for war. Tet has been spoken of at length in these terms. But the lessons of Tet will only become truly clear in the West when Americans begin to view the strategic results of that battle in precisely the same way they view the strategic results of a Stalingrad or Midway. The American bombing and invasion of Cambodia largely accomplished its immediate goals (I barely survived it myself). Nixon and Kissinger justified it then and later as an operation that gained an essential year of time. Yet this "victory" arguably did more to undermine American unity than any other event of the war. The American leaders braced themselves to weather a storm of protest that would, they thought, eventually subside. But how does one judge the cumulative effects on one's own body politic of ingrained distrust and ill will? To achieve a year or so of dubious battlefield grace, Nixon and Kissinger incurred a propaganda defeat whose effects are still apparent (fifteen years later) and, to the extent that they have entered the American national psyche, may well be permanent. Whatever the facts of who infringed first on Cambodian neutrality, the significance of that engagement was that it helped separate the American leadership from its internal support and instilled among many Americans a lasting skepticism about their government's morality. It was—to Vietnam's revolution and to the revolutions that have followed Vietnam—an enduring gift.

The conventional warrior's psychology that governed American strategy allowed us to use the salami-slicing technique of exploiting factional differences to isolate our foe progressively. "Rally all those who can be rallied, neutralize all who can be neutralized," as the slogan phrased it. At the same time, their military orientation deflected American attention away from the internal fissures in our own camp. The Eisenhower and Kennedy administrations had chosen to regard Ho Chi Minh as a tool of Chinese expansionism, ignoring the separate integrity and strength of Vietnamese national aspirations. Just so, the Johnson and Nixon administrations persisted in treating the NLF as part of a North Vietnamese monolith, casually shrugging aside the complex realities of the Vietnamese political world. As a result, the Americans were constantly trying to stamp out fires in their own front yard but never lighting any themselves in our garden. Kissinger was as maddened by this situation as his predecessors had been. More imaginative than they, he responded by striking back through the Soviets and Chinese, hopeful that our allies would eventually pressure us into moderation. But he never went for the jugular. Indeed, his strategic perspective prevented him from seeing where the jugular was.

In the summer of 1972, Nixon and Kissinger's ignorance of Vietnamese political geography led them into an ambush that Le Duc Tho had carefully prepared in Paris. With the military front deadlocked and nothing much to be hoped for from the American presidential elections, the Politburo was ready to resume talks, and this they did, the first meeting taking place on July 19. Kissinger was impressed by Le Duc Tho's conciliatory demeanor, a far cry from the "insolence" the American negotiator had noted on May 2. At subsequent meetings in August and September, Le Duc Tho proved conciliatory in substance as well as in manner. In early August he dropped his insistence on Thieu's immediate removal as a pre-requisite to further progress; eventually he would acquiesce to Thieu's indefinite presence. Finally, in negotiations that began on October 8 and ended on October 12, the North Vietnamese special adviser accepted American formulations for a National Council of Reconciliation and Concord, to be composed of representatives of Saigon, the PRG, and neutralist elements. The council was charged with implementing the agreement and preparing for a future government to be decided by free elections. Tho agreed that this would suffice. There would be no immediate coalition government, and no iron-clad procedures for establishing one.

Kissinger felt triumphant, and it is easy to see why. Back in May he had swallowed the continued presence of the North Viet-namese army. Having done that, he had used a mix of air power, triangular diplomacy, and tough bargaining to force the heretofore tenacious and implacable Le Duc Tho into concessions. Tho had in fact backed away from his two central and previously nonnegotiable demands (Thieu's ouster and an immediate coalition government) with a rapidity that left the American negotiator slightly puzzled as well as gratified. Even the detailed outline for political negotiations between Saigon and the PRG that Tho had handed him at the tail end of the October 9 session seemed perfunctory. Kissinger, testing his adversary, never bothered responding, and Tho never mentioned it again. "Perhaps," thought the American, "his Vietcong colleagues in South Vietnam [had] insisted and he did it for the record."*

Intent on securing a settlement that would insure a Thieu-dominated South, Kissinger had not discerned the entire scope of Le Duc Tho's own meditations on the future. The Politburo's two

* Henry Kissinger, *The White House Years*, Boston: Little, Brown, 1979, p. 1350.

primary objectives had already been satisfied: first, a complete American withdrawal, accompanied by strong Congressional, media, and popular revulsion against further involvement; second, the permanent emplacement of the North Vietnamese army. In our view, these two objectives, by themselves, assured the eventual destruction of the Saigon regime, through a mixture of political and military means whose balance would be determined by circumstances. As a COSVN directive of the period explained it: "We will have new advantages, new conditions, and new capabilities . . . while the enemy contradictions and basic vulnerabilities will become more serious than ever before. This period will be a great opportunity for revolutionary violence, for gaining power in South Vietnam, for troop and enemy proselytizing, and for making great leaps in the balance of forces."* Another analysis concluded that "we will be in an advantageous position over the enemy. Our political superiority especially . . . will be in a position to develop to the highest extent, opening new prospects."

With his bottom-line needs already fulfilled, Le Duc Tho could afford a somewhat more relaxed view of his other priorities. The "anyone but Thieu" ploy had always been considered first as a wedge that might be driven between the United States and its ally ("separate" and "isolate"), then as a catalyst to stimulate the Saigon regime's own internal contradictions. With the American withdrawal agreed to, the wedge was no longer necessary. In addition, Kissinger's stony and persistent rejection of the ploy identified this as an insurmountable barrier to agreement. Unwilling to forgo a basically satisfactory deal in pursuit of a nonessential objective, Tho dropped it. The ease with which this demand, "nonnegotiable" for four years, now slipped off the table suggests the level of importance it had assumed in the special adviser's mind.

The other negotiating priority that Tho dropped—an immediate coalition government—was a more complex issue, which only time and experience have put into perspective. On May 2, Tho had

* Vietnam Documents and Research Notes, Document #108.

reiterated to Kissinger that the actual political situation in South Vietnam was one in which there were three parties, those who supported the Saigon regime, those who supported the National Liberation Front, and those who were neutral. As a broad statement this was accurate, and a coalition government made up of those three elements would have reflected the political reality. Kissinger was determined to circumvent this reality because he was convinced that a coalition government would have been a stepping-stone to NLF, hence North Vietnamese control. But neither did Le Duc Tho regard a formally established tripartite coalition government as a wholly undiluted blessing.

For although constituting such a government would have been the quickest path to toppling the American-backed regime, it also would have given a share of power to the Southern nationalists, and these, to Tho's way of thinking, were not trustworthy people. There were true neutralists in the South, outside the Front but in opposition to Thieu—well-known nationalist political and religious figures, some of them self-exiled to Paris, some living privately in the South, some even forming a bloc in the National Assembly.* There were of course the noncommunist nationalists of the PRG and Alliance, as well as the many Front members whose communism was the thinnest of veneers. There were even—subsequent developments would reveal

---

* Among the best-known "neutralists" were Father Tranh Huu Thanh, the activist priest who directed the People's Movement Against Corruption; Thich Tri Quang, the Buddhist leader who organized opposition to various Southern regimes; and Thich Thien Minh, who was sentenced to fifteen years imprisonment for his anti-Thieu activities. Thanh was arrested after 1975 and remains in detention. Tri Quang is presently under house arrest. Thich Thien Minh died in the unified regime's Ham Tan prison in 1979.

The Dan Toc Xa Hoi (Nationalist Socialist) opposition party was headed by Tran Van Tuyen, a prominent lawyer, who also died in prison after unification. Ho Ngoc Nhuan, the party's deputy chief, was the journalist who publicized Thieu's famous tiger cages. After the war he was allowed to publish the only private newspaper in Vietnam, until the regime shut it down in 1980. His fellow deputy in the National Assembly (and assistant editor until the paper's demise) was Ngo Cong Duc, who achieved a degree of international fame when he was invited by George McGovern on an antiwar speaking tour of the United States during the 1972 presidential elections. Nguyen Cong Hoan was another anti-Thieu assemblyman who subsequently became a deputy in the first Assembly of the unified regime. After this experience he carried out a daring escape by boat and presently lives in the United States.

them—ranking Communists in the COSVN and NLF hierarchy, whose ardent Southern regionalism was especially to be feared.

A government that included types such as these, no matter how liberally riddled with Lao Dong control personnel, would be inherently unpredictable. Had the United States agreed to such a coalition, and then backed it, who would be arrogant enough to foretell where the political chips might fall? The Vietnamese Workers' Party had not spent almost half a century welding patriotism and Marxism into a single revolutionary instrument only to legitimize some other sort of patriotism just as victory came in sight. Despite his many years of proclaiming the justice and logic of a coalition, Le Duc Tho now decided it was time to back away, first from immediately establishing the tripartite entity, then from setting up firm procedures to make sure it would eventually be established. That danger-strewn path he could do without. Meanwhile, sitting across the table and smiling inwardly, Henry Kissinger wondered for a moment if perhaps Tho and the Vietcong were not completely at one on this issue.

It is not altogether fair to accuse Kissinger of being taken in by the North Vietnamese in the summer and fall of 1972. In the first place, my own experiences (and those of the NLF as a whole) are sufficient proof against criticizing anybody else on that account. Moreover Kissinger was faithfully pursuing the policy goals of four American administrations, with their focus on containment and military confrontation—and their peculiar and debilitating blindness toward the imperatives of Vietnam's inner life. Nixon's security adviser did not so much choose to prop up the Thieu regime in preference to exploring the potential of a coalition; he had never considered there was a choice to be made on this issue. To him, a coalition was purely and simply a Communist trap. He did not think of the concept in terms of how it might be used, but only how it might be eviscerated and destroyed. Kissinger's failure in this regard was not his alone; it was the failure of a foreign policy that had long ago surrendered the great motivating passions of a colonized and underdeveloped people to recruitment by America's ideological enemies.

If the consequences of this policy were most evident to the American leaders in the divisions and hatred that racked their own country, neither were they without effect for the PRG. When the time came (as I shall describe in the latter part of my story), we assumed power in South Vietnam, not as a government constituted and guaranteed by international agreements, drawing on various sources of domestic and foreign support—but riding on the back of the North Vietnamese Army's tiger; precarious and tentative guests in our own house.

18

The Aftermath of Paris

These developments, however, were far in the future as Kissinger and Tho moved quickly now to wrap up their deal. Despite the failure to achieve an immediate coalition, the imminent signing buoyed us with excitement and hope. After seven years, the Americans had finally been forced to pull out, vindicating all our sacrifices and opening a new phase in the struggle. The PRG would now be the internationally recognized de jure government in areas under its control, ready to enter into negotiations with Saigon on a basis of equality. In spite of our skepticism about Thieu's willingness to abide by the agreement, the middle of October brought us a mood of relief and exhilaration. When Tran Nam Trung announced that we should prepare to return to Vietnam, we could scarcely restrain our happiness. Breaking our Cambodian exile, moving into possession of our own Vietnamese territory—these were dreams whose fulfillment stirred deep emotions in even the grimmest and most stoical among us.

On October 17 the NLF Central Committee moved out of Kratie, retracing the path of its retreat two years before. Route 7 near Snuol, scene of a fierce blocking action by the NLF 9th Division then, was now littered with the burned-out hulks of Saigon army tanks, personnel carriers, and trucks, casualties of the ARVN's abortive dry-season operations of 1971. Most of the trucks sat on rusting rims;

their tires had long ago been transformed into "Ho Chi Minh sandals" for the guerrillas. Fording the Vam Co, we were once again on Vietnamese soil, the famous Iron Triangle, whose jungles and rubber plantations had shielded us from the B-52s during the deluge years of 1969 and 1970. Finally we stopped, setting up temporary headquarters in Sa Mat and Thien Ngon, small hamlets near the junction of Routes 7 and 22, twenty kilometers from the center of Tay Ninh province. Here we would be near the escape routes and within reach of an International Control Commission post, which we thought might give us some additional security.

Although both the Politburo and our own Foreign Ministry had been sure for some time that Nixon's reelection was a foregone conclusion, the official analysis claimed that the American president needed an agreement to gain the required votes. The information was handed out this way in order to encourage our people by making them think that the revolution had great support in the West. But in fact there was little need for subterfuge of this type. Regardless of the presidential polls, we had every reason to believe that the new American Congress would take up precisely where the old one had left off, with various amendments designed to cut off funds and moves to restrict military involvement. In such developments we saw a realistic hope that the Nixon administration would soon find itself completely hamstrung. With our own forces badly in need of rest and resupply after a grueling campaign, we turned our attention to the political front.

In fact, the Paris Accords created vast new opportunities to bring the Thieu government to an end through political means. However Nixon and Kissinger might have regarded what had happened in Paris, it was clear to us that the concessions were largely in our favor. "The agreement," as the leadership put it, "represents for the Vietnamese people a decisive victory and marks a new turning point for the Vietnamese revolution. It reflects the global balance of forces, both nationally and internationally, and it allows our people to go on toward new successes." More specifically, we could look forward to the progressive demoralization of the Saigon army, and toward provoking a new domestic crisis for the regime.

Despite Le Duc Tho's "failure" to achieve an immediate coalition government, or even to get a meaningful agreement on procedures for setting one up, still the coalition concept was inalienably built into the accords. Article 9 called for the creation of a National Council of National Reconciliation and Concord, which was charged with settling internal matters and organizing elections, preferably within ninety days. The PRG and the Saigon regime were to constitute two equal elements within this council, neutralists a third. Its raison d'être was to resolve Vietnam's domestic problems through political means, publically proclaiming the commitment of all the signatories to the principles of negotiation and elections.

Because the council was to operate on the basis of unanimity (thus giving Thieu a veto), Kissinger might have believed that he had gained some sort of tacit agreement to (in his words) "bury the political issues." But these were hardly issues that would be buried. Thinking in military terms, as was their habit, the American leaders had concluded that Thieu, having been armed to the teeth,* would be able to deal with "moderate [military] violations," while the United States itself could "punish major violations." Having just won a seven-year battle to rid the country of American forces (a feat that far overshadowed our victory over the French or such other contemporary phenomena as Israel's 1967 and 1973 victories), our own outlook on the long-term military prospects was precisely the opposite of Kissinger's.

More to the point, at this stage it was the political front, not the military, that engaged our attention. The accords provided us with a legal political avenue to power. Should Thieu fail to comply with the spirit and terms of Article 9 (as was likely), we now had a weapon ready-made to galvanize our domestic support and to isolate him internationally. Perhaps Nixon's legalistic mind and Kissinger's diplo-

* Before the agreement was signed, the United States had undertaken a massive equipment buildup of the Saigon army, code-named "Enhance Plus."

matic one found comfort in the technical formula that required the Reconciliation Council to proceed only with unanimous consent. We, on the other hand, were sure it was the concept and spirit of coalition and concord that would count—among the disheartened and war-weary Vietnamese as well as in the caldron of Western public opinion. We could in all good conscience clothe ourselves in the ideals of the agreement. As for Thieu, he would face the choice of either dismantling his own government or demonstrating his bad faith to the world. It was no surprise that he choked on the prospect.

Even before the diplomatic process snagged temporarily in Paris, the leadership group of the NLF, PRG, Alliance, and COSVN embarked on a series of meetings meant to clarify the issues involved in "reconciliation and concord." At the same time, similar debates were going on among the mass organizations and military cadres in what was truly a Front-wide attempt to formulate a unified policy on the subject. Our immediate problem was how best to use this issue to rally support from the city bourgeoisie, who were not yet sympathetic, and even from members of the Saigon military and governmental establishment—"to continually sap the inner strength of the Thieu regime." My colleagues and I wished to utilize these discussions first of all to nail down the primacy of "reconciliation and concord," as an unshakable PRG principle. Secondly, we wanted to define methods of conveying our position to the population with the greatest effect.

The Paris agreement, we felt, would give us an unprecedented opportunity to proselytize at the heart of the Saigon regime. With the Americans out, the South Vietnamese could be expected to see the handwriting on the wall. Nixon and Kissinger might feed on visions of a Korean-style equilibrium. But the South Vietnamese, more appreciative of NLF and DRV determination, knew that the war would go on until there was a real resolution, not a paper one. Under these circumstances, Thieu's domestic opposition, both latent and overt, would begin to search more strenuously than ever for a middle path (and the agreement provided an avenue for their participation in government). The business community and even the bureaucracies would be uniquely susceptible to appeals for moderation, which promised a reasonable solution rather than a cataclysm. With a sense of anticipatory excitement, we foresaw that internal pressures for a settlement would begin to mount once the accords were signed. We were determined to take advantage of the moment, by stimulating popular feelings for peace and by doing everything we could to reduce fears of partnership with the PRG.

But as the cabinet meetings opened, it became clear that "reconciliation and concord," despite its unquestioned power as a propaganda weapon (let alone as a humanitarian ideal), was not in universal favor. As we put forward our proposals, we were quickly confronted with precisely the same doctrinaire opposition that we had weathered the previous year in Kratie. The "national bourgeoisie," who had collaborated closely with the puppets and profited from their policies, were not (in the opinion of the Northern cadres) appropriate recipients for a policy of reconciliation. Still less were those who worked directly for the regime or who had fought for it. The revolution could have no interest in making common cause with such people regardless of the circumstances.

And the ideologues were not alone in their position. Their motivating vision of cold, relentless class struggle was complemented in this instance by the emotional arguments of a number of Southerners, mostly people whose families had suffered badly at the hands of the regime or the Americans. It was hard to criticize the feelings of the Vietminh cadres, who had regrouped North in 1954 and returned two decades later to wives and children who had been brutalized (or perhaps killed) in the fighting or government terror. Almost everyone had lost someone close, often under heartrending circumstances. Many of these people were anxious to settle deep scores for their relatives and comrades, and there was something in each of us that responded to their appeals.

Nevertheless, most of the Southern guerrillas, led by the NLF's nationalist intellectuals, pressed hard for a commitment to reconciliation. Those of us who argued its merits felt that this was a case where humanitarian and practical concerns intersected. Regardless of the immediate proselytizing benefits of "reconciliation and concord," we now had an obligation to consider the future. There was not a shred of doubt that the Thieu government, rotten internally and fundamentally separated from the source of its viability, would eventually succumb. (Our confidence on this score may well have been premature.) We would then need a policy of national recovery. That was what this debate was about. With between three and four million casualties, North and South, the wounds of this war would not heal for generations under any circumstances. But with a less-than-determined commitment to reconciliation, they would continue to fester, bringing economic and human consequences that were unacceptable.

Vietnam, we argued, was a wasted country. Even before the French war, its exploited economy had been among the world's poorest. Since then the countryside had been ravaged and the industrial capacity devastated. Both North and South were sustaining themselves on the basis of grotesquely abnormal infusions of loans and aid. Given these circumstances, it was impossible to exaggerate the magnitude of the postwar reconstruction and development task we would face. Only by achieving a unanimity of purpose could the nation be successfully mobilized for the effort. We could not allow our personal and subjective desires for revenge to subvert the interdependent goals of reconciliation and recovery. Nor could we obediently rely on inflexible, ideological preconceptions to resolve the unique difficulties that confronted us as Vietnamese.

Under the present conditions, our need, our obligation, to build the nation ("a thousand times more beautiful," as Ho had said) demanded the reconciliation of differences, not their exacerbation and perpetuation. In the circumstances of the anti-French and anti-American war, we argued, the entire Vietnamese people must be regarded as victims, even including the Southern bourgeoisie, even including those who were working for the Saigon government and fighting in its army. Any other approach would be a desecration of our duty to the nation, as well as a denial of Ho Chi Minh's principles of national unity that had suffused our struggle.

Our Party comrades, however, were not to be persuaded by arguments either of compassion or reason. They had (or so it seemed to me) given up their consciences and pragmatic sense both in return for the certitudes of their political religion. Among their steely and arrogant convictions, compromise could find no room to breathe. Having had an unpleasant foretaste of this crusader mentality the previous year, we were not surprised by the attack we now experienced. But neither were we prepared to back away from our proposals.

As far as my colleagues and I were concerned, reconciliation was not a principle that could be discarded. We had lived through horrors ourselves and had watched the mutilation of our people. We had accepted these things, perhaps even dimly foreseen them, when we first decided to oppose Diem. It was our deepest conviction that the cause of liberation warranted any sacrifice whatsoever; in that we were making no departure from the living tradition of Vietnamese history. But at the same time these sacrifices constituted for us, for the leadership, the heaviest burden of responsibility. What the nation had lived through over the past nineteen years could only be vindicated by what was to come afterward. To accede to the hatred and vindictiveness espoused by the cadres would violate the profound obligations we had assumed. On this issue there could be no retreat.

Here truly were the makings of a fundamental split in the revolution. To prevent it, Secretary General Le Duan was forced to intervene personally. In mid-August the definitive resolution to this bitter debate to decide the revolution's future path came in a directive published over the secretary's signature and addressed to all political and military cadres: "The policy of national concord and reconciliation without reprisal is the long-term strategy, and it is the political line and the political behavior of the Party. It is also the position of the worker class." Reading Le Duan's message, we knew we had won the essential victory. As in Kratie, it seemed that in the end we had been successful in drawing the upper level of the Party's leadership to our side. The entire revolution was now committed—or so it appeared.

At the time no one would have believed that the Party line itself was being used as a vehicle for internal propaganda. Le Duan's directive was not, after all, a statement intended for foreign consumption (subject to the psychological-warfare considerations that governed all such communications), but a declaration of principle meant to determine the conduct and thinking of the entire revolutionary apparatus. Later, when they found themselves in retirement, the NLF leaders would have the leisure to reflect on Le Duan's expertise in manipulating, not just the Party's allies but the Party as well. By then of course it would be too late. On the issue of reconciliation, as on the later problem of national reunification, the first secretary and his immediate circle were to prove adept at surreptitiously twisting the Lao Dong's inner mechanisms to their own purposes. In this instance, the "political line of the Party" and even the "position of the worker class" were effectively manipulated to gain both Party and non-Party support at a crucial moment. But in 1972 the revelation of the first secretary's blatant cynicism was still several years away. And so was the devastation of Vietnam's national life and the refugee disaster that were its legacies.

But even as the after ripples of our debate began to calm down, a test of wills was going on between Washington and Hanoi that threatened to make the entire episode superfluous. Thieu, doing everything he could to obstruct an agreement, induced Nixon to intrude a large number of new items into the virtually completed negotiations. The unexpected stalemate that resulted led eventually to the December bombings of Haiphong and Hanoi. These may indeed have given added credence to Nixon's ability to threaten, but they also exacted a sharp political price. On the world stage Nixon was reviled as a "barbarian" and a "mad bomber." Even the Pope expressed his grief over Vietnam. In the American capital, the

Congress resumed its attack on the administration's warmaking powers. When it was all over, the accords were signed, substantially as Le Duc Tho and Kissinger had agreed to them in October. Foreign Minister Nguyen Duy Trinh and Secretary of State William Rogers signed respectively for North Vietnam and the United States, Madame Binh [Nguyen Thi Binh] for the PRG, and (on a separate page) Tran Van Lam for the Saigon regime.

Despite his foreign minister's signature, Nguyen Van Thieu made it clear immediately that his government had no intention of abiding by the agreement. The war, he declared in a broadcast address, would continue. "The Communists will not be allowed to enter our villages and hamlets. We will fight them anywhere we meet them." There was no ambiguity whatsoever in Thieu's position: The agreement was a disaster which he could compensate for only by demonstrating a redoubled aggressiveness and by ignoring its most damaging provisions. His policy would be one of four noes: no coalition, no negotiations, no giving up territory, no communist or neutralist activities.

For our part, we now launched the political offensive we had been preparing since the fall. In the areas under our control, we distributed the text of the accords and urged people to study it carefully, paying special attention to the subject of national reconciliation and concord. Along with sympathizers and intermediaries, we set up committees throughout the South to disseminate the terms of the agreement—counteracting Thieu's efforts to restrict popular knowledge of what both he and his allies had formally agreed to. (After initial publication of the text in Saigon's newspapers, there had been no further distribution.) We strove to initiate widespread agitation for the "democratic freedoms," which the accords promised, and for cooperation between North and South to bring the bloodletting to an end. We emphasized the agreement's confirmation of the PRG as a lawful and equal party in deciding the future of South Vietnam and we focused attention on the coalition government, which elections stipulated by the agreement would bring about. At the same time, we broadcast in every way we could the PRG's commitment to reconciliation and concord—in leaflets, over Radio Liberation and Radio Hanoi, by word of mouth, in university and secondary-school seminars conducted by sympathizers, a countrywide campaign. In the liberated zones we began a conspicuous program of public assistance, distributing land, agricultural equipment, and supplies, initiating reconstruction projects, and establishing advisory teams to help manage the rubber plantations—demonstrating in concrete and visible terms the PRG's goodwill and intentions.

In the meantime, our military attitude was primarily defensive, as we moved to center attention on the political agreement. The contrast between our posture and Thieu's unremitting and well-publicized aggression could not fail, we believed, to generate anger toward Thieu and support for us. It quickly became apparent, though, that the Saigon forces were capable of using our relative passivity to their advantage, as they launched an ongoing campaign to acquire land and population, particularly in the many isolated areas of PRG control that dotted the provinces. Caught momentarily off balance, the COSVN and the PRG met in March to establish a uniform and balanced military and political strategy to counter these attacks.

The outcome, enunciated in PRG directive 3/CT/73, charted a middle course. On the one hand, it condemned the commonly held view that Saigon's violations had abrogated the treaty and should be met with all-out military violence before our strategic position was threatened. It also rejected the argument that we should strictly maintain the spirit of the Accords regardless of enemy activities, in order to strengthen our hold on the moral high ground and further exploit Thieu's political weaknesses. The correct approach combined elements of both positions. The Paris Accords were to be regarded as a new arm, a lever to use against enemy forces demoralized by the departure of their American field and air support, and untrained in the integrated warfare that would now be demanded of them. The *binh van*, "troop-proselytizing," efforts were to focus on the hopes for peace held out by the Accords and on the subversion of these hopes by Thieu and his corrupt circle. At the same time we would attempt to structure the pervasive civilian discontent into a peace movement, agitating ever more strongly for the cease-fire, democratic rights, negotiations, and release of political prisoners agreed to by the regime.

Meanwhile, we would respond vigorously to Saigon's land-grabbing operations, though in a limited fashion, taking back lost territory and frustrating new initiatives but avoiding major confrontations. The immediate period ahead would be one of predominantly political struggle . . . while our armed forces were being resupplied and rebuilt to meet Saigon's forthright insistence on a military resolution.

As the spring of 1973 progressed, the remarkable events of Watergate attracted more and more interest in Sa Mat and nearby Loc Ninh, which we were now using as a temporary capital. We began to monitor the American news with almost an obsessive curiosity, through regular briefings and radio reports from Hanoi, as well as through daily sessions spent listening to BBC and Voice of America. With the Nixon administration in obvious disarray, the U.S. House and Senate were busy with legislation that would put a definitive end to further sustenance for the Saigon regime. Then, on June 4 the Case/Church amendment passed, blocking funds for Indochina military involvement after August 15. Of course, we could not be sure to what extent these provisions might actually control American conduct, especially if there were to be a major escalation in the level of fighting. But on each front—political, military, and diplomatic—there was no doubt that momentum was building.

For the military front especially, October would prove to be a crucial time. Early in that month, the Politburo met to evaluate the balance of forces and realign strategy accordingly. The conclusions reached in Hanoi fueled the military confrontation that had been fermenting since the spring: "The comparison of forces is more favorable than ever before. . . . The path of revolutionary violence is the path of the revolution in the South." Politburo Resolution 21 envisioned as yet no large-scale offensive, but neither would our forces be excessively restrained in the Gianh Dan/Lan Dat ("Land and People's Struggle"). Our hope (mine, at any rate, and that of my colleagues) was that Thieu would see the thunderclouds mount-

ing, that he would read the omens in Washington as we were reading
them, and find a way to take refuge in the political articles of the
agreement. But while we scanned the horizon for signs of accommodation, the storm of violence broke.

On October 15, the PRG and the NLF general staff broadcast its
justification for intensifying the armed conflict, claiming "the legitimate right to take all measures possible to counteract the Thieu
administration's sabotage of the Accords, to counter their violations
anywhere through the use of appropriate force, to insist on the correct
execution of the Accords and to maintain their integrity." Gradually,
post by post, our forces began pushing back the Saigon troops from
positions they had occupied just prior to the signing and from areas
they had taken since then. Relentlessly but carefully, we liberated
territory, particularly in the Delta, the great rice basket—calculating
the requirements of each situation, striving to avoid a test of American
resolve.

Regardless of what had taken place in Washington, our analysts
urged the general staff to be cautious, predicting the return of American air power. But even while this powerful psychological weapon
constricted our movement, the pressure built on Thieu's troops. Day
by day our strength and confidence grew, while their hopes were
increasingly fixed on a salvation that daily seemed more distant.
Now they were fighting what their generals called a poor man's war,
without the endless supplies, the mobility, and the air cover they had
grown used to. Among the soldiers as well as civilians, rumors of
secret deals and coups d'état proliferated wildly. Ky was about to
overthrow Thieu. Thieu was about to resign. Secret meetings were
being held among the United States, Hanoi, and the NLF. Everyone
was sure the situation would change, though none could say exactly
how.

In Saigon our agents worked overtime to plant the seeds of panic.
At the Givral Café and the Brodard on rue Catinat (the capital's
Fifth Avenue) "Radio Catinat" buzzed with life. Here government
and military people, Saigon's newsmen and the international reporters met to eat and drink and pass on the latest. What they heard

and what they said was a mixture of fact and imagination, some of it a product of the usual grapevines, some of it disinformation created especially for their benefit. We used Nguyen Cao Ky's open talk about replacing Thieu as the basis for rumors of palace plots. American Congressional debates over aid cutoffs to Saigon were sure signs of an impending treaty between Washington and Hanoi.*

Meanwhile, as apprehensions began to mount in Saigon, the rough equilibrium on the military front, which had existed since spring, was about to be ruptured. On November 6, our forces launched a division-sized attack in Quang Duc, overrunning several ARVN positions. From the Americans, there was no response. Congress had passed the War Powers Act just weeks before, giving further proof of the truly pervasive victory we had gained on the American domestic battlefield. As we intensified activities in the Delta around U Minh and on the Cambodian border, our military cadres began reporting a substantial drop in the morale and effectiveness of the Saigon troops. For South Vietnamese generals and common soldiers alike, the significance of their isolation from the Americans was beginning to strike home. The fruit of the "separate and isolate" tactics, which we had pursued so persistently, was about to ripen.

By the beginning of the 1973–1974 dry season, our logistical

---

* A year later the Catinat rumor mill was having serious consequences. A carefully planned whispering campaign spread the news that Kissinger had secretly agreed to partition the country at the 13th Parallel in return for a cessation of hostilities. Feeding on the secretary's well-known penchant for secrecy and the Americans' obvious quandary by then about the military situation, this particular report snowballed, initiating a selling panic among the wealthier people in Hue and Danang.

As the partition rumor took hold, people began to hear that Thieu and many of the top generals and officials were quietly transferring their fortunes out of the country and were making secret preparations to assure their own departures if the need arose. This news (based partly on fact) gained widespread credence; it corresponded only too well with what the Southerners already knew of their venal leaders. As for others who might want to leave, the black-market price of a passport was soaring toward the $20,000 mark. There was no need to publicize this startling figure (and its implications)—the Saigonese knew it the way a stockbroker knows the latest quotes.

By the new year, villas in Saigon began flooding the market at cut-rate prices, as did their owners' factories and businesses. Stories were rampant of well-known pillars of the community who had already fled. It was the Vietnamese equivalent of Americans finding out that the Rockefellers, Kennedys, Hunts, and Murchisons were getting out of the country while the getting was good.

coordination and supply buildup had altered the balance of military forces irreversibly. Our NLF divisions had completed their redeployment around Saigon and in the Delta, and had taken up strong defensive positions protecting Loc Ninh. From North Vietnam to the South, we were expanding and modernizing road systems that could move matériel and mechanized forces at rates unimaginable even a year ago. A thousand-mile oil pipeline over the Truong Son range down to Quang Tri and Loc Ninh was under way to supply the new battlefields. Even as we prepared for modern warfare, the Saigon army began to sink into a defensive posture, increasingly harassed by ammunition deficiencies and gasoline shortages.

As if to underline the meaning of these developments, on December 2 the Nha Be tank farm, by far the largest oil storage facility in the South, was infiltrated and blown up by a dozen men from the 10th Vietcong Sapper Regiment. What Thieu's thoughts were as he watched the oily billows blacken Saigon's horizon, I don't know. At that moment his American friends were listening to a concert of wails from their closest European allies, whose own oil lifelines had been suddenly choked off by the Arab embargo. Richard Nixon, his partner of the past five years (and his sole hope), was fighting for political life. At home, shrewd political manipulations had done nothing to stifle popular anger and discontent, or even the scheming opposition of Thieu's associates. Undoubtedly he had received reports of the discreet contacts several well-known generals had initiated with the Front. Even the military situation, so auspicious for him early in the year, had turned sour. Another man might have begun seeking avenues to a compromise while leverage was still available. But Thieu wholeheartedly shared Henry Kissinger's commitment to an impregnable staunchly anticommunist South Vietnam. His vision could accommodate nothing less. And grasping for everything, he lost everything.

With hindsight, one can speculate on the survival potential of a coalition government, one faction backed by Hanoi, one by the United States, while "third force" neutralists were wooed by both. China, it was clear even then, would have found practical ways to support such a regime, and it is not too imaginative to believe that many Third World and Western nations would have done the same. Whether under such conditions the South's nationalists could have carved out a position of dominance for themselves remains one of the war's most tantalizing (and poignant) questions. But if such thoughts flitted even momentarily across Nguyen Van Thieu's mind as he prepared to lead South Vietnam into the vortex, there is no record of it.

19

The Ideologues
Claim a Victim

With the military struggle heating up, we undertook a carefully coordinated diplomatic campaign to plead the PRG's case in international forums and line up political and material support from foreign governments. Early in the spring of 1974, President Phat asked me to assist with these efforts. My long immersion in French language and culture apparently gave me an adequately cosmopolitan style, and my credibility as a nonideological nationalist would be an advantage in discussions with Third World diplomats. But before joining Madame Binh (our foreign minister) I would travel to Hanoi, then to East Germany to receive treatment for the physical problems that were becoming increasingly troublesome. Malaria had been my unshakable companion for years, and now each attack found me weaker and less resilient. Various intestinal and visual difficulties, legacies from the days spent in Saigon's prisons, also seemed to be worsening. Though reluctant to leave my comrades, I was looking forward to a real convalescence, and then to the endeavors that would follow.

The excitement of leave-taking, though, was marred by thoughts about my old chief, Tran Bach Dang. Dang, I learned, had been removed from his Party position and was now at COSVN awaiting a verdict that would determine his future. This report was deeply shocking, not just to me and the other Saigon intellectuals, but to everyone who knew Dang as a brilliant organizer and one of the Party's rising stars.

Tran Bach Dang had joined both the resistance and the Party during the French war. One of his code names, Tu Meo ("Number 4 Twitch") suggested that his immense energy was not unaccompanied by inner tensions. But despite his overpowering drive and habit of plain speaking, Dang had the knack of winning friendship as well as respect. Slight even by Vietnamese standards, he managed to project waves of warmth and optimism into every situation he dealt with. He was a fountain of intellectual and emotional energy, as blunt and incisive as he was personally supportive. Such was Dang's dynamism that even the revolution couldn't absorb all of his attention; he was in addition a practicing poet, publishing under the pen name "Huong Trieu."

Early on in his career Dang's genius for improvisation and effective organizing caught the attention of the Party hierarchy. He advanced rapidly, and it was understood that Le Duan himself had developed a high regard for his talent. In 1961 at the age of thirty-five Dang had organized the Youth Liberation Association and at about the same time began to mastermind the Front's intellectual proselytizing movement in the cities. Since 1965 he had been permanent secretary for Saigon/Cholon/Giadinh, under First Secretary Vo Van Kiet, with special responsibility for urban mobilization. It was in that capacity that he had met with me in 1966 to formulate plans for organizing Saigon's youth. By then he had been living underground in Saigon for over a decade. Dang's wife I had first seen lying unconscious on the floor of the secret police interrogation room, and she later became my neighbor for a brief time in the isolation row at National Police headquarters. Like almost everyone, I had a great deal of esteem for Dang both personally and professionally. In addition, I felt I owed him my life; he had been responsible for the difficult negotiations with the American embassy that led to my exchange in 1968.

Dang's troubles stemmed from a remark he had made during a COSVN meeting, at which he was giving a report on the mass movements in Saigon. In an informal discussion that followed the various presentations (this according to a mutual friend who had heard him), he allowed his well-known sense of humor to slip its leash for a moment. "You see," he said, "all of the city movements have been wonderfully successful—the intellectuals, students, Buddhists, all of them. It's only the workers' movement that acts like it's out to lunch" —*xe qua*, literally "worse than bad."

This comment turned out to be a strategic blunder. The thought that the workers' movement might be *xe qua* was not acceptable under any guise to the dour leaders of the party of workers and peasants. Allowing such a remark to slip out constituted not just a lamentable violation of etiquette; it argued for a hidden strain of opposition that required thorough investigation. In two seconds Dang had managed to commit the unforgivable crime of lèse-majesté, blighting a career that had seemed among the most brilliant of all his contemporaries. After this unfortunate slip, Dang was instructed to present himself at COSVN to conduct his own self-criticism. There he was forced to give a detailed explanation of why he had deviated from the proper line and the "position of the worker class." At the same time he was removed from his responsibilities and isolated, pending a final disposition of his case.

News of this situation soon began to spread, causing great consternation. To my friends and me, the episode vibrated with reminders of the iron fanaticism of many Party cadres. More unsettling, what had happened to Dang suggested that the ideologues had a very strong grip indeed on the decision-making mechanisms within the hierarchy. This was no simple matter of Party discipline. Though none of us could read all of its implications, certain facts were felt rather than clearly understood. Dang was close to many of the Southern nationalists; he had himself brought not a few of them over to the revolution, and he had directed and supported others. He was a dedicated Communist. But he was also a charismatic Southerner with ties to all the leading urban revolutionaries. And his power in the Party was growing.

There were vague but disturbing similarities in this to an episode involving Tran Buu Kiem several years earlier. Kiem had been one

of the NLF's founders, a charter organizer of the original mobilization committee back in 1958, and the third member (along with
Phat and Nguyen Van Hieu) of the leadership cell, prior to the
Front's formal inauguration. Kiem had from the start been instrumental in decisions about foreign relations, and in 1963 had become
chairman of the Front's foreign affairs commission. In 1968 he had
led the first NLF delegation to Paris, at which time the soon-to-be-
famous Madame Binh served as one of his deputies. Though Kiem
himself had been a Lao Dong member since 1951, a special political
cadre had accompanied that initial delegation to insure Party control.
Not too long after they arrived, a violent argument broke out between
this cadre (Tran Hoai Nam) and Kiem. According to the cadre, Kiem
was making altogether too many unmonitored, self-initiated contacts
in Parisian diplomatic circles and within France's Vietnamese community. Kiem angrily maintained that these interactions were a
normal part of his function as NLF chief of mission and that he
hardly saw any need to submit such activities to the oversight of the
Party.

Before long, Kiem and his antagonist had both been called home,
and Madame Binh found herself elevated to the senior diplomatic
post. (She would later become the PRG's foreign minister.) Back in
Vietnam, Kiem was forced to undergo self-criticism, and few were
expressing any confidence about his future. Fortunately for Kiem,
however, we were just then preparing to organize the Provisional
Revolutionary Government, and he was a conspicuously well-known
Southern personality. Both the NLF and the Alliance of National,
Democratic, and Peace Forces proposed that he be included in the
new government, and the upshot was that he was appointed minister
to the President's Office. But it was quite clear that Hanoi considered
Kiem uncontrollable, one who allowed his regional loyalties to
impinge dangerously on his duty to the Party.

By 1974 Kiem's hopes, like those of the rest of the PRG, were
sparked with optimism. But his own future (had he been able to see
it) was not to bear out that expansive confidence. In 1976 the man
who had been one of the prime movers of the Southern revolution was

performing the duties of a representative in the rubber-stamp unified National Assembly. Shortly afterward he was relieved of even this honorific and his political activities limited to membership in the Fatherland Front (the umbrella mass organization that had absorbed the Alliance and NLF). In the end he was simply retired, his final political emasculation assuaged to some extent by a government pension, a house, and a car—sufficient, it was assumed, to keep the former dissident permanently quieted.

The subsequent history of Tran Bach Dang was not much happier. Following Dang's isolation at COSVN, he was ordered North to study Marxism-Leninism at Hanoi's Nguyen Ai Quoc Cadre Institute, where he previously had given his own lectures as our greatest expert on the techniques of urban struggle. His former students had now become his teachers. When this exercise in humiliation was con-

Tran Buu Kiem, minister to Chairman Huynh Tan Phat.

cluded, the Party sent him to round off his education in Eastern Europe, where he could admire at first hand the realization of working-class principles in the Soviet Union, Bulgaria, and other model socialist utopias. In 1976 Dang finally resurfaced, now as an official of the Fatherland Front. It was a position whose duties gave him plenty of opportunity to cultivate his talent for poetry and no doubt to reflect on the ends as well as the means of revolutionary struggle.

Shortly after Dang returned from Eastern Europe, we met briefly for the last time. But I was reluctant then to ask him about the painful experiences he had gone through. He displayed a similar sensitivity toward my own feelings and inquired politely about the farmer's life I had adopted in my own retirement, about my wife, my cottage, my crops. It was, I thought, an interesting discussion to be taking place between two old revolutionaries, who had once shared events of such moment.

All this, however, was still in the future, as I prepared to leave for Hanoi and my new life as a PRG diplomat. As disquieting as the news about Tran Bach Dang was, I did not allow it to dampen my overall enthusiasm for the unfolding of events and for my place in them. Ho Chi Minh had written somewhere that "the closer the victory, the more difficult the problems." It was with thoughts of this sort that I strove to allay my concerns for Dang and readied myself for a journey up the Ho Chi Minh Trail.

20

PRG Ambassador

From Loc Ninh, a capacious Chinese-made jeep drove me across the Cambodian border and onto the Duong Mon Ho Chi Minh, the famous Ho Chin Minh Trail. I was not to lack for companionship on this trip. A doctor, a nurse, an administrative assistant, and my bodyguard —in addition to the driver—all crowded in with me; together we made an appreciative audience for the wonders of "the trail" as it branched out in front of us. Threading through the jungles and mountains of eastern Cambodia and Laos, the network of all-weather roads we were traveling would not have been recognized by the hardy souls who had pioneered the route.

The first of these had moved southward from Hanoi in May of 1959—Vietminh fighters from South Vietnam. They had regrouped above the 17th Parallel after the Geneva Accords and were now beginning to filter back into their old battlefields. These original trailblazers needed six months for the trip, each person carrying the supplies and equipment he would need. In the suffocating humidity they had climbed and hacked their way through the thick foliage of the mountain jungles, struggling for survival in one of the world's most hostile environments. Malaria, dysentery, and vicious jungle fungus infections were the lot of everyone who came down the Trail in those days, carrying with them only the most rudimentary of medicines, and nothing at all to counteract the venomous snakes or the clouds of mosquitoes. Ten kilometers or so a day [six miles plus] was all they could expect to advance, and those who became too sick to walk were simply left in primitive shelters, which had been constructed by even earlier advance parties. Only half of them survived it, and those who did said that afterward death held no fears for them.

One of these early travelers wrote in his diary:

> We march all day bent under the weight of our packs. In the heat and humidity we are forced to stop often for rest and to get our breath back. In the evening, utterly exhausted, we hang our hammocks and mosquito nets from the trees, and sleep under the stars. At times we have to search far from the trail for a waterfall or spring where we can drink and fill our canteens. There are tigers and leopards in the jungle, and we knew about attacks on stragglers and people who have become separated. We climb mountain faces of over a thousand meters, pulling our headbands down over our eyes to filter the sun's rays. From the summit a spectacle of splendor and magnificence offers itself to us. It is like a countryside of fairytales. Those who get sick we leave at the next way post. The group continues to march. We must have faith in our struggle, in our leaders and in our country to endure these tests of suffering and pain, when we can no longer distinguish the line betwen life and death.

Slowly the original paths were widened and improved until by the time of my trip to Hanoi, the route had become an interlocking system of two-lane roads, their hard-packed dirt beds surfaced with crushed stone. At approximately every hundred kilometers along the route was what amounted to a village for the soldiers and work battalions that protected the lifeline, a largely self-sustaining force that in early 1974 numbered close to one hundred thousand. Barracks, armories, storage and shop facilities, farms, dispensaries, guest houses, fueling stations, everything imaginable for defense, repair, and transportation was available in these places and in the smaller depots and camps that marked the road between them.

The veritable army of workers included youth groups, contingents of Montagnards, and peasant volunteers. Some had lived on the road for eight to ten years without seeing their homes. Several of the

Volunteer Youth I talked to had arrived as teenagers and were now in their early thirties. The magnitude of their task was apparent everywhere one looked. Huge bomb craters pocked the roadside for much of its length, and many bombs had obviously scored near or direct hits. Yet the artery had not only never been closed; it had kept expanding and developing. As soon as each flight of B-52 "steel crows" would finish bombing, large work crews would quickly construct bypasses around those sections that had been destroyed, allowing traffic to keep flowing. At the same time, others would be working feverishly to repair the damaged stretches of main roadway. Over years this resulted in a web of bypasses and cutoffs, which made the system practically invulnerable to air attack.

We drove along this marvel of construction at a constant speed of about thirty kilometers an hour, amidst a continual flow of traffic not much different from what I would later experience heading into the suburbs of an American city during rush hour. At one point we passed a slow-moving convoy of heavy trucks carrying American jet planes (their wings detached) toward the North. Each night an eerie and beautiful spectacle would emerge before our eyes, an endless stream of flickering headlights tracing curved patterns against the blackened wilderness, as far in both directions as the eye could see. Our accommodations during this journey were, literally, royal. The previous year North Vietnam's government had hosted Cambodia's Prince Sihanouk on a strategy-coordinating visit. To demonstrate its solicitude for the Samdek and his cause (temporary solicitude, as it turned out) the Politburo had built a series of well-appointed cottages conveniently placed to receive the princely entourage at the end of each day's progress. What had served royalty was now turned to the use of the revolution, and our eleven nights on the road were passed in unaccustomed luxury. I am sure I was not the only one in our little party to find myself musing on the contrast between our own comfortable journey and the months of torment the Trail had meant for so many of our compatriots.

Our route took us up along the Laotian Cordillera, then back into Vietnam at Khe Sanh and across the demilitarized zone to Dong

Hoi. There we said good-bye to our driver and boarded a two-engine Russian-built plane waiting to take us to the Northern capital. At the Hanoi airport I was welcomed by a PRG official and driven into town to meet with NLF President Tho, my old friend Trinh Dinh Thao, and some other Front and Alliance people who were in Hanoi at the time. Although I was anxious to see my colleagues, I could feel my heart beginning to sink as we drove into the city.

I had last been to Hanoi as a student in 1944, thirty years before. It was then a graceful place, quiet in comparison with Saigon's ceaseless turmoil but agreeably furnished with diversions for a well-off Southern boy just beginning to explore life. Perhaps my nostalgia magnified the dreariness and poverty of what I now saw around me. But there was no doubt that the city had suffered dreadfully in the intervening years. Not only had it not been modernized or beautified in any way; it seemed to have fallen apart. Through the car windows I could see some bomb damage, but nothing seemed to have been done to repair it. Even the most rudimentary maintenance on the city's once lovely French colonial buildings had been neglected; the vista was one of crumbling facades and peeling paint, with only a hint of bygone dignity.

The human landscape was equally wrenching. People walking or biking in the streets shared a look of grim preoccupation. They seemed poorer than they had been three decades earlier. They walked slowly, as if resigned to their lives of poverty and constant toil. Though the streets were crowded, there was none of the bustle or vitality that Asian cities usually display. In its place was an air of melancholy given off by people who seemed to have aged prematurely. The scene was somber and colorless, like the clothes that almost everybody was wearing—both men and women in dark or khaki pants and white shirts (industrial textile dyes were an unaffordable luxury). A surge of pity came over me for what Hanoi's citizens had gone through, for the sacrifices that the war had demanded of them, not just for years but for a full generation.

In each house I visited, several families lived. Often a curtain stretched across the room was all that separated one family's area from another's. Invariably there was an altar set up in the corner with photographs of a husband or children killed in the South. As often as not, even the place of death or burial (if there was a grave) was unknown, a loss of unimaginable proportions for these people, who revered the dead and held their final resting places sacred.

After several days of meetings and visits, I was admitted to the Vietso (Vietnam/Soviet) hospital, caught in a crosscurrent of feelings. I was emotionally drained by what I had seen since my arrival in Hanoi. At the same time I was more determined than ever to see a conclusion to this massive human tragedy, and full of hope for the future of my stricken country. Physically I was exhausted, a most willing candidate for the month of enforced bedrest the doctors had now decreed.

At the end of this time I was pronounced fit enough to undertake the long trip to Dresden, East Germany, for further treatment and an extended period of recuperation. Perhaps unused to seeing the physiological consequences of six years of jungle living, the German doctors seemed reluctant to part with me. (There were hundreds of thousands of similar specimens available in Vietnam.) At any rate, it was several months before I was able to return to Hanoi and November 1974 before I could embark on my mission.

My first and most important stop was Algiers, where I was to lead the PRG delegation at the November 1 celebration of Algerian independence. For two weeks I was the guest of the Algerian government, staying at the city's most luxurious French hotel (now nationalized) and feeling almost at home with the residual French culture that marked this one-time sister colony. Mme. Nguyen Thi Binh, our foreign minister, had had great success in welding a connection between the PRG and her Algerian counterpart Abdelaziz Bouteflika, who proved an exceptionally valuable ally. Among other acts of friendship, Algeria had undertaken to finance all of Madame Binh's diplomacy. On each of her world tours she would stop first in Algiers to arrange for her necessities, staying at the private residence she kept there for just this purpose. At that time Algeria was also the head of the nonaligned nations, and it was partly because of Algerian

In Dresden.

support that our relations with these countries flourished—providing us with "neutral" international platforms for our positions.

The twentieth anniversary of Algeria's uprising against French colonialism was a gala affair, attracting high-level delegations from throughout the Third World. It provided an ideal opportunity to meet and talk with my counterparts from these countries, detailing Thieu's violations of the Paris Accords and attempting to confirm and coordinate diplomatic support for the PRG.

With the Algerians, of course, I was able to discuss material aid as well; I was especially anxious to obtain additional assistance for our international propaganda campaign and for various educational projects. The minister of culture and information, Ahmed Taleb, proved as receptive as he was gracious, agreeing to my requests "with joy and friendship." During our discussions he put into specific terms the general feeling of warmth manifested by all the Algerian officials. It was, he said, the duty of the Algerian people to help the

Madame Nguyen Thi Binh,
minister of foreign affairs.

Vietnamese people. Dienbienphu, as he described it, had been a turning point in Algeria's own revolution. Prior to that battle, only a minority of Algerians had favored a military struggle; France was simply deemed too powerful. But Dienbienphu had vividly demonstrated French vulnerability. Afterward, a wave of confidence developed about Algeria's ability to fight its way to independence. (Subsequently, the Algerian Ministry of Culture and Information printed our *White Book* on violations of the Paris Accords by the Saigon government as well as the other material I had spoken to Taleb about.) Boualem Ben Hamouda, the minister of justice, was equally friendly. With him I spent time discussing Algeria's juridical reforms, and he provided me with documents and a wealth of background information on his country's transition from one legal system to another.

Sihanouk was also in Algiers at the time, and I briefed him on our internal political situation, reaffirming Vietnam's support for the

Khmer resistance. For him, as for us, the upcoming 1974–1975 dry-season campaign would be a turning point. Like me, the prince was hopeful about his country's future—although even then it is likely that his boyish enthusiasm masked anxieties far more profound than my own. Before parting, we reminisced about our schoolboy days at Saigon's Lycée Chasseloup Laubat, where we had shared a bench and desk. Sihanouk had been a brilliant student and a jovial, obliging friend. He was also something of a ladies' man, and we recalled with some merriment the lycée's crusty headmaster and his beautiful daughter, with whom Sihanouk had fallen in love.

This brief personal interlude with Sihanouk provided the only respite from a constant round of meetings and discussions. After two weeks I felt bone tired and quite ready for the short rest visit to Moscow that had been scheduled. A noisy and turbulent flight aboard an Aeroflot Ilyushin did nothing to dispel my fatigue, and by the time we arrived in Moscow, it was apparent that this "vacation" would consist mostly of rest and recuperation. As it turned out, the quiet room and comfortable bed waiting at the PRG embassy proved far more enticing than the tourist attractions of the Soviet capital. My one chance to observe Russian life was thus squandered, for the most part, in a deep and contented sleep.

Having seen nothing of Moscow except the inside of our embassy, I left after seven days to visit Budapest, at the invitation of my Hungarian counterpart. Here I was treated to a round of sightseeing so relentless that it seemed the Hungarians were determined to compensate me for the deprivation I had endured in Russia. Power stations, lake resorts, and historical monuments succeeded each other in a wonderful and seemingly endless profusion. None of it, however, distracted my host from what was uppermost in his mind—not Hungarian support for the PRG but Vietnam's position on the Sino-Soviet dispute. The minister complained bitterly about the Chinese leaders and hoped that we were in agreement with the Soviet Union on this vital matter. I responded carefully that Ho Chi Minh had admonished us to protect international solidarity and that this was our constant endeavor. We were unhappy about the conflict between two socialist brothers and looked forward to a speedy reconciliation.

These innocuous remarks were meant to deflect any more serious probing into a subject I was not at all comfortable with. I knew that the Party had already decided to ally itself with the Soviets. Movement in that direction had begun as far back as 1969, and Ho's death had opened the way to formalizing the decision. Though nothing like an open declaration could be expected while there was still a need for Chinese aid, in fact, by 1974 the bitter infighting had resulted in a clear victory for the pro-Soviet faction led by Secretary General Le Duan and Paris negotiator Le Duc Tho. Such stalwarts as General Giap, long-term Politburo member Hoang Van Hoan, and assistant Paris negotiator Xuan Thuy had already been damaged by their espousal of neutrality in the war between the giants. Other Party leaders, including number two man Truong Chinh and Premier Pham Van Dong, had managed to limit their exposure by steering a middle way between the "neutralists" and the Soviet advocates. (What their actual convictions were they managed to avoid saying. But through most of his long political life, Truong Chinh had been an advocate of friendship with China, and it was rumored that Pham Van Dong harbored deep reservations about a Russian alliance.)

My private belief was that Le Duan and Le Duc Tho were unwise to subvert the principle of even-handedness that Ho Chi Minh had so assiduously maintained, that it was a tragedy in the making. How to manage China was the classic Vietnamese dilemma, and it would become so again as soon as the Western presence in our country was permanently ended. But the thought of relying on the Soviets as a strategic counterbalance to the Chinese gave rise to grave premonitions. First and foremost, would not a Soviet alliance bring permanent tension to the area? Hadn't our problems with the United States grown out of their insistence on viewing Vietnam as a test of their containment strategy? What was the point of freeing ourselves from American neocolonialist visions, I thought, in order to enroll as pawns in the Soviet Union's version of containment? Worse, the vigilance and energy needed to oppose China (as would be required of a member of the Russian camp) would inevitably divert the country's attention from internal reconstruction. In my mind there was a basic connection between partnership with the Soviets and ongoing military priorities. Contrariwise, economic recovery was of necessity linked to neutrality.

These thoughts, of course, I had kept strictly to myself. I knew that, in private, most of the Vietnamese revolutionaries, both Communist and non-Communist, still revered both Ho and his policies and shared the opinion that the leadership was wrong on this issue. But this was not something that could be spoken of openly.

From Budapest I flew to Tiranë for ceremonies marking Albanian independence. Foremost among the celebrators in this mountainous capital was the Chinese delegation, led by Yao Wen Yuan, later to achieve fame as one of the Gang of Four. Yao initially did not realize that I was representing the PRG, and his attitude was glacial, a result of the worsening relations between China and North Vietnam. At some point, however, he recognized that there was also a delegation from Hanoi, on which he could more appropriately vent his distaste for Vietnamese ingratitude.

The Albanians, on the other hand, received me warmly from the beginning. In a meeting with Enver Hoxha, I was treated to an exposition (in Hoxha's excellent French) of the Sino-Soviet schism that was 180 degrees removed from the one I had heard in Budapest. Hoxha explained that he could not accept the Soviet desire for worldwide domination, and he forcefully criticized what he repeatedly referred to as "Soviet revisionism." He recalled his confrontations with Nikita Khrushchev over just these issues, and Khrushchev's mendacious attack on Albania.* Now, said Hoxha, the Soviets had made overtures about resuming diplomatic relations. This he would agree to only if the U.S.S.R. made a public apology for its insults over the years to

---

* Khrushchev, according to Hoxha, had called him "ungrateful." It must have been one of the Soviet leader's milder charges; in his memoirs Khrushchev accused Hoxha of personally strangling to death one of his early political opponents.

the Albanian people. I was no expert in Albanian-Soviet relations, but I understood Hoxha's pride and his determination not to bow to pressure from the superpower.

My last two stops were to be Bulgaria and Syria, whose foreign ministers I met for an exposé of the post-Paris situation in Vietnam. Then I went home. By the time I returned to Hanoi in mid-January, 1975, the military situation had altered radically in our favor. The optimism with which we had undertaken the 1974 dry-season campaign had indeed been borne out. We had consolidated and expanded almost all of our areas, and in addition to numerous local successes, elements of the NLF's 3d, 7th, and 9th Divisions had taken Phuoc Long on January 6, liberating for the first time an entire Southern province.

Both the military and psychological consequences of this victory were enormous. It was, as one of our commanders put it, "a bloodred pillar on the road to victory." As reports from Phuoc Long came in, a joint meeting of the Politburo and Central Military Committee was under way to maintain an up-to-the-minute watch on the situation as it developed and to nail down strategy for the next phase. The news acted like a tonic on everybody present. People were out of their seats, shaking hands and embracing jubilantly. As the room quieted down, Le Duan made an emotional announcement. "For the first time," he said, "a province in South Vietnam has been completely liberated. That province, furthermore, is near Saigon. . . . This event reflects more clearly than anything else our capability and the reaction of the puppets, and especially of the United States."* The long and tense meeting ended on a strong upbeat of optimism for a new two-year plan to complete the revolution. But as the final resolution also declared, "if the opportune moment presents itself . . . we will immediately liberate the South in 1975."†

The "opportune moment" had in fact been prepared for during

* Tran Van Tra, *Vietnam: History of the Bulwark B2 Theatre,* Vol. 5, Ho Chi Minh City, 1982, p. 128 (FBIS translation).

† General Van Tien Dung, "Our Great Spring Victory," in *Monthly Review Press,* New York, London, 1977, p. 25.

the rainy season just ended. By the time Phuoc Long fell, our transport and supply troops had managed to stockpile nearly thirty thousand tons of war matériel in South Vietnam, including eight thousand tons of ammunition for use in the battlefields of the upcoming spring campaign. Not only had Saigon's troops been forced into a defensive posture, they would now be clearly outgunned and outsupplied. General Tran Van Tra, NLF commander in Nambo (essentially the southern half of South Vietnam, including Saigon and the Mekong Delta) left the meeting "extremely enthusiastic and confident," ready to return South and implement plans for a final campaign.* He would be working closely with Van Tien Dung, North Vietnam's energetic chief of staff and the overall field commander.

The hinge of battle was to be the centrally located city of Ban Me Thuot, whose size made it appear an unlikely target. Looking for an attack in the northern region, Saigon forces were caught off guard when on March 8, Ban Me Thuot was suddenly cut off. Thirty-two hours later the last defenders from Saigon's 23rd Division had stopped firing. The city was ours. Understanding the significance of Ban Me Thuot, the Saigon General Pham Van Phu attempted to launch a counterattack, but quickly found that the routes toward the city had been strongly blocked. At this juncture Nguyen Van Thieu made the fatal decision to pull all his forces back from the central highlands and regroup on the coast. This ill-advised pullback turned a bad tactical defeat into a strategic disaster. Columns of retreating Saigon troops were hemmed in and wiped out on the only available jungle escape route.

As the morale of the Southern army began to come apart, so did Thieu's strategy of consolidating his coastal strongholds of Hue and Danang. On March 21, Van Tien Dung severed Route 1, the highway known as the Street Without Joy, which linked Hue with the South.

---

* Tran Van Tra had been chief of the PRG delegation in Saigon after the Paris Accords. He was later to become head of the Military Management Committee that governed the South immediately following the liberation of Saigon. General Tran, like Tran Bach Dang and Tran Buu Kiem, was a Communist revolutionary who had spent decades in the struggle. Like them, he was also a Southerner whose regional loyalties would eventually tell against him.

At the same time he drove home a series of attacks on the coastal cities and enclaves. By the end of March a rout of gigantic proportions had taken place. Hue had fallen on the twenty-sixth, Danang on the thirtieth. Pictures and film footage of what had happened reached us in Hanoi by the beginning of April. They showed masses of refugees and Saigon soldiers frantically trying to escape by ship and clawing for places in the evacuation planes and helicopters. Authority had completely disintegrated; soldiers attempting to save their own lives shot each other and civilians. Half a million refugees swarmed through the area. The briefings and pictures conjured up an image of hellish bedlam.

With the Southern defenses unraveling at such an unexpected rate, the Politburo decided that the "opportune moment" had indeed arrived. To seize the moment, Van Tien Dung was ordered to prepare a plan for an immediate assault on Saigon itself—"with strong determination . . . as soon as possible, during April at the latest," according to the directive.* The motto for the campaign would be "Marvelous Speed, Boldness, Surprise, and Certain Victory." Now Dung wheeled his army southward for what was to be the final battle of ten thousand days of fighting.

I was not to have a firsthand view of these developments. On April 4, I took off once more for Algeria, this time to represent the PRG at the conference of the International Association of Democratic Jurists. As it turned out, however, events followed me to the conference. Excitement generated by news from Vietnam percolated through the left-leaning delegations. They gave it concrete expression by electing me vice president—unanimously. Any doubts I might have had about the sentiments of even the Western participants were dissipated by the standing ovation that followed the announcement that the representative of the Provisional Revolutionary Government of South Vietnam had been elected.

Despite the personal expressions of support for the PRG that I had been hearing since my arrival in Algiers, the fervid public en-

* Tran Van Tra, Ibid., p. 158.

thusiasm shown by these Western delegates at the imminent humiliation of the United States surprised me a bit. It was a striking exhibition
of the rancor American foreign policy had generated among its own.
As I read it, the emotion evident at the conference was not much
different from that which had manifested itself in the streets of the
United States and so decisively in its Congress. It was this force that
resulted in American impotence during the 1974 taking of Quang
Duc and the January assault on Phuoc Long. The final campaign
against Saigon was to be a classic battle of main forces. But such a
climax had been made possible only by the thoroughness of our victories on the political and diplomatic fronts. It had been the gradual
and cumulative erosion of our enemies' internal cohesion that prepared
the way for Saigon's sudden collapse while her protector looked on
helplessly.

The United States was about to suffer the greatest military reversal
in its history, due largely to its inability to cope with the strategies of
people's war. But listening to the Soviet delegate at the conference, it
was evident that the Americans held no monopoly on the arrogance of
power. At one point I found myself standing next to the Russian
representative as he held forth to the Algerians and others on the
subject of Soviet aid to the Third World. "Look at these good hands,"
he was saying, holding out his own open hands. "In these good Soviet
hands you can find good Soviet arms. And with Soviet arms the Third
World can defend itself against the American imperialists." As he
said this, he grasped my own hand in his and thrust it forward, a
graphic symbol of how at this very moment Soviet arms were humbling
the imperialists in Vietnam.

Shocked at this crudeness and by the presumptuous ignorance of
his remarks, I was momentarily deserted by my sense of diplomatic
etiquette. "Look," I blurted out, withdrawing my hand from his large
and sweaty grip, "you gave Egypt the best you had, and that didn't
seem to help *them* much." The startled silence that followed told me
how truly out of place my comment was—in light of both my Algerian
hosts' sensibilities and the Soviet Union's real munificence toward us.
I hastened to add: What I had meant to convey was that Vietnam's

success was hardly a simple matter of arms, that the diplomatic, and especially the political struggle were essential, and that without the support of the people the best weapons in the world could not be sufficient. I can't say to what extent the Russian appreciated any of this. When I returned to the embassy that night, I vowed to rededicate myself in future to the arts of restraint and decorum.

In Algiers, as in the other capitals I had visited, the PRG embassy was a good deal more luxurious than that of our Northern compatriots —bigger buildings, newer cars, finer furniture. All of it spoke of the considerable aid we were receiving from both the Soviet bloc and Third World treasuries. (In addition to Algeria, Syria and Libya were large contributors.) Direct financial subsidies covered all of our diplomatic expenses, including support of the embassy properties plus staff and ambassadorial salaries. These salaries were never touched, however, but were transferred directly into DRV embassy accounts. Even the newspapers and magazines bought for PRG offices eventually found their way to North Vietnamese waiting rooms. (After unification the grim joke went around that the PRG had been the goose that laid the golden egg, but that our Northern brothers had managed to kill the goose.) There was no question that South Vietnam's revolutionary struggle had become a worldwide symbol, inspiring sympathy and support that were not necessarily available to the Northern government.

The actual relationship between North Vietnam's government and the Southern revolution was both more complex and more direct than Westerners liked to believe—more complex than Johnson and the now-departed Richard Nixon thought, and more direct than many antiwar figures believed. But in April of 1975 all debates on this subject had become academic, for the moment at least. By the middle of the month, Dung's final march on Saigon was in high gear. (He would later call this last offensive, the Ho Chi Minh campaign, "the most beautiful product of the age.") The avalanche, once started, could not be contained, and Thieu's government was now entering the last stages of shocked disorientation.

Meanwhile, events in Cambodia were outracing even what was

As PRG ambassador, meeting Norodom Sihanouk.

going on in Vietnam. On April 15 and 16, Phnom Penh came under guerrilla artillery and rocket attack. On April 17, with the last Americans gone, the city fell to the Khmer Rouge. The day before this happened, Madame Binh arrived in Algiers on a stopover during a tour of Africa. Blissfully ignorant of the sea of blood into which Cambodia's new rulers would lead their country, she and I paid a call on the Khmer representative to congratulate him on the victory. It was my last official function in Algeria.

By April 20 I was back in Hanoi, preparing to lead a PRG delegation to Beijing for the funeral of Queen Kossamak, Norodom Sihanouk's mother. Despite his pressing concerns about developments in Cambodia, the prince graciously invited both the PRG and DRV representatives to an intimate dinner, a mark of his expectation that our partnership in struggle would now blossom into a partnership in development. Amidst the evening's cordiality it did not seem an un-

Norodom Sihanouk and Pham Van Dong in happier days.

realistic desire. But Sihanouk's disillusionment on this score would soon be quite as deep as mine was to be on others.*

Another dinner, distinctly less pleasing to our Northern compatriots, was organized in honor of the PRG by Li Xian Nian, then vice president of China's State Council, and Li Quing, minister of commerce. In the course of the banquet, Li Quing announced that the People's Republic had a large freighter loaded with food, medicine, and other necessities, waiting to be sent directly to Danang or Saigon as soon as it was liberated. The implicit meaning of this announcement was not lost on any of those present, from North or South. Throughout our stay the Chinese had treated us with a good deal more cordiality than they had the DRV delegation. They were plainly using this opportunity to express their feelings about Hanoi's already serious romance with the Soviets. At the same time they were signaling to the PRG that they were open to independent contacts.

* I was not to meet Sihanouk again until 1980, when we were both in exile. By that time I had come to feel an odd sense of shared destiny with him. He related to me then that he had written three separate letters to Pham Van Dong, proposing negotiations for a political resolution to the two-year-old Vietnamese occupation of Cambodia. Dong had returned each of them unopened. "He thinks that in this way he is humiliating me," said Sihanouk, "but I think that in light of my contribution to Vietnam, he has really humiliated and disgraced himself."

Though Chinese intentions were clear, they misjudged both our ability and our readiness to respond to overtures of this sort. The overpowering taste of victory was already in our mouths. Nguyen Van Thieu had resigned on the twenty-first and was now in Taiwan lashing out bitterly at the Americans. Van Tien Dung's *bo dois* ("soldiers") were in the suburbs of Saigon, and a lifetime's hopes were on the verge of realization. All the problems and hardships of our struggle were dissolving before a flood tide of anticipation.

21

Joys and Sorrows

On April 28, 1975, immediately after cremation ceremonies for Queen Kossamak, our delegation flew back to Hanoi. There we joined our colleagues in a round-the-clock vigil over the radio news and dispatches from the South. On the morning of the thirtieth many members of the Alliance, PRG, and NLF leadership met in President Tho's house in the expectation that an announcement would come soon. At 11:25, bending over the radio and cupping our hands behind our ears to catch each word, we heard Duong Van Minh ("Big" Minh had been appointed president two days before) announce that all Saigon soldiers would now lay down their arms. A total capitulation. Saigon was liberated—without any house-to-house fighting or the die-hard defense that everyone feared would bring massive destruction to the city. A confusion of joy and emotion filled the room. Everybody was embracing, eyes filled with tears. Trinh Dinh Thao, Dr. Hoa, Lam Van Tet, and the others—all of us were overwhelmed at the thought of going home.

Outside, a tumult had erupted. Rushing into the street, we were caught up in a swirl of delirium. It seemed the entire population of Hanoi had run outdoors. Firecrackers were exploding everywhere; the ordinarily grim and stoic Hanoiese were cheering, singing, hugging each other—many of them sobbing with a force of emotion unimaginable to anyone who had not endured and suffered as they had. Dotting this sea of abandon were hundreds of thousands of flowers whose fragrance sweetened the air. Hanoi's peach and cherry trees seemed to be blooming all around, although I had hardly noticed them the day before. It was as if a springtime of peace had suddenly replaced all the hardship and sorrow that had been their lot as well as ours for so long. We were celebrating the advent of a new world.

Together with my colleagues and friends, I began planning for an immediate return. We could barely control our impatience when the Politburo informed us that the situation in the South was still somewhat unclear and that we should not return until security could be assured. Meanwhile, to assist the newly constituted Military Management Committee achieve firm control, groups of cadres from various Northern ministries were dispatched ahead of us. They were seen off by Premier Pham Van Dong, who admonished them to "strictly maintain the morality of revolutionaries and of the working class," and warned them against the temptations of "poison pills encased in sugar"—that is, the material seductions that would assault them in the dissolute South.

Finally, Truong Chinh and Xuan Thuy called on us to announce that the Party had organized a farewell banquet in our honor on the twelfth and that we would depart the following morning for the grand victory celebration in Saigon. Over the next days it was impossible to think of anything other than our glorious city and the loved ones we had last seen so many years before, but whose memories had sustained us throughout our exile.

At last, on the morning of the thirteenth, after a night of feasting and camaraderie, we boarded our Ilyushin for Saigon. We were in a state of something near ecstasy at the thought of being reunited with our families and friends, and being once more in our own land. It was two weeks to the day since Duong Van Minh had announced the Saigon regime's surrender and more than fourteen years since we had formally launched the revolution in the jungles of Tay Ninh. At Saigon's Tan Son Nhut airfield, we were met by a triumphal welcome, crowds with banners and flowers catching us up in a flood of affection and pride. Dignitaries from the NLF and the Northern government embraced us, some of them crying unashamedly. Our cavalcade drove into the city along streets lined with cheering, flag-waving people.

We were taken directly to the Hotel Miramar, a luxury establishment on Tu Do Street, which was serving as temporary quarters until sufficiently secure residences could be located. Though there was no more fighting, the Military Management Committee's fears were evident in the large and heavily armed contingent of guards protecting the hotel. Whatever residual dangers there might have been, however, were far from my mind. The moment I arrived at the hotel, I found a telephone and dialed my parents, who I knew had been living for some time with my older brother Quynh.

After a number of rings my mother answered, but not with the joy that I was expecting and that I longed to hear in her dear voice. Instead, in words broken by sobs she told me that my father was dead, that he had died less than a month before after a long illness. This news was like a hammer blow. I had last seen my father in late 1967 while I was still a prisoner of the National Police. Emaciated and half-blind, I had tottered unsteadily from my "coffin" to the visiting room, where he was waiting. His expression as we embraced was one of bottomless grief. His words had burned themselves into my memory. "My son," he had said, "I simply cannot understand you. You have abandoned everything. A good family, happiness, wealth—to follow the Communists. They will never return to you a particle of the things you have left. You will see. They will betray you, and you will suffer your entire life." I had answered him then, "My dearest father, you have six sons. You should be content to sacrifice one of them for the sake of the country's independence and liberty." Now, though I had returned as a minister in the government of the new, liberated South, the sorrow of that last parting could never be erased.

I was still distracted by this terrible news when my mother began to spin a tale of further calamities that stunned me into silence. My wife, unable to endure the separation of so many years, had obtained a divorce and was now living in the United States. My children too had left the country—my twenty-four-year-old-son to France [the child my first wife had borne after her return to Vietnam from France], my daughter to the United States where she was studying at a university.* I couldn't think or utter a word into the phone. Around me flowed the fulfillment of a lifetime's hopes—the joyous faces of comrades who had been with me through the years of fighting and enduring. All the feelings brought on by a victory so immense that no one had dared dream of it swept through me, feelings that were challenged now by this sudden revelation of all I had lost. Faces appeared in my imagination: Vo Van Kiet, whose wife and children had been killed in the bombing; Madame Liem, who had been granted five unexpected minutes with her husband before he too had marched off for his appointment with the B-52s. Friends and comrades-in-arms who had not survived, among them Albert Thao with his wandering eye and mocking smile. Those faces of ultimate desolation I had seen in Hanoi's wretched apartments. Among all these, my own losses were nothing special. But this knowledge did not make

---

* My daughter Loan had experienced one of those striking ironies the war was famous for. While I was director of the Société Sucrière, we had enrolled her at the Convent des Oiseaux, an exclusive Catholic private school in Dalat, reserved for the families of high officials. Her closest friend there had been Tuan-Anh Thieu, daughter of the president. During the period when I was busy secretly proselytizing Saigon's intellectuals, Loan was spending a great deal of time at the presidential palace, taking meals with the Thieu family and often staying over. Madame Thieu had grown especially fond of her and treated her almost as if she were a daughter. In 1967 when I was exposed and arrested, Thieu himself had taken Loan aside for a talk. "*Ton ton* ('uncle') and your father are enemies," he told her. "But that makes absolutely no difference as far as your welcome in my home is concerned."

Subsequently, when Loan graduated and expressed a desire to study overseas, Madame Thieu sponsored her, introducing her to the ministers of the interior and education and arranging permission for her to go abroad. Having discovered a flair for mathematics and science, Loan was especially interested in attending the Massachusetts Institute of Technology. While waiting for a decision on her application, she had stayed in the Vietnamese embassy in Washington, where it was believed she was a relation of the president's wife. When MIT's acceptance came, it occasioned a good deal of consternation among Loan's temporary guardians. Boston was one of the more chaotic centers of antiwar activity, home of such agitators as Howard Zinn and Noam Chomsky, who was in fact a professor at MIT. In the end it was decided that Loan's (supposed) relationship with Madame Thieu, no matter how distant it might be, would expose her to threats and possible violence from Boston's militant protestors. Instead of going to MIT, she enrolled at a university in western Pennsylvania, where it was felt she would be safer, graduating four years later with a degree in computer science.

them any less painful. Still, as I looked around the Miramar lobby, I was aware that there was hardly a person there whose joy was not mixed with sorrow or who did not see his own sacrifice as part of the immense suffering of the entire people, North and South.

The next day we returned to Tan Son Nhut to greet the DRV's president, Ton Duc Thang, and others who were flocking in for the victory celebration. Le Duc Tho, General Van Tien Dung, NLF President Tho, PRG President Phat, cabinet members and high cadres, everyone crowded around the plane to welcome the elderly Thang, who had succeeded Ho Chi Minh as chief of state and who would dedicate this historic triumph to Ho's memory. Again, cheering crowds lined the roadside, as we drove back to the Miramar for a day busy with reunions and preparation for the future.

The May 15 victory celebration stand. Le Duc Tho is at center. I am immediately to the left. Nguyen Huu Tho is to my left in the dark shirt. To the right,

On the fifteenth we woke to a clear, sunlit sky. Already at dawn crowds of people were pouring into Independence Palace Square to celebrate this most glorious of events, total victory after thirty years of grim and bloody sacrifice. The immense throng stretched out in all directions opposite the dais—over half a million we were told later, and that seemed a conservative estimate. Together with the rest of the PRG leadership, I climbed to my place on the reviewing stand and looked out on a sea of faces and banners. Our colleagues gathered around us, from the Front, the Alliance, the DRV, the Party, all beaming with happiness, some wiping away tears.

President Thang of the Northern government spoke for all of us, dedicating this day to Uncle Ho, whose spirit seemed all but palpable in the air around the dais. "From this time on," Thang declared, "the

in military dress, is President Ton Duc Thang, Ho Chi Minh's successor.

whole Vietnamese people will share a new happiness, in a new era."
After Thang, Chairman Nguyen Huu Tho of the NLF spoke on behalf of the Front and the Provisional Revolutionary Government,
recalling and celebrating the heroic struggle of the people. Pham
Hung, representing the Workers' Party, then rose to comment on the
earthshaking significance of our historic triumph and to appeal for
national unity and reconstruction.

"Only the American imperialists," he said, "have been defeated.
All Vietnamese are the victors. Anyone with Vietnamese blood
should take pride in this common victory of the whole nation. You,
the people of Saigon, are now the masters of your own city."

With this the parades began. First the mass organizations filed by,
the youth, students, workers, Buddhists, Catholics, representatives of
every group and stratum in the city. Above their smiles waved the
flags of both the Northern republic and the South's proud new government. Portraits of Ho swung down street, sprinkled among thousands
of pennants and banderoles proclaiming "Nothing Is More Precious
Than Independence and Liberty" . . . "Long Live Chairman Ho" . . .
"Unity, Unity, Great Unity," and also "Glory to Marxism-Leninism"
and "Glory to the Workers' Party of Vietnam."

Then the military units came in sight, troops from every North
Vietnamese Army outfit, all of them wearing distinctive new olive-
colored pith helmets. Tank squadrons, antiaircraft batteries and
artillery rumbled by, as did sleek, murderous-looking Soviet missiles.
All the while, air force overflights shook the dais, adding their din to
the martial and patriotic music of the bands.

At last, when our patience had almost broken, the Vietcong
units finally appeared. They came marching down the street, several
straggling companies, looking unkempt and ragtag after the display
that had preceded them. Above their heads flew a red flag with a
single yellow star—the flag of the Democratic Republic of North
Vietnam.

Seeing this, I experienced almost a physical shock. Turning to Van
Tien Dung who was then standing next to me, I asked quietly, "Where
are our divisions one, three, five, seven, and nine?"

Dung stared at me a moment, then replied with equal deliberateness: "The army has already been unified." As he pronounced these words, the corners of his mouth curled up in a slight smile.

"Since when?" I demanded. "There's been no decision about anything like that."

Without answering, Dung slowly turned his eyes back to the street, unable to suppress his sardonic expression, although he must have known it was conveying too much. A feeling of distaste for this whole affair began to come over me—not to mention premonitions I did not want to entertain.

In the days that followed, I became aware that our police and security were being handled exclusively by various DRV departments. Now that I thought about it, I realized that all the arrangements for the victory celebration had also been taken care of by the DRV. We all began to note the extent to which the Northern cadres were filling positions of responsibility on our staffs and handling business of every variety.

This was not a new development. But before this we had been involved in a common struggle, in which our organizations had faced severe manpower and expertise shortages. Now, with victory, it was somehow different.

A new tone had crept into the collaboration. All of the PRG cabinet began to feel uncomfortable, although we strove to put the best face on what was happening, attributing it to "organizational difficulties" (in the push to set up our new administrations and get them running) or our undeniable lack of experienced personnel. And indeed—as we kept reminding ourselves—we did desperately need all the managerial help we could find. Reasoning along these lines, we managed to bury our anxieties in the avalanche of work that engulfed us.

Meanwhile, the Military Management Committee that had been set up to maintain order was still functioning as the government pro tem. The real power in this group was Vo Van Kiet (Kiet at this time was a full member of the Party's Central Committee), who was in constant communication with the Politburo. All of the policies and directives concerned with the problems of victory and transition were in fact devised in the Politburo and administered through Kiet and his colleagues. The Provisional Revolutionary Government, "the sole genuine representative of the Southern people" (as the Party had so felicitously styled it over the years), was still playing a purely subordinate role—although to give these proceedings an air of legitimacy, all decisions were passed through the PRG staffs, to receive an imprimatur from the appropriate ministry. But in the heady and tumultuous days of May, no one gave much thought to this arrangement. Once the chaos of transition had been controlled and a semblance of calm restored, we would of course begin to use more normal avenues of government.

But as the weeks slid by, it became impossible to shut our eyes to the emerging arrogance and disdain of our Party staff cadres—almost as if they believed that they were the conquerors and we the vanquished. Try as we might to ignore the signs, each of us felt it. In the Justice Ministry, my administrators began claiming that they had to carry out orders from their superiors in the Northern government, rather than the directives they received from us. One of my cadres, an official of North Vietnam's High Tribunal, drew up plans to establish branches of the tribunal in each Southern province. Others, employees of the DRV's Supreme Council of Censors and State Juridical Committee, were anxious to confiscate some of the Justice Ministry's buildings for use by their own departments.

At first, I treated these and similar situations as opportunities to delineate the authority of my ministry. Still struggling to suppress the obvious, I reasoned that the entire cabinet could expect attempts to encroach on its jurisdiction and that this was essentially normal bureaucratic infighting. One of our first tasks, then, would be to establish a clear chain of command. I began this process by using the plans for province tribunals and the transfer of property as examples. Since my signature and seal were required for all magistrate appointments, as well as for property transfers, I decided to withhold approval. Such directives, I insisted, would have to originate with the ministry, and I would consider them on their merits. As long as the ministry was my responsibility, I was the one who should be making these and all other substantive decisions.

As the cadres' demands became more and more heated, I remained adamant, continuing to operate on the theory that authority would have to be grasped. Eventually, my obstinacy brought results—visitors from the North. I received word that the chiefs of the High Tribunal, the Censorate, and the Juridical Committee would meet with me to resolve the impasse that had developed. In an afternoon of discussion, my guests succeeded in conveying to me the fundamentality of the North's resolve to control the Provisional Government.

As we talked, the true outlines of power revealed themselves with painful clarity. Suddenly all the creeping fears that, until now, I had succeeded in holding down were released. When my visitors left, I felt all I had managed to retain was the respect due my office, for I had listened to their arguments and pleas as if these people were actually supplicants—the formal charade had been expertly maintained on both sides. But in the end I signed the directives.

By the time this diplomatic encounter was over, I had no illusions about what was happening, and I knew that neither I nor my colleagues would be in office long.

My fellow ministers quickly found their own illusions and rationalizations swept away just as cleanly. Like me, most of these veteran revolutionaries put up an initial fight, refusing to cooperate once they discovered they were involved in a farce. Many just left, keeping away from their offices while they mulled over what to do next. "Let the Northern cadres make the wind and the weather," growled Dr. Hoa as she stalked out of the Ministry of Health. A miasma of disgust hung over most of the NLF and PRG people who stayed.

There were several interesting exceptions to this, though. A few, Presidential Minister Kiem, Professor Nguyen Van Hieu, and Culture Minister Luu Huu Phuoc kept their mouths shut, frightened by the thought of deviating from the Party's will. Meanwhile, NLF President Nguyen Huu Tho and PRG President Huynh Tan Phat took steps to secure their privileges by faithfully expounding the new line: forced reunification and the rapid socialization of the South.

As for me, for the time being I stayed, presiding over a department roiled with controversy. My embittered deputy minister, Le Van Tha, was intent on turning life into a bureaucratic torment for the Northern staff cadres, who, if they had been arrogant as subordinates, were insufferable now that the veil was lifted. Not content with the hard time Tha was giving them, they squabbled incessantly among themselves, chiefly about the best way to insure the demise of the ministry—the three DRV bureaus for which they worked each having its own distinct thoughts on the subject.

It was a time of unalloyed cynicism on the part of the Workers' Party and stunned revulsion for those of us who had been their brothers-in-arms for so long. About this period the Northern Party historian Nguyen Khac-Vien commented, "The Provisional Revolutionary Government was always simply a group emanating from the DRV. If we (the DRV) had pretended otherwise for such a long period, it was only because during the war we were not obliged to unveil our cards."* Now, with total power in their hands, they began to show their cards in the most brutal fashion. They made it understood that the Vietnam of the future would be a single monolithic bloc, collectivist and totalitarian, in which all the traditions and culture of the South would be ground and molded by the political machine of the conquerors. These, meanwhile, proceeded to install themselves with no further regard for the niceties of appearance.

The PRG and the National Liberation Front, whose programs had embodied the desire of so many South Vietnamese to achieve a political solution to their troubles and reconciliation among a people devastated by three decades of civil war—this movement the Northern Party had considered all along as simply the last linkup it needed to achieve its own imperialistic revolution. After the 1975 victory, the Front and the PRG not only had no further role to play; they became a positive obstacle to the rapid consolidation of power.

This obstacle had to be removed. As Truong Chinh, spokesman for the Politburo, put it, "The strategic mission for our revolution in

* Interview from *Vietnam Press,* Foreign Language Publishing House, Hanoi, 1978.

this new phase is to accelerate the unification of the country and lead Front and the PRG not only had no further role to play; they became the nation to a rapid, powerful advance toward socialism." Chinh's phrases were not simple rhetoric. They conveyed policy decisions that were to change the fabric of the South's political, social, and economic life. No longer would South Vietnam be regarded as "a separate case" whose economy and government would have the opportunity to evolve independently, prior to negotiating a union with the DRV. All of the NLF and PRG emphasis on civil rights, land reform, and social welfare was "no longer operative." The program now was to strip away as fast as possible the apparent respect for pluralistic government, neutrality, and national concord and reconciliation in the South that the DRV had maintained with such breathtaking pretense for twenty-one years. We had entered, in Chinh's words, " a new phase."

In mid-July the organizations representing the old phase held one of their last general meetings. The leadership of the NLF, PRG, the Alliance of National, Democratic, and Peace Forces, and the mass organizations were called together to hear relevant portions of the new master plan. In a series of virtuoso speeches, Pham Hung (DRV Politburo member in charge of the South), Huynh Tan Phat, and Nguyen Huu Tho managed to address the subject of a unified Vietnam without once referring to the fate intended for the Front and the PRG, those erstwhile "sole authentic representatives."

While this amazing performance was going on, Presidential Minister Tran Buu Kiem (the former foreign affairs specialist) leaned over and whispered in my ear, "They are burying us without drums or taps. You'd think they would at least have the decency to say prayers for the dead."

"You're right," I whispered back. "We should insist on a formal funeral." During a break in the proceedings, I went up to Tho and said, "Listen, some of us feel we should get a funeral celebration out of this. What do you say?"

Tho stared at me quizzically, unsure that he had detected a note of mockery. After a moment he answered with stony seriousness, "Of course. We can easily arrange that."

Tho was as good as his word, though it turned out to be not quite so easy. The problem was that by this time all the Saigon government buildings and official residences had been appropriated by Party leaders from Hanoi, none of whom were anxious to sponsor such a possibly questionable affair. In the end, Tho hired the Rex Dance Hall for the Vietcong funeral celebration. This sleazy former pleasure land had been one of the magnetic poles of Saigon's demimonde. In its day it had seen deals of every description made by the most corrupt of the city's pre-1975 denizens. Drug transactions, debauchery, and the buying and selling of power had been its daily meat and drink. I am sure it never saw the likes of the gathering that met there for the last rites of South Vietnam's revolution.

About thirty of us were present, from the Front, the PRG ministries, and the Alliance. We ate without tasting, and we heard without listening as some revolutionary music was cranked out by a sad little band Tho had dredged up from somewhere. We even managed to choke out a few of the old combatants' songs. But there was no way to swallow the gall in our mouths or to shrug off the shroud that had settled on our souls. We knew finally that we had been well and truly sold.

22

Concord and
Reconciliation

During this period of rampant disenchantment, I was developing the deepest fears for our policy of national concord and reconciliation. This had been one of the bedrock PRG positions and had gained us substantial support from even nonleftist elements of Southern society. It had enabled us to attract many individuals of reputation and integrity to the Alliance of National, Democratic, and Peace Forces, and had played a major role in assuaging fears of the revolution among ordinary people. Our insistent reiteration of this policy had helped generate among the Saigonese (and Southerners in general) a reluctance to put up a die-hard battle as the Thieu regime began to crumble. Instead, they were willing to greet the victorious armies with a cautiously friendly wait-and-see attitude.

But though this policy of concord and reconciliation had been one of our most potent political weapons, we had not spelled it out in any detail prior to the capitulation of the Saigon government. This was one of the large tasks that had been caught short in the complete collapse of the regime fifty-five days into a campaign that we had anticipated would take two years. All, consequently, was not in readiness when it came to the specifics of just how we were going to deal with our recent enemies. At the beginning of May, a COSVN/ PRG meeting was held to settle the details of what was now a matter of great urgency. Although many of the PRG officials were still in

Hanoi when this meeting took place (myself among them), the directives that came out of it were in keeping with the strong emphasis on moderation and restraint that had clearly emerged from previous policy deliberations.

The directives established at the beginning of May called for all soldiers, officers, and officials of the old regime to undergo a period of reeducation. This included individuals who had participated in the government at every level, as well as the leading members of the various political parties. Common soldiers and low-level employees would enroll in a three-day course near their homes or former offices, to be taught about their own mistakes and about the crimes perpetrated by the Americans. Middle-level officials and junior officers were to undergo a more intensive, ten-day course on the same subjects. For the rest, high officials, leaders of the national parties, senior officers, and members of the National Police, the period would be thirty days. All of these would go through a rigorous curriculum consisting of

1. Their errors
2. American crimes
3. Crimes of the puppet regime
4. The history of Vietnam's heroes
5. The history of the Vietnamese revolution
6. The policies of the revolutionary government
7. The value of labor.

In addition, these individuals would be required to take part in mutual criticism and self-criticism sessions.

Considering the length of the war and its destructiveness, the policy we were about to implement was magnanimous and humane. Many of us felt it was also wise. Treatment of this sort would be likely to reorient people, who had been shocked by defeat and were now experiencing considerable anxiety about their own futures. A humane approach to such psychologically vulnerable individuals would have a good chance of winning their allegiance, or at least securing a loyal tolerance of the new government. Given the thoroughgoing nature of our military and civil control and the absence of any rallying points for those who might be considering opposition, such a policy risked little and stood to gain a great deal. Its effect on the rest of the population, we hoped, would be to mobilize support for the reconstruction of the country, a job that would require the undivided energy of the entire nation. The prerequisite for this was mutual goodwill and trust in the leadership. Concord and reconciliation was not simply a political weapon in the conflict with our enemies; it was an essential ingredient in the new and even more crucial struggle ahead. We had liberated the nation from its neocolonial status. Now we had the task of liberating it from injustice, poverty, and underdevelopment. If we failed at that, the Great Spring Victory would turn to ashes in our hands.

The first step in marshaling the people was to guide them through the infinitely delicate process of reconciling the bitter, often savage enmities that a generation of civil war had left in its wake. I personally encouraged the officials who had worked for the old Justice Ministry to comply with the directive and report for reeducation—the magistrates, attorneys, judges, many of them friends of mine from the years before my second arrest. I myself opened the ministry's three-day course for lower-level employees of the previous administration, relieving as best I could the worries of the clerks and minor bureaucrats who made up most of the former work force.

On June 16, 1975, I also drove two of my brothers, Quynh and Bich, to their own reeducation points. My older brother Quynh was director of the Saigon General Hospital and had been an adviser on health policies to the Nationalist Party. Bich, my younger brother, was head of the foreign exchange division of the National Bank.* They brought with them, as the directive had stipulated, everything they would need for a thirty-day stay, including their own food. Like hundreds of thousands of others, they had convinced themselves

---

* Of my other brothers, Hoang and Due had retired from the Southern air force some time before this and were not called in for re-education. Khue, the Shell executive, had never worked for the government.

that the public announcements were sincere and that after a month they would be welcomed back into a society desperately in need of people with their considerable talents. In addition, they felt, as did my friends, that my position would protect them from any special severity.

Thirty days passed, then thirty more. At home, my mother became more agitated each day. "Why haven't your brothers come back yet?" she asked repeatedly. "You told me for certain that this government of yours was as good as its word. But I have a feeling that you've been tricked. Those Tonkinese [a pejorative Southern term for Northerners] have made dupes out of you and all the rest."

My mother wasn't the only one I was hearing from. Every day someone or other from one of my friends' families would come to my office or stop me in the street to ask what was going on. Their questions were frightened and accusatory. Each person who had turned himself in for reeducation had left at least half a dozen close relatives behind, all of whom were beginning to feel surges of fear and outrage. The family harmony and closeness that are so precious to Vietnamese had scarcely been restored; the great flood of emotional relief at the war's end had scarcely been triggered—and now something ominous and unexplained was in the air. Almost every family was affected. The atmosphere grew heavy with anxiety and foreboding.

As time passed, it became clear that the thirty-day period had not simply been lengthened by some ad hoc decision of the Politburo, made necessary by unforeseen difficulties. Rather, the directive established at the May COSVN/PRG meeting now revealed itself as a ruse intended to mask the Politburo's real policy, which was altogether different and (to my mind) vicious and ultimately destructive to the nation. Finally understanding this patent fact, which I had been so reluctant to face, I decided to confront PRG President Phat directly. Phat, a Party member since 1940, had from the beginning been one of the Politburo's chief agents in controlling the Southern revolution. My discussion with him was far from satisfactory.

"Brother Tam Chi [Phat's nom de guerre]," I began, "Perhaps

My extended family at a Tet celebration in 1972. My father is at center. My mother is seated at the left. My brothers: Due is in a suit and glasses to the rear. Bich is standing next to my father. Khue is in a bow tie at the extreme right.

you can explain to me what is happening. We have promised that these people would spend a month in reeducation. That time is long past. What's going on?"

"Listen, Brother Ba, we never said the term would be limited to thirty days. All we said was that they should report with thirty days' worth of food and clothing."

I stared at Phat incredulously. "What is this, a word game? We don't need it. We've got the power, don't we? You think we have to deceive them and punish them? That's the way weaklings would do it. Are we insecure? Don't you think we've got enough control? I feel as if I have been personally betrayed in this—by you! And because of you, I've betrayed others!"

Phat tried to calm me down. "Brother Ba, we're applying clemency—real clemency—to a great number of people. Most of the

soldiers and officials and junior officers are already back at work.
You've got to distinguish between the criminals and the ones who
were just cannon fodder. Those who were in on decisions, they need
a lot more. And what about the torturers? Would you let them go?
You can't treat all these people alike. Each one is a separate case,
and we've got to deal with each one differently."

"Listen, Brother Tam Chi, you say that they have to be treated
individually. But the truth is that they're all in the same boat, aren't
they? They're all in indefinitely—isn't that so? I'll tell you what I
think. I think we had better keep our word and let them go back
home. If we've got some who need a longer time, we have to let
them know without any ambiguity so that their families can make
arrangements to take care of themselves. There's a lot more at stake
here than punishment."

On this sour note our discussion ended. I was beginning to

Huynh Tan Phat, president
of the PRG.

experience an active sense of despair that was, if anything, worse than the original shock of discovering the duplicity behind the Party's relationship with us over so many years. Now I was well on the road to understanding in concrete terms what Party control of the South was going to mean. This inner turmoil was not calmed by the news several days later that a member of my staff, Hai Thuan, had committed suicide.

Hai Thuan had been an old resister, a Southern cadre of the Vietminh in its war against the French. After the 1954 Geneva Accords, he left his family and went North, along with other particularly dedicated and ideologically minded partisans. Now Thuan was once again in Saigon, reunited with his wife and working in the study and research section of the Justice Ministry. Several days earlier he had come into my office looking haggard and depressed. As I gestured for him to sit down, he began sobbing uncontrollably. It took several minutes before he had regained enough composure to begin begging for my help in getting his son released.

It seemed that this son, whom Thuan had left behind years before, served as an officer in the Saigon army and had dutifully reported himself for thirty days of reeducation. Like all the others, he was still in camp, and the recently reunited mother and father were unable to get any news of him. Now Thuan began to suffer the torments of the damned, fears for his son combined with the sharpest reproaches from his wife and his mother, who also lived with them. They were the ones who had raised this boy and the other children— alone, they reminded him—while he had deserted them for the revolution. They had endured all of it, the poverty, the social ostracism, the police surveillance, because they too believed that victory would give them a better life. "Now you come back and you can't do a thing for your family. You can't even make enough salary to support yourself, let alone us. You're nothing more than an extra mouth. Now we have to take care of you along with everyone else." His life at home, Thuan told me, had become unbearable. Couldn't I somehow intervene for his son?

Needless to say, I could hardly offer Thuan any comfort. I advised him to address a petition to the Politburo, requesting his son's release, reviewing his own record of service to the revolution, and citing the official policy of concord and reconciliation. Thuan took my suggestion, and I transmitted his petition to the Politburo with my comments attached. So far as I knew, there had been no response. Two weeks later Thuan was dead. He had thrown himself out of the sixth floor of a building on Le Loi Street, which I had requisitioned for ministry housing. He left two letters. One was addressed to the Party leaders, criticizing them for their callous insensitivity toward the problems of the South and for their deceitfulness. The second was to his wife and mother, asking forgiveness.

Thuan's story, even his suicide, was by no means unique. But it shook me badly. I was having problems of my own, both in my immediate family with my two brothers, and among more distant relations. Everyone had some family member or other in camp, and even those with the strongest revolutionary credentials were coming up against a wall of silence when they tried to find out anything— where they were being held, how they were, when they would be home. For its own inexplicable reasons, the DRV had instilled a wave of panic that reached throughout the South.

By this time my anxiety about my brothers was becoming acute. I was absolutely determined to find out what was happening to them. Several days later I was able to arrange through Phat a visit to the camp at Long Thanh where they were both being held. My old friend Trinh Dinh Thao, president of the Alliance of National, Democratic, and Peace Forces, was given permission to accompany me; his son-in-law, a former Saigon army doctor, was also interned there.

At Long Thanh we were received by the camp commander with a chilly politeness. He would arrange a car to drive us around the camp area, he said, but we would not be permitted to stop or talk with either our relatives or anyone else. So we were chauffeured through the camp, trying hard to make out our loved ones among the clumps of dazed-looking prisoners. As we drove slowly by one group, I saw Quynh and Bich walking together. Even now their faces haunt me: pale, thin, frightened, their eyes fixed in a glazed stare. For a moment we glimpsed each other. I can't even imagine what they must have thought, seeing me in the back seat of a government car driving around that place.

Four months of persistent effort later, I was able to impose on Pham Hung, the former COSVN chief, to have Bich released. Quynh, however, was transferred to a more secure camp in the North, where he is still incarcerated at this writing, nine years after I drove him to the induction station for his thirty days of reeducation. His crime was in having accepted a consultant's position with a political party whose participation in the old Assembly had offended the Lao Dong. Quyhn's misstep appears to have marked this gifted physician/administrator for perpetual detention, a tragedy not only for him, but for the people who so badly need his skills, as they need the skills of so many others among the permanently damned.

Although the camp situation continued to prey on my conscience, other equally malignant developments were under way, and these would soon claim the bulk of my attention. With no strong central government in the South, various military, Party, and DRV government organs embarked on their own schemes for consolidating the conquered territories. These schemes were most evident in the wave of arbitrary arrests that scythed through the cities and villages. The army, local authorities, and security police all began sweeping up people who had somehow made it onto their respective lists. There was no code of laws governing who was to be taken, no authority to which any of these organs were responsible for their decisions, and no protection for those who were seized. Arrests were carried out much as my second arrest had been—more kidnappings than legal apprehensions. People were simply snatched from their homes or offices, often right off the street. No one knew why a neighbor or coworker had been arrested or where a son or daughter had disappeared to. The Saigonese, already deeply disturbed by the "concord and reconciliation" being meted out in the camps, were seized by new fears. The initial hopefulness with which they had greeted the revolution (what hope there was left) was swallowed up by a frightened hostility. An ugly mood enveloped the city.

Without any means of my own to bring order to this situation, I appealed directly to DRV Prime Minister Pham Van Dong, sending him a detailed report on the lawless rampage that was taking place and urging the quick development of a uniform code of law, with explicit protections against arbitrary arrest. About a month later, the response to my proposal came in a letter informing me that a delegation from the DRV High Tribunal, Censorate, and State Juridical Committee would come to Saigon (now Ho Chi Minh City) to work together with my ministry on a new legal code.

This was not the first time I had met with these gentlemen, and I did not face our initial discussions with much rapturous enthusiasm. As it turned out, however, Dong had made it clear to them that he expected results, and from the first my DRV counterparts were cooperative and efficient. Impelled by the deterioration of morale and by the disruption in production and services brought on by the reign of terror, we worked hard to produce a reasonable body of law. Over a period of two months we drew up a working corpus that covered a number of related areas:

1. Regulations specifying which governmental organs had authority to make arrests.
2. The definition and classification of violations for which arrests could be made.
3. Establishment of a court system to process those who were arrested.
4. Establishment of a uniform sentencing code.

None of this was either comprehensive or flawless, but it would allow us to gain at least some control over the prevailing chaos.

Mr. Phat, however, was highly annoyed that I had gone directly to Prime Minister Dong, and he indicated the extent of his displeasure by refusing to sign this brief code into law. Again I had

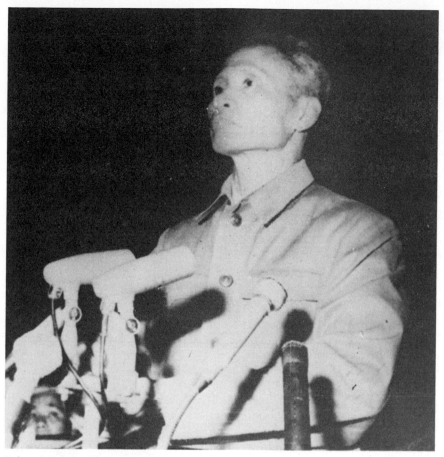

Prime Minister Pham Van Dong.

no recourse but to go back to the Prime Minister. Perhaps Dong
interceded, or perhaps in the end Phat simply decided that he had
made his point. I never found out. But whichever the case, in March
of 1976, almost a year after victory and more than four months after
I had originally written to Hanoi, Phat set his hand to our work,
and the South finally had a basic uniform code of justice. It was a
year that had seen outrages of every description perpetrated by a
government whose priorities called for the ruthless consolidation of
power rather than the reconstruction of the country. A historic opportunity had been squandered, one that would not come to us again.

As for our poor legal code, even after it was promulgated, it
didn't fare well. The laws were ostensibly to apply throughout South

Vietnam, but administrative units outside Saigon simply ignored them. Throughout the entire country, administration was in the hands of Party cadres accustomed to taking their orders from the Politburo. These people felt quite comfortable disregarding directives emanating from the Southern government, especially those that seemed to them somehow deviant from the Party line. Restrictions regarding who could arrest whom and for what reasons, restrictions about what could be done with the arrestees—such restraints, to their way of thinking, were clearly not in keeping with the requirements of the times. And since the Southern government lacked the means to enforce its decisions, the local authorities had little incentive to accept them as binding. Even in Saigon there was no way to insure that the code was being implemented, and the continuing flood of arbitrary arrests loudly proclaimed that in most cases it wasn't.

In the first year after liberation, some three hundred thousand people were arrested—a figure based solely on the number of officers, state officials, and party leaders who were summoned for thirty days of reeducation. To my knowledge, none of these had returned after a month or even after a year. Up until the time I retired from government in the summer of 1976, not a single one had been freed. This figure of course does not include people who were arrested in the sweeps by governmental organs and military authorities that terrorized both Saigon and the provinces during that period. It is simply impossible to estimate the number of such people. This all happened during my tenure as minister of justice.

One Nation

As the reconciliation policy expired in the reeducation camps and prisons, another of the revolution's ideals was also in its death throes: a careful approach to the unification problem. "Haste never breeds success," runs the old Confucian adage. But a year after our Great Spring Victory, whatever relevance this proverbial wisdom might have had for Vietnam's unification had long since been a dead letter. So had the PRG and Alliance formulas for eventual confederation: "on the basis of equality and respect for the characteristics of each zone" (the Alliance in its Political Program), "without coercion by either side" (the PRG's Action Program). Ho Chi Minh had written that "Vietnam is one, the Vietnamese people are one. Though the rivers may run dry and the mountains crumble, this verity is eternal." Whatever the reality of Ho's words, there is another reality equally profound. And that is the political, psychological, moral, and economic differences between the North and the South and among Vietnam's various peoples.

It was this latter truth that had been incorporated into the PRG's vision: a slow and careful reunification that would maintain and protect these characteristic differences. Over a period of fifteen years, this had also been the vision that the Lao Dong had expressed in the Party's internal deliberations on the subject. The Central Committee's position had consistently been what Ton Duc Thang had announced it to be at the Third Party Congress back in September 1960:

> Owing to the differences in the situation of the two zones of the country (North and South), the South must work out a program that, while in accord with the general program of the Fatherland Front, is suitable to its own situation. The South is carrying out the people's national democratic revolution, the North a socialist revolution.

These sentiments were of course reemphasized for Western consumption. "How could we have the stupid, criminal idea of annexing the South?" said Pham Van Dong to various foreign visitors. "We have no wish to impose communism on the South," said Le Duc Tho to the international press in Paris. But both the solemn internal line and the somewhat less solemn public assurances had been discarded like trash within months of victory. By then it was clear that there was no further need for subterfuge—either toward the Western media or antiwar movements, or toward the Southern revolution itself.

With North Vietnam's People's Army firmly in charge, there was in fact no further need for any of the techniques of seduction or covert control that circumstances had previously called for. There was no further need for anything other than the forthright exercise of power by those who held it. This, at least, was the conclusion of the Twenty-fourth Plenum of the Central Committee, which was held at the beginning of the summer of 1975 in Dalat, former mountain playground of South Vietnam's bourgeoisie. Who, after all, could now object to the rapid unification and socialization of the South?

The plenum decision was put into effect at the Political Conference for the Reunification of the Country, convened at the former Independence Palace on November 15. Ostensibly called so that Northern and Southern representatives could exchange views on reunification, it was actually intended only to ratify the reunification program already decided on by the Northern leadership. Politburo Number Two Man Truong Chinh headed the Northern delegation. The Southerners were led, not by NLF President Tho or PRG President

Phat, but by Pham Hung, former deputy prime minister of North Vietnam and the Politburo's number four man. These, as it turned out, were the two whose "views" were to be "exchanged."

Leading figures of the Southern movement did attend, but as deputies of Pham Hung. I was one of these lucky delegates, and I had the privilege of voting "yes." (In Vietnamese such a gathering is called a "yes conference.") To my colleagues and me, it was like being among the unfallen dead, watching a farce strangely gotten up for our benefit. I have to admit that I was curious as to exactly how the Party would manage this blatantly illegal gathering. But we had faith in the leadership's ability to brazen it through without batting an eye, and this faith was not disappointed. The Politburo's Truong Chinh spoke for the North, declaring that "whatever differences still exist between North and South must be reduced and leveled" and that "the first and most important step is to establish a unified government." Responding for the South, the Politburo's Pham Hung let it be known that "the Southern delegates totally support and unanimously agree with the proposals and measures of the Northern delegates." The phrase "total support" did not suffer from disuse; delegate after delegate, called on to express "views," employed it lavishly: total support for unification as fast as possible . . . total support for the establishment of socialism in the South . . . total support for forgoing the now unnecessary phase of "national, democratic revolution." The final step, it was unanimously agreed, would be countrywide elections for a unified National Assembly to be held in the spring.

The story circulated later on in our circles that someone had warned Pham Hung that perhaps some of the Southern cadres and government officials were not "totally" satisfied with what had happened. Pham, according to this story, had laughingly answered, "It doesn't matter; fifty-one percent of the vote is all we need to put unification across." The joke of course lay in Pham's sudden concern over a bare majority. In the event, the nationwide elections that were held on April 25, 1976, 99 percent of the people voted as expected. They hadn't much choice. The penalty for not voting was confiscation of the abstainer's ration card, without which he and his family could not buy anything to eat.

By the end of June the unification of the North and South was complete, except for its final act. To confirm and ratify this incorporation, a Reunification Assembly was convened in Hanoi, to which I was invited. One day during these proceedings, as the delegates and Party officials were taking a break for refreshments, I felt a tap on my shoulder. Turning around, I found Truong Chinh looking at me curiously. I had seen Chinh at the unification conference the previous November, but my last personal contact with him had been just after liberation, on the night before the PRG ministers had left Hanoi for the victory ceremonies in Saigon. That night the Party had thrown a grand banquet of celebration for the Southern leadership. Most of the Politburo and many other Central Committee members had attended, giving the occasion a festive spirit of solidarity and brotherhood. When the speeches and feasting were over, there were tears of gladness and embraces all around. Chinh had hugged me warmly as he said good-bye, wishing me great success in the undertaking I and the others were about to embark on. Now, fifteen anguished months later, Chinh was again staring me in the face, this time with a thoughtful and puzzled look in his eyes.

"Excuse me, comrade," he said. "You look familiar to me. Who are you again?" For a moment I was nonplussed—to say the least. When I answered that I was the minister of justice for the South, Chinh's eyes lit up. "Oh, really?" he said. "What's your name, and what are you doing now?"

I don't think there was anything intentionally malicious in this, only an old man's forgetfulness. But as a final comment on the South's revolution, the remark spoke volumes.

Shortly after this encounter, I was approached by Ngo Minh Loan, the DRV's minister of food and supply, who invited me to join the new unified government as his vice minister. I had no intention of taking any part in a regime that was imposing itself on the South after the betrayal of so many promises, but as a courtesy

I told Loan that I would give the offer my consideration. Very few PRG or Alliance people were being taken into the new government, and Loan was perplexed by my apparent lack of enthusiasm. He simply could not believe that one of us would turn down such an invitation.

Several weeks later, Loan flew to Saigon to renew the discussion. My experience in the sugar industry, he argued, would be tremendously beneficial, especially in consideration of Vietnam's potential to develop a strong sugar-exporting capacity. Prime Minister Dong himself had approved my nomination, Loan said, and had asked him to insist that I accept the position.

Perhaps my interactions with Dong over the previous fifteen months had suggested to him that I would be willing to work with the new regime. It is possible too that he felt my joining the government might somewhat alleviate the prevailing bitterness among PRG and Alliance leaders. But whatever Dong thought, my only ambition was to get out. I was in the throes of a devastating disillusionment, and I was looking hard for the best way to retire. To Loan, I said that I was honored by the nomination, and I asked him to convey my gratitude to the prime minister. Unfortunately, my health, as he knew, was not good, and I had been separated from my family for so long that I was determined not to leave them again (the post would have required moving to Hanoi).

Loan regarded this nomination as a rare distinction, but to me continued association with the government was a stigma I was feeling more and more keenly. Over a year had passed since the initial sabotage of our reconciliation policy, and still the wave of official terror continued to swell. At home, my mother, seventy-eight years old but still as perceptive and outspoken as ever, would ask why I had brought this "specter" with me. What had possessed me to inflict this misery on my family and my people? "Your Communist friends are full of double-talk—lies and violence. They're sowing the wind," she said, "and they'll reap the whirlwind." She had applauded the liberation of Saigon in April 1975, but in the intervening year her sympathy for the revolution had turned to repugnance.

My mother's feelings were hardly unique. Talk about what was happening enveloped Saigon, which had always been a garrulous place. And among my friends, at least, much of it seemed directed at me. "At least under Diem and Thieu [I would hear] there was honor among thieves. But these Party people are wolfing down everything in sight."

"Do you think it was such a wonderful idea to chase the Americans out? Now we're going to get the Russians stuffed down our throats. At least when the Americans were here, we had food. Now what do we have? International solidarity?"

"The cadres are always talking about serving the people. At last we're supposed to be the masters of our own country. Funny how the masters are walking barefoot, and the servants are riding around in cars."

The arrests and uncertainty had generated hostility toward the government, but the breathtaking rapacity of the Northern soldiers and cadres filled the Saigonese with contempt and brought out their talent for scurrility. For days at a time, it seemed, I heard nothing but scathing complaints, mixed with reports of the most disquieting personal and family tragedies. I couldn't walk down the street without friends of mine, old schoolfellows and former colleagues, accosting me. Finally I just couldn't stomach it anymore. I shut myself up in my house and refused to go back to the office. Some other PRG ministers and NLF officials had already secluded themselves long before; still others continued to endure daily scenes that seared their consciences, perhaps because they felt their presence might exert a moderating influence on events—or perhaps because they had simply grown inured to it.

But by the summer of 1976, paralysis was definitely in the air. It was not just the officials who felt it, but people everywhere. Office and factory workers stopped coming in to work, or would show up and spend their days talking with their equally sullen and depressed coworkers. They had seen the great moment finally arrive—Peace—after thirty years of continuous violence and a hundred years of hated foreign domination. But peace, which they had so passionately desired, had brought with it not blessings but a new and even more insidious warfare, this time a warfare practiced by the liberators against their own people.

As this ultimately desperate message sank in over the first year or so of independence, a deep malaise began to come over people, a malaise that showed up in their personal lives and in their working lives. Even the Party was forced to acknowledge it. Articles began appearing in *Nhan Dan* (*The Party Daily News*) referring to absenteeism and the decline in productivity. One editor wrote: "Our industrial plant is only being used at fifty percent capacity. Effective work is only going on four or five hours a day. All the agricultural plans are failing, and many peasants are abandoning their land."

In response, the Party propaganda mills began churning out a new generation of slogans, whose stridency pointed up the nervousness with which economic and political planners were viewing this new and threatening public mood. "We have defeated the Chinese, Japanese, French, and Americans, the greatest powers in the world," one headline blared. "We will certainly overcome all our difficulties." But the truth was that the problems had been precipitated by ideological ruthlessness and a contemptuous disregard for human dignity and rights. And these attitudes, firmly embedded in the mental world of the Party leaders, would prove even less tractable than had Vietnam's external antagonists. As Pham Van Dong was later to acknowledge to the journalist Stanley Karnow, "Waging a war is simple, but running a country is very difficult."

One large difficulty continued to be the thousands of Northern cadres who had come south to govern. Accustomed to the extremes of austerity, they seized voraciously on the opportunities offered by westernized and decadent Saigon. They fought each other over houses, cars, prostitutes, and bribes. Soldiers and officials brought up in the bleak poverty of North Vietnam and subjected for years to the rigors of military life were suddenly confronted with what seemed to them an almost fairy-tale richness, theirs for the taking. It was as if the city had been invaded by a swarm of locusts.

Caught in the middle of this, by the summer of 1976 I found that

As minister of justice in 1976.

I couldn't stand to see any of the people in the government. I had
developed something very close to a physical revulsion for them. I
didn't even want to talk to my friends in the PRG and Alliance, who
were suffering the same agonies I was. I simply wanted to get away,
to someplace where I could think and chart out for myself some
way of existing in this unwelcome new world.

Exile

Near the end of 1976 I realized my ambition for seclusion. In the summer of that year I had married a close family friend of Trinh Dinh Thao, whom I had met shortly after my return to Saigon. Now I moved with my new wife to our little family farm in Go Vap, just outside Saigon. It is something of a Vietnamese custom, left over from the old Chinese-style bureaucracy, to keep a small plot in the countryside to retire to should official affairs become excessively problem-filled. I found this traditional precaution a godsend.

The cottage my wife and I moved into had no water or electricity. We cultivated rice and planted coconut palms; we raised fish and a few pigs. Occasionally I would bicycle into the city to visit my mother or to look in at the villa that was still my official residence and which my bodyguards now inhabited by themselves. At my official villa my salary would be waiting for me (the government had not acknowledged my resignation), as would my ration card. The pay rate for ministers was 210 piasters (about $40) a month, but my card allowed me to shop in the special-privilege stores reserved for foreigners and high officials. At that time the food ration was fourteen kilos of rice per month (jungle rations were twenty kilos—conditions had worsened), four cans of condensed milk, and two kilos of sugar. We eked out this diet with whatever we were able to raise on the farm.

I found the physical work pleasant and relaxing; it helped me concentrate on the problem at hand. Slowly it became clear that I would be forced to make a decision of the most profound consequences. I could choose one of two paths. I could simply acquiesce in what had happened, stay in retirement, and die quietly by degrees. Or I could continue to struggle for the political and social ideals to which I had devoted three decades of my life. But if I continued the struggle, then how? On the other side was a Party organization controlling brutal and thorough organs of repression and a powerful military machine. And what allies could I look to in such a struggle? There was no network of energetic and capable resisters to join. There was no ready-made guerrilla movement in the jungle. There was no world opinion to look to for support, as there had been in our opposition to Diem and his successors. The Western antiwar movements had contributed much to our victory, but they were hardly prepared to set off on a new crusade, which would have to be based on a recognition of what had really happened. And how was that recognition to take place? Slowly I came to the conclusion that no struggle could be realistic. But neither was I going to resign myself to the life and death of a frightened rodent. I would get out.

Since shortly after the first days of liberation, escape by boat had been the single great topic of conversation throughout the South. Everyone talked about it, but actually making the arrangements was a dangerous business. First you had to find a boat and a pilot. Of course you never knew if your contact, which had been arranged through some friend's friend, was legitimate or a thief—or, worse, a provocateur or security agent. A host of unsavory elements discovered they could profit from what rapidly turned into a mass movement. Losing your money (quite likely your own life's savings together with every cent you could scrape together from friends and relatives) was the least of many unpleasant risks. You might, for example, lose your money and also find yourself in prison. Even assuming you did manage to locate a relative with access to a boat— or some honest entrepreneur looking to arrange his own escape and willing to take you along—your future would then be even more uncertain. To Thailand you faced a voyage of at least several hundred miles. To Malaysia or Indonesia it might be twice that distance. The seas were infested with pirates, and beyond the pirates lay a string of squalid refugee camps already filled to overflowing. From these unhappy places the best you could hope for was the chance to start up your life again in some foreign land, which might have the compassion to take you in, but whose language, customs, and people would be alien and forbidding.

Escape was truly a decision that could only be made out of desperation. Once made, though, there was no choice but to put your faintheartedness aside and plunge into the shadowy world of boat arrangements.

In my own case, escape was complicated by my position. I knew that my retirement had not been viewed favorably, and even though I had pleaded health, the move had marked me for suspicion. The first step, then, was to mask my intentions from the surveillance of the Party and its security organs. Before anything else, I had to quit my rustication, which was itself a visible gesture of nonconformity. So in the autumn of 1977, my wife and I moved back to the city and into my mother's house.

It wasn't long before things began to happen. Shortly after we got settled, I received a visit from Vo Van Kiet, first secretary of the Saigon Party organization and a Central Committee member. Kiet's attitude was friendly and conciliatory. "You know," he told me, "the Party and our friends are worried about you. Everyone understands what kind of contribution you made during the war, and most of us hoped that you'd take on some of the burden of making our way through this difficult period."

With Kiet I felt I could be straightforward; my views were no secret anyway. "I've given my life to the struggle," I told him. "You know that. But it looks to me like the leadership isn't very concerned about Uncle Ho's ideas on reunification or revolutionary morality— or very much else for that matter. In my view, there have been a lot of serious mistakes. Everything has gone much too quickly. As far as I can see, the bureaucrats and cadres are running the whole show. Given what the people are going through, I don't feel I can do a thing. Tell me, isn't your conscience bothering you about what's happened?"

Kiet wasn't eager to pursue this line of discussion. On the other hand, he thought he might still lure me out of my recalcitrance. "Look, Ba, if you don't want to go North, I could use your help right here, with our own industry. You know the situation as well as anybody. I don't have to tell you what it would mean to get things mobilized again."

Kiet had considerable charm and persuasiveness, and I admired his skill in using them. Moreover, he was an energetic and pragmatic person, a man I respected. His wife and children had been killed by a B-52 attack during a visit to him in the jungle, and I felt a good deal of sympathy as well as affection for him. But despite his personal qualities, as he talked, I couldn't help thinking to myself that this one swallow doesn't mean it's summer.

On the other hand, a job with Kiet would make superb cover for my escape plans. With this in mind I moved the discussion along, meeting with Kiet a number of times over the next several weeks. In the end, I accepted an appointment as director of the National Rubber Industry, a position that provided a degree of protection from unwanted scrutiny and also allowed me to intensify my search for a way out.

But tracking down a boat owner in whom I might reasonably put some trust proved to be a nerve-racking proposition, especially since I was forced to deal through indirect contacts—and even then only with the most elaborate precautions. Eventually, however, a break came. One of my wife's brothers-in-law, a doctor named Ton, had fought with the Vietminh during the French war and had moved to Hanoi in 1954. Now he was back in the South, having taken a job as senior medical officer for Long Xuyen Province. According to the family grapevine, Ton was deeply unhappy and was laying plans for his own departure. Apparently the contrast between the propaganda picture of the South that he had imbibed during his twenty year sojourn in Hanoi and the actual conditions in Long Xuyen had incensed the doctor. He had expected to be received as a savior by a poverty-stricken people used to laboring under the heel of American oppressors. Reality had turned out to be quite another story. Feeling thoroughly betrayed and humiliated, Dr. Ton was surveying his possibilities.

In the same province, Ton had a cousin, a wealthy businessman, who was looking around for a boat himself and who agreed to include the doctor in his plans. Through my wife we got in touch with Ton, who then approached his cousin on our behalf. For his part, the businessman was happy to have us along. Typically in these situations, a group of people would pool resources to buy a boat, and the organizer was just as much at hazard as the people buying in. Any one of the "shareholders" might turn out to be an agent, and months of tense effort could easily end in disaster.

Overjoyed at our luck in making this connection, my wife and I managed to borrow enough to cover our share, and we immersed ourselves in preparations. Meeting with Ton, I urged him to persuade his cousin to buy a riverboat instead of an ocean-going trawler. Vietnam was in the throes of a mass exodus, and all boat-buying transactions were attracting the closest official attention. A riverboat was not nearly as likely to raise suspicions, and once we bought it, we could reinforce the hull and substitute a stronger engine to make it seaworthy. Of course there were a host of other difficulties. Necessities for the trip had somehow to be acquired: sufficient fuel, extra rice, drinking water for a minimum of two weeks, binoculars, a compass—all items that were on the restricted list. Whoever showed an interest in such things would immediately become suspect. Attempting to buy them would land the customer-to-be in prison.

It was a happy day when we heard that Ton's cousin had found and bought a little river freighter about thirty-five-feet long. Using his contacts in Long Xuyen, the businessman immediately began to outfit the boat and was able to bribe some local officials to acquire a contract for hauling crushed stone downriver to the coastal province of Ca Mau and charcoal back up the Long Xuyen—a round trip of about 250 miles. With this contract in hand, he was given an operator's permit, and with the permit he went about hiring a crew, all of whom qualified by dint of their desire to get out of the country rather than by their seamanship. By now the whole affair was taking on a serious cast.

Fortunately, Long Xuyen was an ideal place to launch such a venture. Located on the Mekong River about eighty miles from the sea, it was not as carefully watched as the coastal areas, from which most of the hopeful refugees began their flight. Nevertheless, in light of the international publicity surrounding the Boat People, the government was exercising considerable vigilance even on the inland waterways. At intervals along the river were checkpoints, six or seven of them between Long Xuyen and the coast, at each of which the boat pilots would stop to get their papers stamped and pay the obligatory mulct. To familiarize himself with the river's ways, Ton's cousin became a full-time freighter captain, studying the navigation charts, the traffic patterns, the habits of the police units. He learned how to check in at the patrol posts rather than wait for the patrols to come out to him. He learned the etiquette for bribes—not too little (which would irritate the police), not too much (which would arouse their suspicions).

Over a two-month period the ex-businessman-turned-riverboat captain made perhaps ten trips from Long Xuyen to Ca Mau and back. For each trip he received an official allotment of fuel, rice, and drinking water, which he and his impatient crew hoarded mercilessly. Other supplies they picked up on the black market. By late August of 1978, everything was ready. It had been more than a year since my original decision to leave.

On Wednesday, August 22, my wife's sister came to Saigon to tell us to be ready to leave that Sunday, four days later. Sunday had been chosen for two good reasons. In his trips up and down the river, Ton's cousin had discovered that the police considered weekends a time for relaxation and enjoyment rather than revolutionary vigilance. Unexpected checks or thorough inspections were a good deal less likely then. More significant still, the monsoon season was under way, with its intermittent gales. Typically, a storm lasting many days would be followed by a brief intermission before the next blast hit, but our little boat was never built to withstand the ocean conditions produced by these storms. So we had been waiting for a break in the weather, knowing that, once embarked, we would have to make land before the next squall came down on us. By the middle of the week it had become obvious that the current monsoon was winding to a close.

Saturday the twenty-fifth dawned clear. My wife and I gathered the few personal things we had decided to take and said a painful farewell to my mother. Then we took the bus to Long Xuyen, arriving at the home of Dr. Ton's parents late in the afternoon. Soon after we got there, one of our coconspirators came by to go over the plans, the rendezvous point, the timing, what to do if we ran into trouble. Tense and worried, we settled down in a darkened back room to avoid any surprise visitors. The wait seemed interminable.

At 4 A.M. we heard muffled talk in the outer rooms; one of the crew had come to lead us to the boat: my wife, myself, Ton, his wife, and their five-year-old boy. Through the darkened town, down to the river and the boat we followed our guide, as silently as we could—five very frightened people. On board, we made our way down to the hold and through a trapdoor in the fake deck that Ton's cousin had built in. In the bowels of the boat we sat down among water barrels and sacks of rice and tried to find comfortable positions. As my eyes grew accustomed to the dark, I began to make out other people in the hold, about twenty of them, adults and a few children—our fellow passengers on this journey. The adults sat with their backs against the side walls, the children in the middle. Below us was the ballast; a foot above our heads was the false floor that would conceal us—if we were lucky—from prying eyes.

After a few minutes the engine began throbbing, and the boat moved slowly off, easing into a steady motion downriver. What with the slightly fetid air and the boat's gentle roll, I soon fell into an exhausted sleep. It must have been several hours later that I dragged myself awake to the knowledge that the throbbing had stopped and the boat was lying still in the water. Suddenly the trapdoor opened, and one of the crew poked his head in to tell us in a stage whisper that we should make room for more passengers. I couldn't believe what I was hearing. But before anyone had time to do more than register shock, another twenty-five people were climbing down through the opening and squeezing themselves in among us. All the adults sat hunched in, their backs to the walls, knees drawn up and arms crossed over their chests to make a few extra inches. It seemed almost like a drill that we had practiced before. The children sprawled in the middle space, what there was left of it. How we might survive huddled up like this for the whole trip was beyond me. The air, which had been stale before, now turned heavy and hard to breathe. As the boat resumed its motion, everyone seemed nervous and fatigued. Children began to complain. But the discomfort took second place to our fear of the police and anxiety for the safety of this overloaded craft. I don't know how many of the others were aware—as Ton and I were —that there wasn't a single professional sailor on board.

At about midnight, some twenty hours after we had left Long Xuyen, the boat arrived at the river's mouth. In the hold, we sensed a change in the rhythm of the swells and guessed that we must be passing Dai Ngai, ready to break into the open sea. Though none of us were aware of it at the time, the Mekong's estuaries have difficult and occasionally treacherous tidal currents. Unfortunately, the former businessman who was our pilot knew very little more about it than the most ignorant of his passengers. His two brief months of self-taught navigation had not included any midnight practice runs, and now his inexperience proved almost fatal. Misjudging the channel in the dark, he ran the boat right up onto a sandbar, which had been brought near the surface by the low tide. Under us, the bottom growled, then gently shuddered as the boat stopped dead.

Among the passengers, the feeling of drugged torpor changed instantly to fright. The men climbed up through the hatch to see what had happened and arrived on deck to find that most of the crew were already in the shallow water trying to push the vessel free. Following their example, the stronger passengers threw off their pants and shirts and jumped over the side in their underwear to add their strength to the effort. They worked desperately, twenty or twenty-five people straining in the black water to muscle the boat back off the sandbar. But the bottom was lodged fast. Heaving with all their strength, the engine whining in reverse, they couldn't budge it an inch. When it was finally obvious that no effort they could make would help, the pilot told everyone to form a chain down into the hold to get rid of the rocks that were used for ballast. Quickly the line formed, and the heavy stones were passed up on deck and boosted over the side.

Unable to help because of my physical weakness, I stood and watched, trying to calm myself enough to decide what to do. Even though the ship was lightening steadily, there was still no movement. Every once in a while, the men in the chain would break off and scramble into the water to begin heaving again. But nothing seemed to work. It began to appear that no effort, no matter how frantic, would succeed. We were stuck. We would be sitting in exactly the same place when dawn came and brought with it the early-morning fishing boats and police patrols.

As I thought about this, I realized that I could not allow myself to be captured. It would be far preferable to commit suicide by drowning. I was sure that if they caught me, they would go to special lengths to humiliate me and subject me to mental torture. That was their way. I thought about what had happened to Tran Duc Thao, the great Vietnamese philosopher, who had been Sartre's classmate and friend and whose fate weighed on my mind with sudden relevance. After World War II Thao had joined the Communists, and in 1954 he had established himself in Hanoi, already a renowned phenomenologist. But two years later the Party made several "mistakes," one of which was to have truly diabolical consequences for the philosopher.

The mistake best known outside Vietnam was the bloody Northern land-reform program, which involved the execution of thousands of so-called landlords. Most of these had simply been poor peasants who happened to own slightly larger plots than their neighbors—all the holdings being minuscule to begin with. The anger raised by these outrages had led Ho Chi Minh to cancel the program and punish those who were directly in charge. Ho had then taken the unusual step of personally apologizing to the people, admitting that "injustices had been committed."

A second mistake, for which no one had ever apologized, was the 1956 campaign to suppress intellectuals, a sort of Vietnamese-style Cultural Revolution. Thao had been the most prominent of many victims. He was neither physically harmed nor incarcerated, but the security police threw a cordon sanitaire around him, isolating him from all human contact. Thao continued to live in his Hanoi apartment and take care of himself. He could shop for his food and other necessities. He could walk through the city. But no one was permitted to communicate with him. If Thao approached someone himself, say a friend on the street, that person would be arrested and interrogated. To all outward appearances the philosopher went about his normal business. But in reality he was living like Robinson Crusoe, totally alone—though surrounded by people. Not even his relatives were allowed to speak with him. For an intellectual, whose life depended on the exchange of ideas and interaction with his colleagues, it was fiendish torture. Sartre, who had supported our struggle, reportedly requested Thao's release on a number of occasions, but there had never been a response. In 1974 Lucien Pham Ngoc Hung, a member of the Alliance and an old friend of Thao's, had received permission to visit him.* Thao, he told me afterward, "was like a man on the moon," demi-fou ("half-mad").

Memories of my own isolation in the National Police prison and the disorientation I had experienced there were still far too acute. I was not going to be subjected to that kind of experience again, not in any form—about that I was quite clear.

These reveries were interrupted by a commotion that had broken out around the pilot. When I joined the little group that was with

---

* Although Lucien Pham Ngoc Hung was Albert Pham Ngoc Thao's brother, he is no relation to Tran Duc Thao.

him, I saw that he had begun to tremble uncontrollably, as if he were having a malarial fit.

"Oh my God, oh my God," he was saying to Ton, "if we get caught, they'll kill me. They'll say that I seduced people. And that I brought a high cadre along, that it was all my doing."

Ton tried to soothe him, telling him that if we couldn't get free he (Ton) and I and all the former officers in the group would swim ashore—before any patrol boats came out.

"At least don't worry about that," he said.

"Anyway," I put in, "you can be sure *I'm* not going to let those ghouls capture *me*."

Slowly the pilot's shivers subsided. "Well," he said, "we'll all have to decide what to do before the sun comes up."

Daylight, in fact, was only a couple of hours away. The work went on, more frenzied than before, if that was possible, though some of the men were now obviously near exhaustion. The ship seemed embedded. An hour later, even the most optimistic were beginning to wonder out loud what would happen to us when we were arrested. Then, around four o'clock, someone noticed that the water near the boat was beginning to deepen. The tide was coming in. A surge of excitement went through all of us at once. The men who weren't already in the water jumped overboard for a giant final effort. The boat began to rock. Then, just as traces of light began to reveal the eastern horizon, it came free, and the engine went into gear, moving us off as the men scrambled over the rail and onto the deck. A spontaneous cheer went up. *"Hoan ho"*—"Hurrah, Let's go!"

Our excitement, though, was short-lived. Light had come, and with it we could see the first of the hundreds of fishing boats that work the estuary and coastal waters. In the summer of 1978 each of these boats carried along a *bo doi* ("government soldier"), put there to prevent the crew from joining the outpouring of refugees and to convert each little trawler into a patrol craft. These first boats would quickly be followed by others; then the rest of the river traffic would start up, and with it the regular police patrols doing their spot checks.

As slow as our old river freighter was, all this activity would be on us before we knew it. Wisely, the pilot decided that our safest course would be to hide until dark, then try again the next night. But hide where? The only option was to go back upriver, pretending to be on a return run.

Heading slowly inland to deflect attention, we began retracing our path toward Long Xuyen. In the sun and humidity of the day, the rancid hold became hotter and more oppressive hour by hour. Adults were slumped against each other in fatigue—the children, who had been given barbiturates to keep them from crying, sleeping fitfully in their laps or jumbled in the middle. In this condition, we continued upriver until dark, then turned once more for a second try. Near midnight we arrived again at the river's mouth, expecting at every moment the same growl we had heard last night as the ship's bottom scraped onto the sandbar. But this time there was only the choppier pitch of the sea as the pilot steered us safely through.

Half an hour offshore our luck ran out. We heard one of the crew scream, *"Day, day"* ("Stop, stop!"), and a few moments later the boat shuddered to a halt. This time we had run straight into one of the permanent guy nets the fishermen erect off this part of the coast. These nets are stretched out along cables anchored to posts that are planted in the shallow seabed. Often they are spread out one after the other to increase their effectiveness. We now found ourselves immobilized in one of these net systems, unable to go forward or back. After the anxiety of the previous night and the disheartening trip back upriver, it hardly seemed real that we were going to go through another seige. Again we knew we had perhaps four hours to find a way out before the early trawlers with their *bo dois* aboard would make an appearance. Attempting to break free, the pilot threw the engine into full ahead, then full reverse. The boat wallowed back and forth in its own wash, straining against the nets. Then, by chance, the propeller bit into one of the cables and cut through. Carefully, the pilot maneuvered free, and we headed for international waters.

Our troubles, however, were hardly over. The course we had planned to follow was approximately due south into the South China

Sea and toward the trade lanes, where we hoped to be picked up by a freighter or tanker, or perhaps by one of the U.S. Seventh Fleet Ships, which we had heard were in the area. But our pilot's inexperience again led us into danger. Uneventfully we sailed through the darkness, but as the sun rose, we saw in front of us the black outlines of an island, which one of the crew identified as Poulo Condore. This was the infamous prison island that had been used in turns by the French, the Saigon government, and now by the new regime. Instead of leaving it far to our east, as we had supposed, we were now headed straight at it. As the boat turned to skirt the island, we apprehensively scanned the waters around it for the inevitable security patrols. Miraculously, the sea was empty under our anxious eyes. The prison at that hour appeared to be still asleep—as we passed less than a kilometer away, in what seemed to be slow motion.

After this last scare, the ship settled into a steady rolling motion—heading finally, we hoped, in the right direction. The passengers, those who wanted to, were now able to take turns on deck to breathe the fresh air and survey the empty horizon. Under the glaring sun the water appeared calm, but the long, soft swells had a bad effect on quite a few, especially those who were experiencing the sea for the first time. I was slightly nauseated myself, but no discomfort could suppress the elation I felt at having escaped from a series of such desperate situations. And now we were in international waters, safe from pursuit and likely to be rescued at any time. Even the weather seemed to be holding. I felt a sense of inner calm and confidence in the future, as vague as that might be.

All day we ran without sighting another vessel. Then shortly after dark, as I was on deck staring into the night, one of the crew pointed out a glimmer of light barely visible in the east. The pilot immediately altered course toward it, and word spread quickly through the ship that we might soon be picked up. As people climbed up from the hold, the talk was full of hope that this might be an American naval vessel, one of those that President Carter had ordered into the South China Sea to rescue whatever boat refugees they could find. As we chugged on toward the distant light, I had ample time to reflect on the irony of fate that had overtaken me. Beside me at the rail, Dr. Ton was silent, his gaze fixed on the tiny twinkling beacons. I knew he was indulging in reflections similar to my own, caught up in a crosscurrent of emotions. Neither of us spoke as the immense bitterness we shared was crystallized in the moment, a bitterness we knew was far better left unacknowledged.

For most of our fellow passengers, however, there was nothing nearly so complex about what was happening. It was full speed ahead toward liberation. Or so everyone thought. Three hours later the glimmer had become a ship sitting in the water with all its lights on, not an American warship after all but a large trawler. As we moved in closer we could see a flag at the mast, a red flag, caught momentarily in the glare of a searchlight.

On our deck someone yelled, *"Bo doi!"* and there was sudden panic. I saw Dr. Ton pull a pistol from his pants pocket and throw it overboard, afraid of being caught with a weapon. Stumbling to the far side of the boat, I readied myself to jump overboard, hoping that I could disappear under the water before anyone noticed that I was gone. I struggled to compose myself, wanting to face these last seconds with courage. Then I took a final glance at the trawler, which was now directly alongside. Above the rail I could see men holding machetes and hammers, ready to jump down onto our boat. In an instant I realized that these weren't Vietnamese soldiers at all but Thai. We were about to be boarded by Thai pirates.

Oddly, the thought filled me with a sudden relief. As I watched, twenty or so young Thais clambered onto our boat, grasping a variety of weapons, long knives, hatchets, hammers, but no guns. Looking at their faces, which appeared simple rather than vicious, it registered on me that these were fishermen-pirates rather than the professional cutthroats who terrorized the Boat People. Everyone knew that many poor Thai fishermen supplemented their meager livings by robbing refugees who happened near their boats. Encounters with thieves of this sort always left the refugees poorer, but seldom resulted in the butchery and rapine that were the trademarks of the professionals. Our pirates rounded everybody up on deck and threatened us. Then they searched us and the boat, taking our money, jewelry, and a few shirts that caught their fancy. They also liberated our compass and binoculars. But they left us food and water, and they pointed us toward the sea lanes before climbing back on their trawler and sailing off. Afterward we called them our honorable pirates.

After this, our journey assumed a monotonous routine as we slowly made our way toward the international trade routes. The bright clarity of our first few days at sea had now given way to hazier weather, which hinted that the time before the next storm was growing short. But one day followed the next without any sightings. Then, on the sixth day we saw a ship, a freighter passing miles off in front of us. Soon we spotted others, some of them coming a good deal closer. We had entered what we thought must be the main sea-lane between Singapore and Hong Kong. Whereas before we had seen no one, now numbers of ships began to pass by, huge tankers in addition to cargo ships. To each one we signaled our distress, waving shirts, gesturing, imploring. We even lit fires on the deck. Some of the sailors on board these ships would stare. Some waved back. None stopped.

By this time we badly needed to put in somewhere. Everyone was filthy and exhausted; many of us were sick, especially the children. The food and water left to us by the Thais were running low, and it was increasingly evident that our grace period between monsoons was coming to an end. But still the ships just passed by, rocking us in their long wakes. Then, on the night of August 31 we saw lights on the horizon, stationary lights that appeared to be on land.

By the next morning we had arrived—not at a coast as it turned out, but at an Indonesian oil-exploration station, consisting of an anchored drilling ship with a second vessel attached to it by gangways and mooring cables. We pulled up as near the station as we dared, and our pilot called in English to the Indonesian captain to allow us aboard. The answer came shouted back through a bullhorn that they could give us some food, water, and fuel, but they were not permitted to take us on. Their government, they said, was flooded with refugees and had issued firm orders that no more would be accepted.

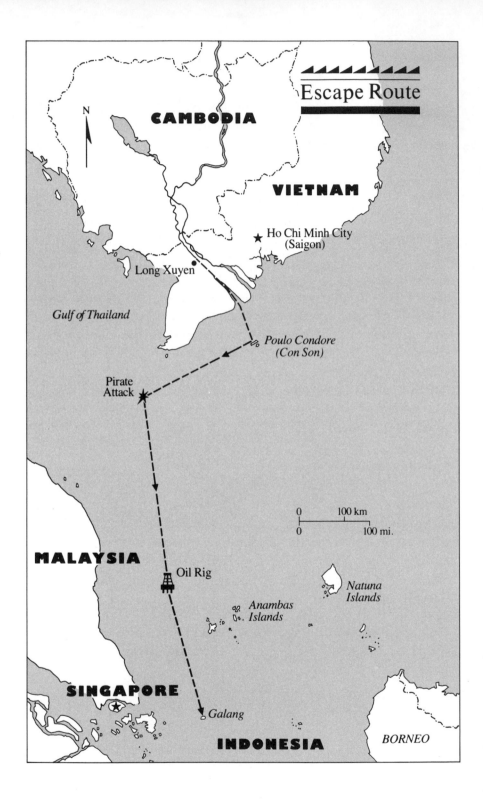

At this our pilot began pleading with the captain, telling him that the women and children were seasick and near collapse. Would he not at least allow them on the station to take showers and rest for a few hours. The Indonesian captain was clearly a compassionate man, and it was evident that our pilot's words—together with our truly pitiable appearance—had affected him. We could see him thinking the situation over. Then, after what seemed an age, he agreed to take them on. While the women and children were being helped up the ladders, several Western technicians who were leaning over the rails—we later learned that they were American and Dutch—began making odd and extraordinarily animated gestures at us, repeatedly poking their index fingers into their palms and hammering their palms with their fists. At first we stared at them stupidly, which seemed to spur them into even more dramatic efforts, clearly exasperated by our obtuseness. Finally it dawned on us that they were telling us to sink our ship—smash holes in the bottom and sink it so that the Indonesians would be forced to save us. As soon as we realized what they meant, the pilot sent several of the crew into the hold with hammers and crowbars to try to break through the hull. But the Indonesian captain had seen this interchange, and he quickly ordered some of his own crew onto our boat and down into the hold to stop what was going on and get our young men up on deck.

But now the captain faced a dilemma. If he forced us to leave, he had no doubt that we would immediately sink ourselves. But his orders forbade him to take us aboard. We could see him trying to puzzle out a solution that would satisfy his conscience and his duty at the same time. Finally, he solved this riddle by ordering all of us onto the station under guard, while he went to discuss this situation with his superiors by radio. While he was gone, the pilot asked Ton and me to tell the women that whatever happened, they and the children should refuse to leave the ship. Even if we were forced back onto our boat at gunpoint, they should resist in whatever way they could. If we could sink the boat near the station, we would. If not, we wouldn't have a chance in the approaching storm anyway.

While Ton and I were explaining this quietly to the women, the captain returned, his face wreathed in smiles. We were welcome, he said. We could stay. Our escape was over. Two days later, a Singaporan freighter arrived to take us to the United Nations refugee camp on Galang Island. Our exile had begun.

My exile took me, over a period of six months, from the Galang Island refugee camp to France, the country where thirty years before my sense of patriotism was born and my political values shaped. I had arrived in Paris as a young student, intent on bettering myself by creating the kind of comfortable personal future my upbringing had taught me was my birthright. It was in France that I had chosen to follow a political star instead.

There was nothing unique about my decision. A host of my contemporaries, intellectuals and peasants, shopkeepers and businessmen, had done the same. For so many of them, that decision had cost them their lives. Others had made sacrifices they would consider only a degree less extreme. These—the survivors—now have a chance to reflect on the trajectories their lives have taken. My own seems to have described a kind of circle. Living in Paris once more, I am back where I started out, though a great revolution and its aftermath have made up the experiences of the intervening years.

As a result of this upheaval Vietnam has indeed freed itself from its former colonial masters. But the national liberation that the revolution achieved was not the only liberation for which it was fought. "We must fight a war not just against colonialism, but against hunger and ignorance" was how Ho Chi Minh had put it. Many of us also believed we were fighting for the human dignity of our people, not just a *national* revolution, but a *national* and *democratic* revolution (the terms are those of the NLF and PRG) that would have insured free political and cultural expression among the variety of ethnic groups, religions, and regions—and among the commonwealth of individuals—that make up the nation.

But the national democratic revolution itself became a casualty, choked by the arrogance of power among those who were responsible for the nation's fate. Instead of national reconciliation and independence, Ho Chi Minh's successors have given us a country devouring its own and beholden once again to foreigners, though now it is the Soviets rather than the Americans. In the process, the lives that so many gave to create a new nation are now no more than ashes cast aside. That betrayal of faith will burden the souls of Vietnam's revolutionary leaders—even as surely as their rigid ideology and bellicose foreign policies have mortgaged the country's future.

But nothing, of course, disappears entirely. The leader of the Japanese constitutional movement from the 1890s on, Prince Saionji Kinmochi, died on the eve of World War II, having seen a lifetime's work ruined and a warlike autocracy in the ascendant. Yet who is to say that his long struggle did not prepare the way for Japan's adoption of a democratic government when the war was over.

Perhaps the struggle of those who had a vision of an independent Vietnam at peace with its neighbors, glorying in its own cultural and political diversity, and achieving the dynamic economy its people are capable of creating, has not been completely in vain. To the revolutionaries who died, to those who now live in a huddled and oppressed silence, and to those who have been dispersed throughout the world—who can say whether or not the seed they injected into the founding of a new nation will yet bear fruit.

In Vietnamese usage there are commonly three names, the family or surname first, the given name last. In polite address, the appropriate term or title (e g , Mr., Mrs., general, president, etc.) precedes the given name: Nguyen Van Thieu is referred to as President Thieu, Vo Nguyen Giap is General Giap. This custom avoids confusion in a country where certain family names such as Pham, Tran, Nguyen, Huynh, and others are common. In general, woman are known by their own names. Duong Quynh Hoa is the wife of Huynh Van Nghi. She would most often be referred to as Dr. Hoa, though Mrs. Nghi might also be used in polite address.

Complicating this system is the universal custom of nicknames. These almost always reflect place in family. A first son or daughter would be called Hai (Number Two)—that is, second to the father. Second children are "Ba" (Number Three), and so on. In order to differentiate all the number twos, threes, etc., an identifying characteristic is commonly added to the nickname. Thus Tran Bach Dang's nickname was Tu Meo—Number Four Twitch (for his facial tic). Often such nicknames accompany a person from childhood on. New ones might be acquired later in life, though, especially when circumstances required a code name to mask an individual's identity. The revolutionaries' penchant for multiple code names (at times making use of their wives' or children's names) was meant to sow confusion among American intelligence analysts, and often did.

Ba Cap The provocative Northern cadre who was chief of administrative services for the Alliance of National, Democratic, and Peace Forces in mid-1970.

Ba Tra Liaison cadre for the Saigon/Cholon/Giadinh urban proselytizing movement. His arrest and confession in 1967 exposed much of the NLF's Saigon network.

Bao Dai Vietnam's last emperor. Known as "The Playboy King," he was the country's nominal ruler from 1949 until 1955, when Vietnam became a republic with Ngo Dinh Diem as its first president.

Bui Thi Nga Huynh Tan Phat's wife. One of the revolution's bourgeois members who embraced communism.

Cao Van Bon PRG minister of economy and finance.

Do Mau Saigon military security chief who played an essential role in the 1963 coup against Ngo Dinh Diem.

Duong Huynh Hoa PRG minister of health. She formally joined the resistance in 1968.

Duong Van Minh Saigon general known as "Big" Minh. He was one of the leaders of the 1963 coup against Ngo Dinh Diem (along with Tran Van Don and Le Van Kim) and served as a member of the military triumvirate that ruled the South briefly in 1964. In April 1975 Minh was appointed South Vietnam's last president, and it was he who formally surrendered to the North Vietnamese and Vietcong forces.

Duy Lien An NLF urban cadre who was arrested in 1967 in the wake of Ba Tra's confession and was exchanged along with Truong Nhu Tang in 1968. Her husband, a Vietcong officer, was killed in a B-52 raid shortly after her release.

Hai Thuan Veteran resistance fighter who worked for the PRG ministry of justice after 1975. He committed suicide after his son was sent to reeducation camp by the revolutionary government.

Ho Chi Minh Vietnam's Mao Tse Tung. Founder and leader of the Vietnamese revolution, he became North Vietnam's first president after defeating the French in 1954. Ho died in 1969 at the age of 79, six years before the final victory of the movement he founded.

Hoang Van Hoan Early associate of Ho Chi Minh and long-term member of North Vietnam's Politburo. He opposed the pro-Soviet policies of Le Duan and Le Duc Tho and defected to China in 1979.

Hoang Van Thai North Vietnamese military commander in the South, a member of the COSVN secretariat.

Huynh Tan Phat (code name "Tam Chi") Chairman of the Provisional Revolutionary Government. Phat, an architect by profession, had been a secret member of the Communist Party (Lao Dong) since 1940. In 1958 he was one of those Saigon intellectuals who took the lead in the formation of the NLF. Throughout the war he played perhaps the most important role in maintaining Party control over the diverse group of individuals who formed the political core of the Southern Front and its related organizations. After 1975 he was rewarded for his services to the Party by an appointment as one of the vice-ministers of the unified government.

Huynh Van Nghi An official of the Alliance of National, Democratic, and Peace Forces. Husband of Dr. Duong Huynh Hoa.

Le Duan (code name "Comrade Ba") Secretary general of the Communist Party (Lao Dong). He succeeded Ho Chi Minh as leader of the Party and most powerful individual in North Vietnam.

Le Duc Tho North Vietnamese Politburo member who negotiated with Henry Kissinger in Paris. Along with Le Duan, Tho was the architect of North Vietnam's lean toward the Soviet Union. He is presently chairman of the Central Military Party Committee and wields authority equal to that of Le Duan.

Le Thi Rieng A leading cadre of the NLF's Saigon/Cholon/Giadinh proselytizing committee. She was Truong Nhu Tang's neighbor in the isolation row at the national police prison and was executed in January 1968.

Le Van Tha   Vice minister of justice in the PRG.

Mai Chi Tho   Brother of Le Duc Tho and second in command of the Saigon/Cholon/Giadinh Party organization. After the war he became chairman of the administration committee for Ho Chi Minh City (the new name for Saigon).

Ngo Ba Thanh   Southern opposition activist who was a member of the Peace Committee in 1965. After the war she became a member of the unified government's National Assembly.

Ngo Dinh Diem   Anticommunist nationalist who became prime minister under the emperor Bao Dai whom he deposed in 1955. The first president of South Vietnam, Diem was killed during the coup of 1963.

Ngo Dinh Nhu   Diem's younger brother and the regime's chief strategist, widely regarded as his evil genius. Nhu was killed along with his brother.

Ngo Dinh Thuc   Roman Catholic archbishop of Hue and Diem's oldest brother. One of Diem's closest advisors, Thuc was a key figure in the strife between Buddhist's and Catholics that created such problems for the Saigon government. Thuc was also Albert Pham Ngoc Thao's patron.

Nguyen Anh Tuan   Undersecretary for economic planning and Truong Nhu Tang's superior while he was director of the Société Sucrière.

Nguyen Cao Ky   Southern air force marshal who was instrumental in overthrowing Nguyen Khanh in 1965. Subsequently he became prime minister, then vice president under Nguyen Van Thieu.

Nguyen Huu Tho   President of the National Liberation Front. Saigonese lawyer who had been jailed by Ngo Dinh Diem in 1954 for opposition activities. A figurehead leader throughout the war, afterward he was chairman of the unified government's national assembly, a nominal position.

Nguyen Khanh   Southern general who came to power through a coup in January 1964. He was overthrown a year later.

Nguyen Long   Saigon lawyer and opposition leader, jailed in 1965 after participating in the Peace Committee.

Nguyen Ngoc Loan   South Vietnamese chief of police during period of Truong Nhu Tang's imprisonment. Famous for his street execution of a Vietcong prisoner during Tet of 1968.

Nguyen Thi Binh   The PRG's foreign minister. After the war she became minister of education.

Nguyen Thi Dinh   Vice commander of the NLF armed forces. Her position was largely for show; in fact she knew little about military affairs. After the war she became deputy secretary of veteran's affairs.

Nguyen Van Hieu   A Saigon lycée teacher who was one of the original NLF organizers. A secret member of the Communist Party since 1951, he was an important liaison agent between the Northern leadership and the Front during its early years.

Nguyen Van Kiet   PRG minister of education.

Nguyen Van Linh   COSVN secretary and chief of propaganda.

Nguyen Van Thieu   South Vietnamese military strongman who became president in 1967. His policies and leadership, particularly after the American withdrawal in 1973, led to the fall of the Saigon government on April 30, 1975. Shortly before this event Thieu resigned the presidency and fled Vietnam, eventually taking up residence in Great Britain.

Lon Nol   Cambodian defense minister who led the successful coup against Prince Norodom Sihanouk in 1970. His government fell to the Khmer Rouge on April 17, 1975.

(Albert) Pham Ngoc Thao   Son of a wealthy South Vietnamese Catholic family, he joined the Vietminh in 1945, serving as field commander in the Ca Mau peninsula, then as undercover agent in Saigon. After 1954 he ostensibly joined the Saigon government, becoming province chief, head of the strategic hamlet program, and eventually chief of military security. In fact, he had never given up his position in the resistance and was perhaps the NLF's most successful agent. In 1965 Thao was killed during factional fighting within the South's military leadership. As far as is known, his Front identity was still intact.

(Lucien) Pham Ngoc Hung   Albert Pham Ngoc Thao's brother and an official in the Alliance of National, Democratic, and Peace Forces.

Pham Van Dong   One of Ho Chi Minh's earliest associates, he served as North Vietnam's prime minister, then as prime minister of unified Vietnam.

Phung Van Cung   A doctor who was one of the early members of the NLF and later became the Provisional Revolutionary Government's minister of the interior.

Norodom Sihanouk   Cambodian prince and political leader, he was overthrown in a March 1970 coup led by his minister of defense. Subsequently he joined forces with the communist Khmer Rouge, though in fact he served only as a figurehead in the antigovernment civil war. Since Vietnam's invasion of Cambodia in 1978, he has been active in the Cambodian opposition to Vietnamese occupation.

Ton That Dinh   Saigon general who commanded the Third Military Region (around Saigon) at the time of the successful coup against Ngo Dinh Diem.

Tran Bach Dang (code name "Tu Meo")   A resistance organizer in the South during the anti-French war, he became head of the Youth Liberation Association in 1961 and chief of the Party's urban mobilization program in the mid-1960s. He was later purged for excessive Southern regionalism and retired to a sinecure in the mass organization known as the Fatherland Front.

Tran Buu Kiem   A secret Party member, he was one of the NLF's original organizers and its foreign affairs specialist. In 1968 he was purged from his leadership position (like Tran Bach Dang) for excessive Southern regionalism. After unification he was retired from active political participation.

GLOSSARY OF NAMES

Tran Duc Thao   Vietnam's leading philosopher, Thao joined the Communist Party in 1954. During North Vietnam's suppression of intellectuals two years later he was purged and isolated.

Tran Kim Quan   Saigonese pharmacist and leader of the anti-Diem Peace Movement in 1954. Offered the presidency of the NLF in 1960, he declined and subsequently retired in France.

Tran Kim Tuyen   Ngo Dinh Diem's secret police chief, he left Vietnam shortly before Diem's overthrow.

Tran Nam Trung   Commander-in-chief of the NLF's military forces and one of COSVN's second secretaries.

Tran Thien Khiem   Saigon general. Khiem was a conspirator in several coups d'état during the mid-1960s. He later served as interior minister, defense minister, and prime minister under Nguyen Van Thieu.

Tran Van Don   Leader of the 1963 coup against Ngo Dinh Diem. The military government he led was in turn overthrown by Nguyen Khanh three months later.

Tran Van Tra   NLF military commander. In 1982 his history of the war's final stages was withdrawn from circulation for its ardent Southern national feeling and implicit criticism of the Northern-led Party.

Trinh Dinh Thao   Saigon lawyer and political activist who became president of the Alliance of National, Democratic, and Peace Forces in 1968. After unification he was retired from active political participation.

Truong Chinh   Northern Politburo member and one of the Party's chief theoreticians.

Vo Nguyen Giap   An early colleague of Ho Chi Minh, Giap led the Vietminh army and was the chief strategist of the French defeat at Dienbienphu. Politburo member and minister of defense, he was the leading North Vietnamese military personality during the anti-American war as well.

Vo Van Kiet (code name "Sau Dan")   Communist Party secretary for Saigon/Cholon/Giadinh during both the anti-French and anti-American wars. After 1981 he was elevated to the Politburo as chief of economic planning.

Xuan Thuy   Nominal leader of North Vietnam's negotiating team during the Paris peace talks, in fact subordinate to Le Duc Tho.

The Provisional Revolutionary Government
of the Republic of South Vietnam

Manifesto and Program of the
National Liberation Front of South Vietnam

Political Program of the Vietnam Alliance
of National, Democratic, and Peace Forces

Action Program of the
Provisional Revolutionary Government
of the Republic of South Vietnam

THE PROVISIONAL REVOLUTIONARY GOVERNMENT
OF THE REPUBLIC OF SOUTH VIETNAM

Chairman	Architect Huynh Tan Phat
Vice Chairman	Dr. Phung Van Cung
Vice Chairman	Prof. Nguyen Van Kiet
Vice Chairman	Nguyen Doa
Minister to the Chairman's Office	Tran Buu Kiem
Minister of Defense	Tran Nam Trung
Minister of Foreign Affairs	Mme. Nguyen Thi Binh
Minister of the Interior	Dr. Phung Van Cung
Minister of Economy and Finance	Engineer Cao Van Bon
Minister of Information and Culture	Composer Luu Huu Phuoc
Minister of Education and Youth	Prof. Nguyen Van Kiet
Minister of Health, Social Action and Disabled Soldiers	Dr. Duong Quynh Hoa
Minister of Justice	Truong Nhu Tang
Vice Minister to the Chairman's Office	Ung Ngoc Ky
Vice Ministers of Defense	Dang Van Cong
	Nguyen Chan
Vice Ministers of Foreign Affairs	Le Quang Chanh
	Hoang Bich Son
Vice Minister of the Interior	Prof. Nguyen Ngoc Thuong
Vice Minister of Economy and Finance	Nguyen Van Trieu
Vice Ministers of Information and Culture	Writer Hoang Trong Qui (pen name: Thanh Nghi)
	Writer Lu Phuong
Vice Ministers of Education and Youth	Prof. Le Van Tri
	Ho Huu Nhut
Vice Ministers of Health, Social Action and Disabled Soldiers	Dr. Ho Van Hue
	Prof. Bui Thi Nga
Vice Minister of Justice	Prof. Le Van Tha

MANIFESTO AND PROGRAM OF THE
NATIONAL LIBERATION FRONT OF SOUTH VIETNAM

MANIFESTO OF THE SOUTH VIETNAM
NATIONAL LIBERATION FRONT*

Compatriots in the country and abroad!

Over the past hundred years the Vietnamese people repeatedly rose up to
fight against foreign aggression for the independence and freedom of their
fatherland. In 1945, the people throughout the country surged up in an armed
uprising, overthrow the Japanese and French domination and seized power.
When the French colonialists invaded our country for the second time our
compatriots, determined not to be enslaved again, shed much blood and laid
down many lives to defend their national sovereignty and independence. Their
solidarity and heroic struggle during nine years led the resistance war to
victory. The 1954 Geneva Agreements restored peace in our country and
recognized "the sovereignty, independence, unity and territorial integrity of
Vietnam."

Our compatriots in South Vietnam would have been able to live in peace,
to earn their livelihood in security and to build a decent and happy life.

However, the American imperialists, who had in the past helped the French
colonialists to massacre our people, have now replaced the French in enslaving
the southern part of our country through a disguised colonial regime. They
have been using their stooge—the Ngo Dinh Diem administration—in their
downright repression and exploitation of our compatriots, in their maneuvers
to permanently divide our country and to turn its southern part into a military
base in preparation for war in Southeast Asia.

The aggressors and traitors, working hand in glove with each other, have
set up an extremely cruel dictatorial rule. They persecute and massacre democratic and patriotic people, and abolish all human liberties. They ruthlessly
exploit the workers, peasants and other laboring people, strangle the local industry and trade, poison the minds of our people with a depraved foreign culture,
thus degrading our national culture, traditions and ethics. They feverishly increase their military forces, build military bases, use the army as an instrument
for repressing the people and serving the U.S. imperialists' scheme to prepare
an aggressive war.

Never, over the past six years, have gunshots massacring our compatriots
ceased to resound throughout South Vietnam. Tens of thousands of patriots
here have been murdered and hundreds of thousands thrown into jail. All sections of the people have been living in a stifling atmosphere under the iron heel
of the U.S.–Diem clique. Countless families have been torn away and scenes
of mourning are seen everywhere as a result of unemployment, poverty, exacting taxes, terror, massacre, drafting of manpower and press-ganging, usurpa-

*Source: *South Viet Nam National Front for Liberation, Documents,* South Vietnam:
Giai Phong Publishing House, December 1968, pp. 11-31.

tion of land, forcible house removal, and herding of the people into "prosperity zones," "resettlement centers" and other forms of concentration camps.

High anger with the present tyrannical regime is boiling among all strata of the people. Undaunted in the face of barbarous persecution, our compatriots are determined to unite and struggle unflaggingly against the U.S. imperialists' policy of aggression and the dictatorial and nepotic regime of the Ngo Dinh Diem clique. Among workers, peasants and other toiling people, among intellectuals, students and pupils, industrialists and traders, religious sects and national minorities, patriotic activities are gaining in scope and strength, seriously shaking the U.S.–Diem dictatorial regime.

The attempted coup d'état of November 11, 1960, in Saigon in some respects reflected the seething anger among the people and army men, and the rottenness and decline of the U.S.–Diem regime. However, there were among the leaders of this coup political speculators who, misusing the patriotism of the army men, preferred negotiation and compromise rather than to overthrow Ngo Dinh Diem. Like Ngo Dinh Diem, they persisted in following the pro-American and traitorous path, and also used the anticommunist signboard to oppose the people. That is why the coup was not supported by the people and large numbers of army men and, consequently, ended in failure.

At present, our people are urgently demanding an end to the cruel dictatorial rule; they are demanding independence and democracy, enough food and clothing, and peaceful reunification of the country.

To meet the aspirations of our compatriots, the *South Vietnam National Liberation Front* came into being, pledging itself to shoulder the historic task of liberating our people from the present yoke of slavery.

The *South Vietnam National Liberation Front* undertakes to unite all sections of the people, all social classes, nationalities, political parties, organizations, religious communities and patriotic personalities, without distinction of their political tendencies, in order to struggle for the overthrow of the rule of the U.S. imperialists and their stooges—the Ngo Dinh Diem clique—and for the realization of independence, democracy, peace and neutrality pending the peaceful reunification of the fatherland.

The *South Vietnam National Liberation Front* calls on the entire people to unite and heroically rise up as one man to fight along the line of a program of action summarized as follows:

1. To overthrow the disguised colonial regime of the U.S. imperialists and the dictatorial Ngo Dinh Diem administration—lackey of the United States— and to form a national democratic coalition administration.

2. To bring into being a broad and progressive democracy, promulgate freedom of expression, of the press, of belief, of assembly, of association, of movement and other democratic freedoms. To grant general amnesty to all political detainees, dissolve all concentration camps dubbed "prosperity zones" and "resettlement centers," abolish the fascist 10–59 law and other anti-democratic laws.

3. To abolish the economic monopoly of the United States and its hench-men, to protect home-made products, encourage home industry and trade, expand agriculture and build an independent and sovereign economy. To pro-vide jobs for the unemployed, increase wages for workers, army men and office employees. To abolish arbitrary fines and apply an equitable and rational tax system. To help those who have gone south to return to their native places if they so desire, and to provide jobs for those among them who want to remain in the South.

4. To carry out land rent reduction, guarantee the peasants' rights to till their present plots of land, redistribute communal land and advance toward land reform.

5. To do away with enslaving and depraved U.S.-style culture, build a na-tional and progressive culture and education. To wipe out illiteracy, open more schools, carry out reforms in the educational and examination system.

6. To abolish the system of American military advisers, eliminate foreign military bases in Vietnam and build a national army for the defence of the fatherland and the people.

7. To guarantee equality between men and women and among different nationalities, and the right to autonomy of the national minorities; to protect the legitimate interests of foreign residents in Vietnam; to protect and take care of the interests of Vietnamese living abroad.

8. To carry out a foreign policy of peace and neutrality, to establish diplo-matic relations with all countries which respect the independence and sover-eignty of Vietnam.

9. To re-establish normal relations between the two zones, pending the peaceful reunification of the fatherland.

10. To oppose aggressive war; to actively defend world peace.

Compatriots!

Ours are a heroic people with a tradition of unity and indomitable struggle. We cannot let our country be plunged into darkness and mourning. We are determined to shatter the fetters of slavery and wrest back independence and freedom.

Let us all rise up and unite!

Let us close our ranks and fight under the banner of the *South Vietnam National Liberation Front* to overthrow the rule of the U.S. imperialists and Ngo Dinh Diem—their henchman.

Workers, peasants and other toiling people! The oppression and misery which are now heavily weighing on you must be ended. You have the strength of tens of millions of people. Stand up enthusiastically to save your families and our fatherland.

Intellectuals! The dictatorial rulers have stripped us of the most elementary human rights. You are living in humiliation and misery. For our great cause, stand up resolutely!

Industrialists and traders! A country under the sway of foreign sharks cannot have an independent and sovereign economy. You should join in the people's struggle.

Compatriots of all national minorities! Compatriots of all religious communities! Unity is life, disunity is death. Smash all U.S.–Diem schemes of division. Side with the entire people in the struggle for independence, freedom and equality among all nationalities.

Notables! The interests of the nation are above all else. Support actively the struggle for the overthrow of the cruel aggressors and traitors.

Patriotic officers and soldiers! You have arms in your hands. Listen to the sacred call of the fatherland. Be definitely on the side of the people. Your compatriots have faith in your patriotism.

Young men and women! You are the future of the nation. You should devote your youthful ardor to serving the fatherland.

Compatriots living abroad! Turn your thoughts toward the beloved fatherland, contribute actively to the sacred struggle for national liberation.

At present the movement for peace, democracy and national independence is surging up throughout the world. Colonialism is irretrievably disintegrating. The time when the imperialists could plunder and subjugate the people at will is over. This situation is extremely favorable for the struggle to free South Vietnam from the yoke of the U.S. imperialists and their stooges. Peace-loving and progressive people in the world are supporting us. Justice is on our side, and we have the prodigious strength of the unity of our struggle to free South Vietnam from the yoke of the U.S. imperialists and their stooges. Justice is on our side, and we have the prodigious strength of the unity of our entire people. We will certainly win! The U.S. imperialist aggressors and the Ngo Dinh Diem traitorous clique will certainly be defeated. The cause of liberation of South Vietnam will certainly triumph.

Compatriots around the country!

Let us unite and march forward confidently and valiantly to score brilliant victories for our people and our fatherland!

South Vietnam National Liberation Front

PROGRAM OF THE SOUTH VIETNAM
NATIONAL LIBERATION FRONT

Since the French colonialists invaded our country, our people have unremittingly struggled for national independence and freedom. In 1945, our compatriots throughout the country rose up, overthrew the Japanese and French and seized power, and afterwards heroically carried out a resistance war for nine years, defeated the French aggressors and the U.S. interventionists, and brought our people's valiant resistance war to a glorious victory.

At the Geneva Conference the French imperialists had, in July 1954, to undertake to withdraw their troops from Vietnam. The participating countries to the Conference solemnly declared their recognition of the sovereignty, independence, unity and territorial integrity of Vietnam.

Since then we should have been able to enjoy peace, and join the people throughout the country in building an independent, democratic, unified, prosperous and strong Vietnam.

However, the American imperialists, who had in the past helped the French colonialists to massacre our people, have now plotted to partition our country permanently, enslave its southern part through a disguised colonial regime and turn it into a military base in preparation for aggressive war in Southeast Asia. They have brought the Ngo Dinh Diem clique—their stooges—to power under the signboard of a fake independent state, and use their "aid" policy and advisers' machine to control all the military, economic, political and cultural branches in South Vietnam.

The aggressors and traitors have set up the most dictatorial and cruel rule in Vietnam's history. They repress and persecute all democratic and patriotic movements, abolish all human liberties. They monopolize all branches of economy, strangle industry, agriculture and trade, ruthlessly exploit all popular strata. They use every device of mind poisoning, obscurantism and deprivation in an attempt to quell the patriotism of our people. They feverishly increase their military forces, build military bases, use the army as an instrument for repressing the people and for war preparations in accordance with the U.S. imperialists' policy.

For more than six years, countless crimes have been perpetrated by the U.S.–Diem dictatorial and cruel rule: terrorizing gunshots have never ceased to resound throughout South Vietnam; tens of thousands of patriots have been shot, beheaded, disemboweled with liver plucked out; hundreds of thousands of people have been tortured, and thrown into jail where they died a slow death; countless people have been victims of arson, house removal and usurpation of land, and drafted for forced labor or press-ganged into the army; innumerable families are in distress or torn away as a result of the policy of concentrating people in "prosperity zones" and "resettlement centers," of exacting rents and taxes, terror, arrest, plunder, ransom, widespread unemployment and poverty, which are seriously threatening the life of all popular strata.

There must be *peace!* There must be *independence!* There must be *democracy!* There must be *enough food and clothing!* There must be *peaceful reunification of the fatherland!*

That is our most earnest and pressing aspiration. It has become an iron will, and a prodigious strength urging our people to unite and resolutely rise up so as to overthrow the cruel rule of the U.S. imperialists and their stooges, and to save our homes and our country.

In view of the supreme interests of the fatherland, with the firmness to struggle to the end for the people's legitimate aspirations and in accordance with the progressive trend in the world, the *South Vietnam National Liberation Front* comes into being.

The *South Vietnam National Liberation Front* undertakes to unite people from all walks of life, social classes, nationalities, political parties, organizations, religious communities, and patriotic personalities in South Vietnam, without distinction of political tendencies, in order to struggle for the overthrow of the rule of the U.S. imperialists and their henchmen and for the realization of *independence, democracy, improvement of the living conditions, peace and neutrality* in South Vietnam pending *peaceful reunification of the fatherland.*

The *program of the South Vietnam National Liberation Front* comprises the following 10 points:

I.—To Overthrow the Disguised Colonial Regime of the U.S. Imperialists and the Dictatorial Ngo Dinh Diem Administration—Lackey of the United States— and to Form a National Democratic Coalition Administration

The present regime in South Vietnam is a disguised colonial regime of the U.S. imperialists. The South Vietnam administration is a lackey which has been carrying out the U.S. imperialists' line and policies. This regime and administration must be overthrown, and a broad national democratic coalition administration formed, including representatives of all popular strata, nationalities, political parties, religious communities, and patriotic personalities. We must wrest back the people's economic, political, social and cultural interests, achieve independence and democracy, improve the people's living conditions, carry out a policy of peace and neutrality and advance toward the peaceful reunification of the fatherland.

II.—To Bring into Being a Broad and Progressive Democracy

1. To abolish the current constitution of the Ngo Dinh Diem dictatorial administration—lackey of the United States. To elect a new National Assembly through universal suffrage.

2. To promulgate all democratic freedoms: freedom of expression, of the press, of assembly, of association, of movement, etc. To guarantee freedom of belief; to do away with discrimination against any religion on the part of the State. To grant freedom of action to the patriotic political parties and mass organizations, irrespective of their political tendencies.

3. To grant general amnesty to all political detainees, dissolve all concentration camps under any form whatsoever. To abolish the fascist 10–59 law and other anti-democratic laws. To permit the return of all those who had to flee abroad due to the U.S.–Diem regime.

4. To strictly ban all illegal arrests and imprisonments, tortures and corporal punishment. To punish unrepenting cruel murderers of the people.

III.—To Build an Independent and Sovereign Economy and Improve the People's Living Conditions

1. To abolish the economic monopoly of the United States and its henchmen. To build an independent and sovereign economy and finance, beneficial to the nation and people. To confiscate and nationalize the property of the U.S. imperialists and the ruling clique, their stooges.

2. To help industrialists and traders rehabilitate and develop industry and handicraft, and to encourage industrial development. To actively protect home-made products by abolishing production taxes, restricting or ending the import of those goods which can be produced in the country, and reducing taxes of import on raw materials and machinery.

3. To rehabilitate agriculture, modernize farming, and animal husbandry. To help peasants reclaim waste land and develop production; to protect crops and ensure the consumption of agricultural products.

4. To encourage and accelerate the economic interflow between towns.

5. To apply an equitable and rational tax system. To abolish arbitrary fines. To develop trade with foreign countries without distinction of political regimes, and on the principle of equality and mutual benefit.

6. To promulgate labor regulations, that is: to prohibit dismissals, wage cuts, fines and ill-treatment of workers and office employees, to improve the living conditions of workers and public employees, and to fix wages and guar-antees for the health of teen-age apprentices.

7. To organize social relief:

—Jobs for the unemployed.

—Protection of orphans, elderly and disabled persons.

—Assistance to those who have become disabled or without support due to the struggle against U.S. imperialism and its stooges.

—Relief to localities suffering from crop failures, fire and natural ca-lamities.

8. To help those who have gone south return to their native places if they so desire, and to provide jobs for those who decide to remain in the South.

9. To strictly prohibit forcible house removals, arson, usurpation of land, and the herding of the people into concentration centers. To ensure for the country folk and urban working people the opportunity to earn their living in security.

IV.—To Carry Out Land-Rent Reduction and to Advance Toward the Settlement of the Agrarian Problem so as to Ensure Land to the Tillers

1. To carry out land-rent reduction. To guarantee to the peasants the right to till their present plots of land and ensure the right of ownership for those who have reclaimed waste land. To protect the legitimate right of ownership by peasants of the plots of land distributed to them.

2. To abolish the "prosperity zones" and the herding of people into "resettle-ment centers." To permit those forcibly herded into "prosperity zones" or "resettlement centers" to return home freely and earn their living on their own plots of land.

3. To confiscate the land usurped by the U.S. imperialists and their agents, and distribute it to landless and land-poor peasants. To redistribute communal land in an equitable and rational way.

4. Through negotiations, the State will purchase from landowners at equi-table and rational prices all land held by them in excess of a given area, fixed

in accordance with the concrete situation in each locality, and distribute it to landless and land-poor peasants. This land will be distributed free of charge and with no conditions attached.

V. To Build a National and Democratic Education and Culture

1. To eliminate the enslaving and gangster-style American culture and education; to build a national, progressive culture and education serving the fatherland and the people.

2. To wipe out illiteracy. To build sufficient general-education schools for the youth and children. To expand universities, vocational and professional schools. To use the Vietnamese language in teaching. To reduce school fees, and exempt poor pupils and students from school fees; to reform the examination system.

3. To develop science and technology and national literature and art; to encourage and help intellectuals, cultural and art workers to develop their abilities in service of national construction.

4. To develop medical service, physical culture and sports.

VI. To Build an Army for the Defense of the Fatherland and the People

1. To build a national army for the defense of the fatherland and the people. To cancel the system of U.S. military advisers.

2. To abolish the press-ganging regime. To improve the material life of the army men and ensure their political rights. To prohibit the ill-treatment of soldiers. To apply a policy of assistance to families of poor army men.

3. To award and give worthy jobs to those officers and soldiers who have rendered meritorious services in the struggle against the rule of the U.S. imperialists and their henchmen. To display leniency toward those who have collaborated with the U.S.–Diem clique and committed crimes against the people but, having repented, are now serving the people.

4. To abolish all the military bases of foreign countries in South Vietnam.

VII. To Guarantee the Right of Equality Between Nationalities, and Between Men and Women; to Protect the Legitimate Rights of Foreign Residents in Vietnam and Vietnamese Living Abroad

1. To ensure the right to autonomy of the national minorities.

To set up, within the framework of the great family of the Vietnamese people, autonomous regions in areas inhabited by minority peoples.

To ensure equal rights among the nationalities. All nationalities have the right to use and develop their own spoken and written language and to preserve or change their customs and habits. To abolish the U.S.–Diem clique's present policy of ill-treatment and forced assimilation of the minority nationalities.

To help the minority peoples to catch up with the common level of the people by developing the economy and culture in the areas inhabited by them, by training skilled personnel from people of minority origin.

2. To ensure the right of equality between men and women. Women to

enjoy the same rights as men in all fields: political, economic, cultural and social.

3. To protect the legitimate rights of foreign nationals in Vietnam.

4. To defend and take care of the interests of Vietnamese living abroad.

VIII. To Carry out a Foreign Policy of Peace and Neutrality

1. To cancel all unequal treaties signed with foreign countries by the U.S. henchmen which violate national sovereignty.

2. To establish diplomatic relations with all countries, irrespective of their political regimes, in accordance with the principles of peaceful coexistence as put forth at the Bandung Conference.

3. To unite closely with the peace-loving and neutral countries. To expand friendly relations with Southeast Asian countries, first of all with neighboring Cambodia and Laos.

4. To refrain from joining any bloc or military alliance or forming a military alliance with any country.

5. To receive economic aid from any country ready to assist Vietnam without conditions attached.

IX. To Establish Normal Relations Between the Two Zones and Advance Toward Peaceful Reunification of the Fatherland

The urgent demand of our people throughout the country is to reunify the fatherland by peaceful means. The *South Vietnam National Liberation Front* undertakes the gradual reunification of the country by peaceful means, on the principle of negotiations and discussions between the two zones on all forms and measures beneficial to the Vietnamese people and their fatherland.

Pending national reunification, the Governments of the two zones will negotiate and undertake not to spread propaganda for secession or war preparation, not to use military forces against each other. To carry out economic and cultural exchanges between the two zones. To ensure for the people of both zones freedom of movement and trade, and the right of mutual visits and correspondence.

X. To Oppose Aggressive War, Actively Defend World Peace

1. To oppose aggressive war and all forms of enslavement by the imperialists. To support the national-liberation struggles of peoples in other countries.

2. To oppose war propaganda. To demand general disarmament, prohibition of nuclear weapons and demand the use of atomic energy for peaceful purposes.

3. To support the movements for peace, democracy and social progress in the world. To actively contribute to the safeguarding of peace in Southeast Asia and the world.

Compatriots throughout the country!

All Vietnamese patriots!

Following nearly a century of struggle and nine years of resistance our people who have shed much blood and laid down many lives are determined not to be enslaved again!

For peace, independence, freedom and the unity of our fatherland, for the destiny of our people, for the sake of our lives and future and the future of our descendants.

Let all of us rise up!

Let all of us unite!

Let us close our ranks and march forward to fight under the banner of the *South Vietnam National Liberation Front* to overthrow the cruel domination of the U.S. imperialists and the Ngo Dinh Diem clique, their henchmen, in order to save our country and our homes.

We will surely win because the union of our people is an invincible force, because justice is on our side, and obsolete colonialism is now disintegrating and heading for total collapse. In the world, the movement for peace, democracy and national independence is expanding widely and strongly, and is winning more and more successes. This situation is very favorable to our struggle for national salvation.

The U.S. imperialists and their henchmen will certainly be defeated!

The cause of national liberation in South Vietnam will certainly triumph!

Let us unite, be confident and struggle heroically! Let us go forward and win a glorious victory for our people and our fatherland!

South Vietnam
December 20, 1960

POLITICAL PROGRAM OF THE VIETNAM ALLIANCE OF NATIONAL, DEMOCRATIC, AND PEACE FORCES*

1. National Salvation

Unite all patriotic forces and individuals in resolutely opposing the aggressive war, overthrowing the lackey puppet regime, setting up a national coalition government and regaining independence, democracy, and peace.

A—National salvation is a common undertaking of the entire people and the strength to insure its success is that of the all-people great solidarity bloc. The Vietnam Alliance of National, Democratic, and Peace Forces advocates the solidarity of all patriotic forces and individuals, regardless of political tendency, nationality, religious belief, or social origin in the present phase of struggle for independence and national sovereignty as well as in the future phase of national reconstruction.

B—The South Vietnamese people are eager for peace—a peace in honor and freedom. The Vietnam Alliance of National, Democratic, and Peace Forces advocates the regaining of independence and sovereignty for South Vietnam, demanding that the U.S. Government end the war, withdraw all the troops of the United States and its allies from South Vietnam, dismantle all U.S. military bases and respect Vietnam's independence and sovereignty as stipulated by the 1954 Geneva Agreements on Vietnam. South Vietnam's national independence and sovereignty and territorial integrity must be recognized and respected by all the governments in the world. The Vietnam Alliance of National, Democratic, and Peace Forces is ready to discuss these problems with the U.S. Government.

C—The South Vietnam National Liberation Front, a patriotic force having made great contributions to the task of mobilizing, organizing and leading the antiaggression struggle during the past years, cannot be absent from the settlement of problems concerning South Vietnam. The Vietnam Alliance of National, Democratic, and Peace Forces advocates contacts and debates with the NLFSV in order to cooperate with it in regaining national independence, restoring peace, building the country and bringing a free and happy life to the entire people.

On the basis of the united action of patriotic forces and individuals participating in the national liberation task, including the patriotic individuals in the lackey administration and army, it is necessary to set up an enlarged democratic, national coalition government composed of representatives of people of all strata, nationalities, religions, and political groups, progressive political parties and patriotic notables, with a view to achieving independence, democracy, peace, neutrality, and prosperity for all South Vietnam.

2. National Reconstruction

To build South Vietnam into an independent, free, democratic, peaceful, neutral and prosperous state. After winning back independence, sovereignty and peace

* Source: Hanoi Radio, April 27, 1968.

for the country, the Vietnam Alliance of National, Democratic, and Peace Forces advocates always uniting with patriotic forces and individuals in order to heal wounds, to achieve national reconstruction and to build South Vietnam into an independent, sovereign, free, democratic, peaceful, neutral and prosperous state.

A—Internal affairs.

(1) Political Regime. To eradicate all vestiges of the colonial regimes, old and new, in South Vietnam; to overthrow the entire lackey, puppet administration; to disband the Senate and House of Representatives set up by fraudulent and deceitful elections; to abolish the Constitution drafted by the previous constituent National Assembly; not to recognize any treaty signed between the puppet South Vietnamese administration and foreign countries —treaties which are illegal and unequal and run counter to national interests and world peace; to abolish all people-betraying and country-harming laws enacted by the puppets and all decree-laws, decrees and court sentences of the puppets, which unreasonably and illegally violate the citizens' lives, property, dignity, and other interests; to establish a truly democratic and free republican regime; and to organize general elections in accordance with the principles of equality, universal, direct suffrage, and a secret ballot in order to elect a constituent National Assembly that truly represents the people.

This National Assembly will work out a democratic Constitution which fully embodies the aspirations and interests of the people. The Constitution will set forth conditions for establishing and organizing a healthy and truly democratic state structure of broad national coalition character. All citizens will enjoy equality in all respects. The people will enjoy all truly democratic freedoms: freedom of speech, freedom of the press, freedom of religious belief, freedom of movement, freedom of assembly, freedom of association, freedom to travel abroad and so forth. There will be no discriminatory treatment of any citizen. Inviolability of the human person, freedom of residence and secrecy of correspondence will be respected for all citizens. The inviolability of National Assembly deputies will be guaranteed. All persons detained under any form by the U.S. and lackey authorities in South Vietnam on account of their patriotic activities or of their opposition tendencies will be set free. Those who have been sent into exile or have fled to foreign countries because of the lackey administration's terrorist and repressive policy are free to return to the country.

To reexamine all inappropriate verdicts pronounced in violation of common rights in order to grant amnesty or reduce sentences; to exercise equality among men and women in the political, economic, cultural and social fields; to exercise equality among religions and not show favoritism for any religion; to oppose all the divisive plots of the U.S. imperialists and their lackeys; to protect and rehabilitate or repair all pagodas, churches, holy sees, and temples that were destroyed by enemy bombs and bullets; to exercise a policy of solidarity and equality among all nationalities in the Vietnamese national community; to care for overseas Vietnamese compatriots' interests, encourage and create conditions for overseas Vietnamese compatriots to return to the Fatherland and engage in national reconstruction; to respect the legitimate interests of foreigners residing in South Vietnam, and abolish the U.S.-puppet policy of assimilating Chinese residents through pressure.

All the units or individual officers, troops, policemen and civil servants of the Southern puppet administration who have carried out patriotic acts and engaged in the struggle to oppose the U.S. war of aggression and the puppet lackey regime through uprisings, military revolts, deserting the enemy ranks, returning to the people with weapons and singlemindedly supporting the South Vietnamese people's struggle for independence, democracy and peace, or all those who did not carry out these acts but still refused to execute enemy orders that were harmful to the people, will be acclaimed, will have their achievements registered and will be commended, rewarded, and well-treated accordingly. Those who have committed crimes against the people and have repented and sincerely returned to the people will be forgiven. Those who earned merits to compensate for past faults will be rewarded accordingly. After independence is wrested back, those who want to continue to serve in the new administrative machinery will be accepted and none will be favored more than others.

(2) Economic Regime. To build an independent, self-governing economy, which will not be subordinated to the U.S. imperialists or any country. After peace is restored, to do our utmost to care for and heal all the wounds caused by war, solve the danger of unemployment and restore the people's normal life on the basis of strongly developing the economy and making the country prosperous. To respect and protect the citizens' right of ownership of the means of production and other property, to pay attention to creating conditions for rehabilitating and developing agricultural production, carry out a credit policy to lend money to the people for the cultivation of crops, improve technology, develop irrigation networks, carry out a price policy, encourage agricultural production and finely solve the consumption of agricultural products.

To carry out an equitable and rational agrarian reform, create bases to develop agriculture and reduce rent. On the basis of negotiation, and based on a certain limit of acreage, the Government will buy surplus acreage from landlords, and parcel it out to peasants who have no land or not enough land to cultivate. To recognize the ownership of land which the NLFSV has parceled out to peasants for the needs of the resistance. As for the land of absentee landlords which the NLFSV has parceled out to peasants, it will be reexamined according to the political attitudes of these landlords to find a reasonable solution.

To respect the legal ownership of land by churches, pagodas, and holy sees. To encourage the management of plantations growing industrial crops and fruit trees. To restore and develop the handicraft industry and commerce. To carry out a policy of free trade useful to the country and people and encourage transportation, industry and commerce enterprises aimed at making the people rich and the country powerful. To eliminate monopolies. To encourage the production and consumption of home-made products. To build a system of stable and independent currency. To bring about an equitable tax policy. To broaden the market at home and abroad. To realize economic exchanges with the North so that the two parts of our country may support and assist each other to develop. To promote commerical relations with foreign countries. To appeal for economic and technological aid, for capital and specialists from all foreign countries regardless of their political or social systems, on the basis of equality and mutual interests, without any mandatory conditions, but based on the respect of the independence and sovereignty of South Vietnam.

In the development of the economy, to care for the laboring people, workers and civil servants, promulgate labor laws and provisions safeguarding the interests of government and private employees. To improve living conditions in laboring people's housing areas and alleys, carrying out the policy of mutual interest between capitalist people and laboring people.

(3) Policy on Culture, Education, Science, Technology, and Public Health. To eliminate all influences of deficient, degenerating, and mixed cultures. To build a progressive and national educational culture, and make efforts to develop the fine traditions of our ancient national culture. To safeguard and develop good morals and customs. To make efforts to raise the level of culture of the people. To solve illiteracy. To build more schools of each level. To open courses for cultural and professional improvement. To create conditions leading to compulsory education. To develop science and technology to serve life, national construction and protection of the country. To reform the whole system of study and examinations. To use Vietnamese as the teaching language in all branches of the universities. To cultivate and take care of qualified people. To secure occupations for graduate students. To exempt private schools from taxation and reduce tuition for school and university students. To eliminate fees and grant scholarships to poor students in schools and universities. To help intellectuals in scientific, technical and cultural branches, and artists by providing conditions to develop study, creativity and inventiveness. To improve the system of going abroad for study, aimed at serving national construction. To care for the health of the people. To develop public health services. To improve existing hospitals and build more hospitals, maternity wards and dispensaries in cities and in the countryside so as to broadly serve the masses, and at the same time give impetus to movements of hygiene and disease prevention, and realize a new life for the people. To bring about cultural relations with the North and advance to establishing cultural relations with foreign countries.

(4) Social Relief Policy. To pay the greatest attention possible to social

interests and to take care of the lives and health of old people, women, wounded and sick combatants, orphans, disabled people, and others. To eradicate social ills, which are detrimental to human dignity and to the health of women, and to provide relief for the compatriot victims of the war, including the needy families of the puppet army soldiers.

B—Foreign relations.

To carry out a foreign policy of peace, nonalignment with any bloc and non-affiliation with any military alliance. To establsh diplomatic relations with all nations, regardless of their political regimes, on the principle of equality, mutual respect for one another's independence, sovereignty and territorial integrity, non-intervention in one another's internal affairs and peaceful coexistence. To attach special importance to friendly relations with our neighboring countries, Cambodia and Laos. To develop friendly relations with nationalist countries in Asia, Africa and Latin America. To positively support the national independence movement conducted by the peoples of various Asian, African and Latin American countries. To make a positive contribution to the protecting of peace and security in Southeast Asia and in the world. To expand trade relations with foreign countries and to call upon other countries to provide South Vietnam with economic assistance according to the principle of equality, mutual benefits and no strings attached, and on the basis of respect for the independence and sovereignty of South Vietnam. To establish cultural relations with foreign countries.

3. The Problem of National Reunification

The Governments of the South and the North will conduct negotiations conducive to the peaceful reunification of the Fatherland. To reunify the country is the earnest aspiration and sacred duty of our people. At present, our country has in fact two different political systems in the South and the North. National reunification cannot be achieved overnight. Therefore, the South and the North should hold talks on the basis of equality and respect for the characteristics of each zone, in order to proceed toward the peaceful reunification of the country.

Since the country has not yet been reunified, it is necessary to establish economic, cultural and postal relations and to allow movement between the two parts of the country. The Southern compatriots regrouped to the North and the Northern compatriots evacuated to the South will be free to return to or remain in either part of the country in accordance with their desires.

To allow businessmen and producers in the South and the North to move freely between the two parts of the country to do business and to exchange raw materials and goods, in order to make the Vietnamese economy develop rapidly and become prosperous. To exchange educational, scientific, technical, literary and artistic cadres between the two parts of the country, in order to exchange experiences and develop education, science, technology and culture. College students in the two parts of the country will be free to enroll in various university facilities in either part of the country in accordance with their desires.

Our South Vietnamese people are encountering the great peril arising from foreign aggression. As a result of the U.S. Government's extremely catastrophic war of extermination, an immeasurable amount of our compatriots' blood has been spilled, an immeasurable amount of our compatriots' rice paddies, gardens and houses have been destroyed and a countless number of people have been living in shame and destitution. Our country is engulfed in blood and flames, from the rural to the urban areas. No one could help feeling heartbroken and nursing hatred for the enemy, who has perpetrated countless towering crimes and has caused immeasurable suffering and mourning to the country. Our Vietnamese people have indomitable and heroic traditions. They have always been prepared to side with one another when the Fatherland is endangered. The memory of the Dien Hong conference of elders is still vivid in the minds of those who love the country and the people.* Enhancing these traditions, our southern people have united with one another, have stifled the aggressive determination of the enemy and have driven him into a situation in which he is faced with destruction and the danger of collapse. However, the greater victories we win, the greater difficulties and hardships we encounter.

Although it has suffered many serious and successive defeats, the U.S. Government has not yet agreed to draw practical and timely lessons in order to find a satisfactory solution to the Vietnam war. On the contrary, in its hopeless stalemate the U.S. Government has dashed even more precipitately along the criminal path and has used a large additional amount of murderous equipment, which is unprecedentedly cruel and barbarous. In this situation, it is all the more necessary for our compatriots to further tighten their ranks, to surge forward and to hold aloft the banner of solidarity and victory. In the face of the situation's requirements and in the present critical and historical moments, the Vietnam Alliance of National, Democratic, and Peace Forces solemnly proclaims its political program, which serves as a basis for further enlarging the all-people's great solidarity bloc, further strengthening the ranks of patriotic people and forming a comprehensive anti-U.S. national salvation national unified front, in order to direct decisive blows at the aggressive enemy.

In the present period of desperate struggle, the Vietnam Alliance of National, Democratic, and Peace Forces constantly sides with the NLFSV, in order to fulfill the glorious national salvation task and to restore independence, freedom and peace to the people. The Vietnam Alliance of National, Democratic, and Peace Forces earnestly calls on compatriots in the cities and the areas still under enemy terrorism in South Vietnam, on intellectuals, youths, university and high school students, women, workers, laborers and peasants, merchants and industrialists, compatriots of the various religions, and noted personalities, and on the various patriotic and progressive forces and organizations to further develop and strengthen their unity, thousands like one man, to develop together

* The Dien Hong "conference" was a meeting of the nations' most prominent individuals, convoked in the year 1270 to decide whether or not to forcibly resist the recent invasion from China. The decision was positive, leading to a series of campaigns that were not finally successful until 1287.

the strong and winning posture of our people, and to rush forward like tidal waves to completely defeat the U.S. aggressors and overthrow the puppet regime in order to regain national independence and sovereignty and other democratic freedoms and restore peace and happiness to all our people.

The Vietnam Alliance of National, Democratic, and Peace Forces calls on all civil servants, officers and soldiers of the puppet administration to clearly distinguish the glorious path of justice and victories of our people against the U.S. aggressors from the issueless path of shame and dark prospects of the puppets, to be clearsighted enough to realize the obligations and interests of the Vietnamese people, to definitely return to the national ranks to save themselves and the country, and, together with all the people, build the nation. Since its creation, the Vietnam Alliance of National, Democratic, and Peace Forces has never ceased enjoying the warm sympathy and active participation of compatriots in and outside the country, and the full support of progressive people's organizations throughout the world. The Vietnam Alliance of National, Democratic, and Peace Forces pledges to show itself worthy of the sympathy and confidence of compatriots, to resolutely assume and fulfill its historical mission and to contribute its most active part to the just struggle of all our people. United, thousands like one man, under the anti-U.S. national salvation banner of our people, let all compatriots bravely march forward.

> The Vietnam Alliance of National,
> Democratic, and Peace Forces
> South Vietnam
> July 31, 1968

ACTION PROGRAM OF THE PROVISIONAL REVOLUTIONARY GOVERNMENT OF THE REPUBLIC OF SOUTH VIETNAM*

1. To lead all people and armed forces who are united and of the same mind; to intensify military and political struggle to defeat the U.S. imperialists' aggressive war, to frustrate their scheme of Vietnamizing the war and to demand that the United States seriously talk with the Provisional Revolutionary Government of the Paris Conference on Vietnam on the basis of the ten-point overall solution of the NLFSVN; to force the U.S. Administration to unconditionally withdraw all U.S. troops and the troops of the countries of the U.S. camp from South Vietnam in order to quickly end the war, to reestablish peace and to achieve the Vietnamese people's fundamental national rights—that is, independence, national sovereignty, unification, and territorial integrity which are recognized by the 1954 Geneva Agreements on Vietnam.

2. To eradicate the camouflaged neocolonialist regime set up by the U.S. imperialists in South Vietnam; to topple the whole puppet administration organization; to abolish the constitution and all anti-people and anti-democratic laws of the puppet administration which encroach on the lives, properties, prestige, and other interests of the people.

To build a truly democratic and free republican regime; to organize elections in accordance with the principles of equality, freedom and democracy and without intervention of foreign countries.

3. With a broad national concord spirit and for the sake of the supreme interests of the nation and people, the Provisional Revolutionary Government is ready to consult with the political forces representing the various people's strata and political tendencies in South Vietnam, including people who, for political reasons, have to live abroad, which sympathize with peace, independence, and neutrality, for the formation of a provisional coalition government based on the principle of equality, democracy and mutual respect. The provisional coalition government will organize general elections to elect a national assembly, to build a democratic constitution fully reflecting national concord and the broad unity of people of all walks of life.

4. Strengthen the people's resistance force in all respects.

To consolidate and develop revolutionary administrations at all echelons, to build and consolidate revolutionary armed forces, unify patriotic armed forces, and consolidate and broaden liberated areas.

5. Realize broad democratic freedoms.

Release all persons detained by the U.S. imperialists and the puppet administration because of their patriotic activities.

* Source: Joint U. S. Public Affairs Office (JUSPAO), *Viet-Nam Documents and Research Notes No. 101*, Part II, (n.d.). Saigon: U.S. Mission in Vietnam, October 1967–), pp. 31–37.

Prohibit every terrorist and revenging act and any discriminatory treatment of those who have collaborated with this side or the other side living at home or abroad.

Realize the equality of sexes in every respect.

Implement a policy of solidarity and equality among nationalities; ethnic minorities have the right to use their own spoken and written languages to develop their national culture and art and to maintain or to change their customs and habits. Respect freedom of faith and freedom of worship, practice equality among religious communities. Protect interests of Vietnamese residents abroad and just interests of foreigners living in South Vietnam.

6. Pay great attention to the interests of urbanites of all strata, especially the right to a decent life and democratic rights.

Improve the living conditions of workers and laborers. Revise the labor law and set up a system of minimum wages; oppose mistreatment, fines, and dismissal of workers and laborers. Workers are entitled to participate in managing enterprises and are free to join trade unions.

Oppose the forcible recruitment of youths and students into the puppet army, guarantee studies of youths and students.

Personalities, intellectuals, professors, writers and artists, and journalists are entitled to freedom of thought, freedom of speech, and freedom of press.

Industrialists and businessmen are entitled to freedom of business. Oppose oppression by foreign capitalist monopolists. Urbanites of all strata are entitled to participate in political activities and in all struggles for peace, independence, sovereignty, and the right to live. Oppose all repressive and terrorist U.S.-puppet activities.

7. Accelerate production to provide supplies for the frontline and improve the people's strength, creating conditions for advancing toward the building of an independent and self-supporting economy. Take care of the laboring people's lives. Give due consideration to the interests of other strata.

Implement an agrarian policy in consonance with the practical circumstances in South Vietnam.

Improve the peasant's living standards, restore and develop agricultural and industrial production.

Encourage bourgeois industrialists and businessmen to contribute to developing industry, small industries, and handicrafts.

Guarantee the right to ownership of production means and other property of citizens according to state law.

8. Eliminate the U.S.-type enslaving and depraved culture and education now adversely affecting our people's fine, long-standing cultural traditions.

Build a national democratic culture and develop science and technology.

Improve the people's cultural standards, eradicate illiteracy, promote complementary education, and open more general education schools.

Develop medical, hygienic, and prophylactic activities.

9. Encourage, welcome, and appropriately commend and reward puppet officers and enlisted men, police agents, and civil servants who render services and return to the people; in particular, encourage and commend and reward puppet army or police units who return to the Provisional Revolutionary Government.

Those who have committed crimes but are now repentant and sincerely return to the people will be pardoned and enjoy equal treatment. They will be rewarded accordingly for their meritorious deeds.

10. Positively solve the problems left by the aggressive U.S. war and the puppet administration regime, heal the war wounds, and stabilize the people's normal life.

Wholeheartedly care for and help wounded soldiers and families of war heroes.

Provide the people with jobs, positively solving unemployment.

Concerning the compatriots who were herded by the enemy into concentration camps or strategic hamlets, those who want to stay there will be entitled to the right of mastership of land and rice fields and will be assisted in carrying on business activities on the spot; and those who want to return to their native places will be also aided.

Give relief to the victimized compatriots and care for young orphans, debilitated and lame oldsters.

The wounded and crippled puppet troops and policemen and the poor and helpless families of killed-in-action puppet troops and policemen will also be taken care of.

Help those who were driven by the U.S. imperialists and their lackeys into debauchery to rebuild their lives.

11. Reestablish normal relations between the South and North, guarantee the freedom of movement, correspondence, and residence, establish economic and cultural relations in accordance with the principle that both zones have interests, help each other, agree on the demilitarized zone status, and prescribe procedures for crossing the temporary military demarcation line.

The unification of the country will be achieved step by step through peaceful methods and one the basis of discussions and agreement between both zones, without coercion by either side.

12. Struggle for the sympathy, support, and aid of various countries and progressives worldwide, including the American people, for the South Vietnamese people's anti-U.S. national salvation undertaking.

Positively support the national independence movements of the Asian, African, and Latin American peoples opposing imperialism and neocolonialism.

Positively coordinate with the American people's struggle against the U.S. imperialists' aggressive war in Vietnam. Positively support the U.S. Negroes' just struggle for fundamental national rights.

Implement a peaceful, neutral foreign policy.

Establish friendly relations and a good-neighbor policy toward the Cambodian Kingdom on the basis of respect for the independence, sovereignty, and neutrality of Cambodia, recognize and pledge to respect the territorial integrity of the Cambodian Kingdom according to the present borders.

Implement a good-neighbor policy toward the Laotian Kingdom on the basis of respect for the 1962 Geneva Agreements on Laos.

Establish diplomatic, economic, and cultural relations with all countries, the United States included, regardless of the political and social systems, on the basis of the five principles of peaceful coexistence, respect for each other's independence, sovereignty, and territorial integrity, without infringement upon each other, without interference in each other's internal affairs, equality, mutual benefits, and peaceful coexistence. Accept aid in capital, technique, and experts from any country without political conditions attached.

Join no military alliance, accept no military bases, troops, or military personnel of foreign countries on South Vietnam territory. Accept no foreign protection or military alliance.

The Provisional Revolutionary Government of the Republic of South Vietnam earnestly appeals to all the armed forces and people to closely unite, millions as one, around the government to achieve the program of action, to advance the General Offensive and Uprisings movement toward greater victories, to defeat all dark schemes and cunning maneuvers of the U.S. imperialists and their henchmen, and to create new changes in our people's sacred resistance.

The Provisional Revolutionary Government warmly welcomes and praises the absolutely brave, self-sacrificing spirit of our armed forces and people who are always worthy to be the children of a heroic nation in the anti-U.S. national salvation struggle for independence and freedom.

The Provisional Revolutionary Government of the Republic of South Vietnam expresses its profound gratitude to the DRV government and compatriots of kith-and-kin North Vietnam for fulfilling wholeheartedly and to the best of their ability the duties of the great rear toward the great frontline.

The Provisional Revolutionary Government of the Republic of South Vietnam expresses its profound gratitude to socialist and peace-loving countries, world progressives, and Americans for their sympathy and great support for the South Vietnamese people's anti-U.S. national salvation struggle.

Let all our armed forces and people rush forward bravely, overcome all obstacles, struggle persistently, heighten vigilance, resolutely defeat the U.S. imperialists' aggressive war, overthrow the lackey puppet administration, force the U.S. government to unconditionally withdraw all U.S. and allied troops and to let the South Vietnamese people achieve their real right to self-determination, gloriously complete the national liberation task, and create basic conditions for building an independent, democratic, peaceful, neutral, and prosperous South Vietnam and advance toward the peaceful reunification of the Fatherland.

Let our southern compatriots advance valiantly!
Glorious victories are waiting for us.
The South Vietnamese people will surely win!

South Vietnam
June 10, 1969
Provisional Revolutionary Government of
The Republic of South Vietnam
Chairman, Architect Huynh Tan Phat

Alliance (of National, Democratic, and Peace Forces): history and goals of, 130–44, 270–71, 283; and Lao Dong, 186–89; mentioned, 85, 106, 147. *See also* Nationalists

Anti-war movement (in France), 21–23, 26

Anti-war movement (in USA): NLF goals concerning, 142–43, 145–57, 292; and Cambodian invasion, 183, 211–12; as product of NLF efforts, 210–12, 214, 231, 253, 284; mentioned, 254. *See also* International publicity

Association of Vietnamese in France, 19–20, 23, 25

August Revolution (Saigon, 1945), 7, 14–15, 27, 42–43, 105

Au Truong Thanh, 37

Ba Cap, 186–89

Ban Me Thuot, 65, 251

Bao Dai government, 25, 27, 30, 32, 33

Ba Tra, 105–6, 109–11, 118, 119, 121, 131

Ba Xuyen, 75

Ben Hamouda, Boualem, 246

Ben Tre, 9–10, 49

B-52 bombers. *See* Bombers

Binh, Madame. *See* Nguyen Thi Binh (Mme.)

Binh Gia, 59

Binh Xuyen, 63, 85

Blum, Leon, 20

Boat People, 292–308

Bombers (American): attacks on COSVN, 158, 177–80, 182, 192, on Cambodia, 182–83, 185, 211–12, on Hanoi and Haiphong, 205, 208, on Ho Chi Minh Trail, 242; description of bombardment by B-52, 167–68, 170–71

Bouteflika, Abdelaziz, 244

Buddhists: and Diem, 50, 89–90; and NLF, 55, 66, 92, 195, 202

Bui Thi Nga, 198

Bundy, McGeorge, 58

Bunker, Ellsworth, 203, 208

Cambodia: at Geneva Conference, 30; NLF sanctuaries in, 176–77; American invasion of,

Cambodia (*cont.*)
182–83, 185, 211–12; falls to
Khmer Rouge, 254–55. *See
also* Khmer Rouge; Kratie
Province; Sihanouk, Norodom
Cao Dai Sect, 4, 69, 75, 85n
Cao Minh Chiem, 96, 99, 100
Cao Van Bon, 133
Cao Van Vien, 136
Carter, Jimmy, 303
Case/Church Amendment, 229
Catholics (in Vietnam), 36
Central Office, South Vietnam. *See*
COSVN
Chasseloup Laubat. *See* Lycée
Chasseloup Laubat
Chau Doc province: author teaches in,
27–30, 35
Chiem. *See* Cao Minh Chiem
Chi Hoa Central Prison: and author,
. 61, 99–101
China: 25, 30–31, 176, 200, 204, 232.
See also Sino-Soviet dispute
Chin Chien, 186
Coalition government (in Vietnam):
NLF hopes for, 215–19,
221–22, 227, 232
Colonialism (in Vietnam): and
author, 5, 18–19, 21, 26, 36
Committee to Defend the Peace, 57,
69–70, 95–99, 101, 105, 111
Conein, Lucien, 90
Confucianism, 3–4, 136–37, 195
COSVN (Central Office, South
Vietnam): location of, 127–29;
as liaison between DRV
and NLF, 128, 138, 140,
155, 168, 195, 198–99, 215;
moves headquarters, 177, 182;

strain between PRG and, 193,
195, 198–99, 216, 222, 228,
234–36, 238; mentioned, 132,
156
Cung, Dr. *See* Phung Van Cung

Dalat, 4, 107, 284
Danang, 95, 101, 252
Dang Van Ky, 96
de Gaulle, Charles, 55
Democratic Republic of Vietnam
(DRV). *See* North Vietnam
Diem. *See* Ngo Dinh Diem
Dienbienphu, 30, 246
Dinh, General, 52–53
Dinh Xang, 121–22
Do Mau, 52–54
DRV (Democratic Republic of
Vietnam). *See* North Vietnam
Duong Quynh Hoa (Dr. Hoa): as
Alliance member, 66, 132–33;
background, 132–33, 135; as
PRG minister, 149, 258, 267;
gives birth in jungle, 180–81;
mentioned, 197
Duong Van Minh ("Big" Minh), 52,
57, 202–3, 258–59
Duy Lien, 123–27, 261

Ecole Nationale des Sciences
Politiques (Paris), 18, 20
Elections (in Vietnam): Diem's, 39,
44; Thieu's, 202–3; after
Spring Victory, 285–86

Fatherland Front, 238–39, 284
France: its effect on author, 18–19;
and Vietnam, 10, 145–46, 191.
See also Vietminh

French College Chasseloup Laubat.
    See Lycée Chasseloup Laubat
French Communist Party, 23
French School of Naval Supply, 30, 32

Galang Island, 308
Geneva Accords, 35, 70, 95, 240
Geneva Conference (1954), 30–32
Giap, General. See Vo Nguyen Giap
Go Vap: author's farm at, 291–92
Great Britain, 30, 46
Great Spring Victory (1975), 198,
    258–64
Guerrillas. See Jungle life; Maquis;
    NLF; People's wars; Vietminh
Gulf of Tonkin, 58, 94–95

Hai. See Vo Van Hai
Haiphong, 20, 205, 226
Hai Thuan, 277–78
Hai Xe Ngua, 77, 83
Hanoi, 6, 205, 226, 243–44
Hieu. See Nguyen Van Hieu
Hoa, Dr. See Duong Quynh Hoa
Hoa Hao Sect, 85n
Hoang Bich Son, 155
Hoang Cam, 164
Hoang Van Hoan, 248
Hoang Van Thai, 129, 179
Ho Chi Minh: and North Vietnam,
    30, 31, 300; negotiations with
    France, 10, 17, 19, 20; author
    meets, 10–17; background,
    11n; slogans of, 12, 15, 26,
    164, 196, 224, 239, 264, 283;
    and war with France, 20–21,
    25; and Sino-Soviet relations,
    34–35, 247–49; author's view
    of, 36, 190–91; as spiritual

father of NLF, 68, 71, 72,
    140–41; American view of,
    213; mentioned, 43, 157, 189,
    262–63
Ho Chi Minh Trail, 240–42
Ho Gia Ly, 93, 99
Ho Huu Nhut, 140
Ho Ngoc Nhuan, 216
Hoxha, Enver, 249–50
Hue, 136, 154–55, 252
Huyen, Dr. See Pham Van Huyen
Huynh Tan Mam, 202
Huynh Tan Phat: and rise of NLF,
    66, 77, 79, 82–86, 95, 154,
    237; as Lao Dong member,
    68–69, 189, 193; frees Nguyen
    Huu Tho, 70, 73–75; writes to
    author, 100, 130; as PRG
    president, 149, 156, 180, 189,
    195, 201–4, 234, 284;
    mentioned, 147, 198
Huynh Van Nghi, 180, 197

Imperialism. See Colonialism
International Control Commission, 51,
    96–97, 220
International publicity: and Vietnam
    war, 95, 146–47, 150, 155,
    202–3, 234; and Boat People,
    296. See also Anti-war
    movement (in USA)

Japanese Communist Party, 157
Jeunesse d'Avant-garde, 7–8, 42, 105
Johnson, Lyndon, 58–59, 93, 143,
    204, 209, 254
Jungle life (for NLF), 156–75
Justice, legal. See Laws

Karnow, Stanley, 289
Khanh, General. *See* Nguyen Khanh
Khe Sanh, 142, 192
Khiem, General, 48–50, 56–57
Khmer Rouge, 185, 201, 247, 254–55
Khrushchev, Nikita, 249
Khue. *See* Tran Huu Khue
Kiem. *See* Tran Buu Kiem
Kiet. *See* Vo Van Kiet
Kieu. *See* Tran Van Kieu
Kim, General, 52
Kissinger, Henry: and Thieu, 137,
    210, 232; and Cambodian
    invasion, 183, 212; and Paris
    negotiations, 194, 203–9,
    213–17, 219–22, 226;
    mentioned, 127, 182, 231n
Korean troops (in Vietnam), 202
Kossamak (Queen of Cambodia),
    255, 258
Kratie Province (Cambodia): and
    PRG, 176–85, 219–20
Ky. *See* Dang Van Ky; Nguyen Cao
    Ky; Ton That Duong Ky; Ung
    Ngoc Ky

Lam Van Tet, 133, 134, 138, 150, 258
Lansdale, Edward, 37
Lao Dong (Workers' Party): and
    NLF, 68–69, 73, 80, 83, 118,
    128–29, 147n, 216–17; its
    mistreatment of Southerners,
    186–99, 234–39; its internal
    propaganda, 224–26, 283; and
    Sino-Soviet dispute, 247–49;
    after Spring Victory, 264–70,
    274–77, 279, 289. *See also*
    Nationalists (Southern):
    conflicts between Lao Dong
    and

Laws: concerning communists in
    South Vietnam, 109, 140;
    revolutionary, in Hue, 154–55;
    PRG's, 171–73; after Spring
    Victory, 271–82, 185–86;
    conference on, 252–54
Le Duan, 104, 135, 197, 225–26, 235,
    248, 250
Le Duc Tho: and Paris negotiations,
    194, 203–6, 213–17, 219, 221,
    226; and Party line, 248, 284;
    mentioned, 127, 262
Legend of the Three Kingdoms,
    136–37
Le Loi, 14
Le Thi Rieng (Mme.), 118, 120–21,
    123
Le Van Giap, 139
Le Van Phong, 70, 75
Le Van Tha, 84, 171, 268
Lien, Mme. *See* Duy Lien
Li Quing, 256
Li Xian Nian, 256
Loan, General, 108
Loan, Madame, 83–84
Lodge, Henry Cabot, 50, 58, 89–90, 93
Long. *See* Nguyen Long
Lon Nol, 177, 179, 183, 201
Luu Huu Phuoc, 267
Ly. *See* Ho Gia Ly
Lycée Chasseloup Laubat, 2, 4–5,
    42–43, 247

McGovern, George, 194, 216
Mai, Colonel, 54
Mai Chi Tho, 127, 129
Malaysia, 46
Maquis: author's first experiences
    with, 28–29; and Albert Thao,
    43, 55; defined, 125. *See also*

NLF; Resistance Committee for the South

Military conflict. *See* NLF: its three-pronged approach

Military Management Committee (DRV), 142, 194, 259–60, 265–66

Minh, "Big." *See* Duong Van Minh

Molotov, V. M., 31

Montagnards, 65

Moutet, Marius, 19, 20

Movement for Self-Determination, 92–93, 95–99, 101, 105, 111

Movement in Defense of Peace, 3, 38n

Mung, Major, 85

Muoi Tri, 85

Mytho, 43–44, 48–49, 81

National Council of Reconciliation and Concord, 214, 221–26, 271–82

Nationalists (Southern): on partitioning, 31–32; on Diem, 40–41; conflicts between Lao Dong and, 69, 137–38, 166n, 186–99, 216, 223–26, 234–49. *See also* Alliance; NLF; PRG

National Liberation Front. *See* NLF

National Revolutionary Party (Nhu's), 40, 63

National School of Political Science (Paris), 18, 20, 37

Neutralists (in South Vietnam), 55, 216n

Ngo Ba Thanh (Mme.), 95–96, 99

Ngo Cong Duc, 216n

Ngo Dinh Diem: his regime, 32–40, 81–82; and Albert Thao, 44–52, 54, 62; overthrow and death of, 54, 89–90; his policies, 46–49, 55, 63–65, 72; mentioned, 68, 70, 71, 288. *See also* To Cong campaign; USA: its support for Diem

Ngo Dinh Nhu, 40, 45–48, 50–52, 54, 62, 63

Ngo Dinh Thuc (Bishop Thuc), 45, 46

Ngo Khac Tinh, 40

Ngo Minh Loan, 286–87

Nguyen Ai Quoc Institute (Hanoi), 195, 238

Nguyen Anh Tuan, 88

Nguyen Ba Nghe, 93

Nguyen Cao Ky: and Albert Thao, 54, 60–62; mentioned, 37n, 57–58, 119, 202, 230

Nguyen Chi Thanh, 192

Nguyen Cong Hoan, 216n

Nguyen Co Tam, 78

Nguyen Doa, 155

Nguyen Duy Trinh, 226

Nguyen Huu Khuong, 66, 133

Nguyen Huu The, 78

Nguyen Huu Tho: exiled by Diem, 38; freed, 70, 73–75; as leader of NLF, 70, 86, 147–48, 183, 243, 264; and PRG, 150; after Spring Victory, 258, 262, 267, 269–70, 284

Nguyen Khac-Vien, 268

Nguyen Khanh (General Khanh): in Diem's regime, 48–50; in his own regime, 55–62, 90–92, 94, 96; mentioned, 133

Nguyen Long, 66, 93, 97, 99, 101, 152–53

Nguyen Ngoc Loan, 108

Nguyen Ngoc Suong, 101

Nguyen Tat Thanh. *See* Ho Chi Minh
Nguyen Thi Binh (Mme. Binh), 149,
    206, 226, 234, 237, 244, 255
Nguyen Thi Dinh, 78, 180
Nguyen Trai, 14
Nguyen Van Hieu, 66, 68–71, 78, 79,
    237, 267
Nguyen Van Kiet, 133, 186–87
Nguyen Van Linh, 129, 198, 204
Nguyen Van So, 77
Nguyen Van Tai, 84
Nguyen Van Thieu (President Thieu):
    and Albert Thao, 61; loyalty
    of, 136–37, 261n; his regime,
    138–39, 202–3, NLF's goals
    concerning, 172, 204, 212,
    245; after Paris Accords,
    219–33, 245, 251, 254; and
    Vietnamization, 146–47, 155;
    as subject of Paris negotiations,
    214, 217; resignation of, 257;
    mentioned, 48, 62, 101, 119,
    192, 216, 271, 288
Nguyen Van Tho, 38
Nhu. *See* Ngo Dinh Nhu
1966 Resolution, 104, 122
Nixon, Richard M.: and Thieu
    regime, 137, 203, 217, 220–23,
    232; and "Vietnamization,"
    143–47, 155, 200; his Asian
    policies, 183, 204–12, 254
NLF (National Liberation Front):
    and Diem, 50–51; view of
    American involvement in war,
    55, 58–59, 93–95, 200–204;
    author's positions in, 56; its
    relation to sentiments in the
    South, 56, 133–35; rise of,
    63–87; its anthem, 71, 78; its
    flag, 71, 78, 264; its objectives,
71, 86, 91; its three-pronged
    approach, 86–87, 94–95, 103,
    145, 192, 204, 210–13, 254;
    prisoner exchange with
    Americans, 119; American
    view of, 213; its military
    successes, 250–52; as stumbling
    block to forced reunification,
    268–70. *See also* Alliance;
    Anti-war movement (in USA);
    Coalition gov't; International
    publicity; Nationalists
    (Southern); PRG
North Vietnam (Democratic Republic
    of Vietnam): and NLF, 72–73,
    80, 94, 103, 130–31, 133,
    254; denies claims on South,
    133, 284; its army, 164, 166,
    204, 218, 284, 288–89; its
    propaganda strategy, 203;
    takes over South, 205–9,
    214–15, 222, 264–70; and
    forced reunification, 271–90.
    See also COSVN; Hanoi;
    Military Management
    Committee; Politburo

Paris Accords, 220–23, 226–33, 245.
    See also Kissinger, Henry; Le
    Duc Tho
Peace Committee (or Movement).
    See Committee to Defend the
    Peace
Peasants: 46–49, 62, 64–65, 201–2,
    299–300
People's wars, 209–13, 253
Pham Hung, 129, 182–83, 264, 269,
    279, 284–85
Pham Khac Suu, 57, 96

Pham Ngoc Hung, Lucien, 133, 134, 300
Pham Ngoc Thach, 160
Pham Ngoc Thao, Albert: and Jeunesse d'Avant-Garde, 7–8; his brother Gaston, 42–45; as master spy, 42–62; his coup attempts, 52–54, 60–61, 100–101; mentioned, 81, 95, 133, 135–36, 261
Pham Van Dong: as DRV prime minister, 135, 183, 259, 280, 284, 287, 289; on Soviets, 248; and Sihanouk, 256n; mentioned, 11, 155
Pham Van Huyen, 95–97, 99, 100
Pham Van Lieu, 97
Pham Van Phu, 251
Pham Xuan Thai, 78
Phan Huy Quat, 99, 102
Phan Van Dang, 129
Phat, General, 61
Phat, Madame, 198
Phat (NLF leader). See Huynh Tan Phat
Phoenix program, 201–2
Phung Van Cung (Dr. Cung), 78, 79, 105, 151
Phuoc Long, 250–51, 253
Politburo (DRV): and NLF, 138, 142; and PRG, 155; and war strategy, 194, 220, 229, 242, 252; aims in Paris, 214–15; after Spring Victory, 259, 265–66, 268–69, 274, 277, 281
Political war (in Vietnam): author's role in, xiii–xiv, 25–26, 29; NLF's strategy in, 58–59, 72–73, 209–16, 220–23,

227–33. See also NLF: its three-pronged approach
Poulo Condore, 303
PRG (Provisional Revolutionary Government): aims of, 145–55, 219, 222, 227–28, 283; author as justice minister for, 151–53, 155–57, 171–73, 193, 252–53, 266–82; after Spring Victory, 217–18, 266–70; author as ambassador for, 234, 236, 244–57; world support for, 244–47, 254; mentioned, 140, 189
Prisoner exchange (between NLF and USA), 123–29
Provisional Revolutionary Government. See PRG

Quan. See Tran Kim Quan
Quang Cong, 136–37
Quang Trung, 14

Radios, 72, 80, 157, 227, 229
Reeducation camps, 272–79
Resistance Committee for the South, 43–44
Resistance Veterans' Association, 72–73
Reunification of Vietnam. See Vietnam: reunification of
Rex Dance Hall, 206, 270
Rieng. See Le Thi Rieng
Rogers, William, 226

Saigon/Cholon/Giadinh zone: and Tran Bach Dang, 103–5, 235; and author, 138; mentioned, 79, 82–84, 118, 123, 127, 129, 131

Saigon-Cholon Peace Committee, 38n
Sainteny, Jean, 10
Sartre, Jean-Paul, 299–300
Sau Cang, 70
Sau Ha, 119, 120
Sau No, 123, 124
Self-Determination Movement, 92–99,
     101, 105, 111
Sihanouk, Norodom (Prince of
     Cambodia), 176–77, 183, 185,
     201, 242, 246–47, 255–58
Sino-Soviet dispute: and Vietnam,
     247–50, 256
Société Sucrière, 54, 88–89
South Vietnam. See Alliance;
     Nationalists (Southern); NLF;
     PRG; Key figures in
Soviet Union: at Geneva Conference,
     30–31; its role in Vietnam,
     168, 170, 176, 204; mentioned,
     25, 200, 208, 288
Spellman, Francis Cardinal, 35
Spring Victory. See Great Spring
     Victory
Strategic-hamlet program, 46–49

Ta Ba Tong, 105
Taleb, Ahmed, 245–46
Tao Thao, 136–37
Taylor, Maxwell, 55, 58, 90–91
Tet Offensive (1968): author's
     experience of, 122–23; as
     mobilizing force, 133, 190–92;
     and anti-war movement (in
     USA), 142–43, 183, 212–13;
     in Hue, 153–54
Thang, President (DRV). See Ton
     Duc Thang
Thanh, Mme., 95–96, 99
Thanh Loan (Mme.), 83–84

Thanh Nghi, 133, 134
Thao. See Pham Ngoc Thao, Albert;
     Tao Thao; Trinh Dinh Thao
Thao, Mme., 140–41
Thich Don Hau, 138
Thich Thien Minh, 216
Thieu, President. See Nguyen Van
     Thieu
Third Force. See Alliance
Tho. See Le Duc Tho; Mai Chi Tho;
     Nguyen Huu Tho; Nguyen
     Van Tho
Thorez, Maurice, 23
Thuc, Bishop, 45, 46
Thuy Ba, 130
To Cong campaign (Diem), 45,
     63–64, 66
Ton, Dr., 294–95, 297, 301, 304,
     307–8
Ton Duc Thang, 262–64, 283–84
Ton That Duong Ky, 96, 99, 100, 138
Tran Bach Dang, 103–5, 118–20, 133,
     234–36, 238–39
Tran Bach Dang (Mme.), 110n, 111,
     120–21, 235
Tran Buu Kiem, 66, 68–70, 78,
     236–38, 267
Tran Duc Thao, 299–300
Tranh Huu Thanh, 216n
Tranh Nghi, 133
Tran Hoai Nam, 237
Tran Hung Dao, 14
Tran Huu Khue, 93, 99, 101
Tran Huu The, 40
Tran Kim Quan, 69, 70
Tran Kim Tuyen, 45
Tran Nam Trung, 128–29, 155, 182,
     198, 219
Tran Te Duong, 37
Tran Thien Khiem, 48–50, 56–57

Tran Van Don, 50–55, 90
Tran Van Kieu, 118, 120–21, 123
Tran Van Lam, 226
Tran Van Tra, 174–75, 251
Tran Van Trung, 136
Tran Van Tuyen, 216
Trich Tri Quang, 216n
Trinh Dinh Thao: as NLF member,
    66, 69–70; as Alliance leader,
    138, 140–41, 148, 150, 278;
    mentioned, 243, 258, 291
Trinh Dinh Thao (Mme.), 140–41
Trung, General. See Tran Nam Trung
Truong Bich (author's brother), 1, 3,
    27, 32, 151, 273, 278–79
Truong Cao Phuoc, 70, 82, 170
Truong Chinh, 248, 259, 268–69,
    284–86
Truong Due (author's brother), 151,
    273n
Truong Hoang (author's brother),
    151, 273n
Truong Khue (author's brother), 32,
    151, 273n
Truong Loan (author's daughter), 29,
    30, 261
Truong Luong, 101
Truong Nhu Tang (author): family
    background, 1–8; his father,
    1–2, 6, 9, 14, 19–28, 32, 260;
    his mother, 2, 4, 28, 61, 136,
    260–61, 274, 287, 291, 297;
    his grandfathers, 3–5, 40; his
    education, 8–25; his wives:
    first, 9–10, 19, 21–24, second,
    29–30, 99–101, 108, 115–16,
    119, 260–61, third, 291,
    293–308; his children, 29, 30,
    260–61; his imprisonment and
    torture, 97–101, 108–26; his

jungle life, 126–29, 156–85; as
    PRG justice minister, 151–53,
    155–57, 171–73, 193, 252–53,
    266–70, 273–82; as PRG
    ambassador, 234, 236, 240–57;
    escape from Vietnam by boat,
    292–308
Truong Quynh (author's brother), 1,
    3, 6, 27, 32, 151, 260; in
    reeducation camp, 273, 278–79
Tuan, Undersecretary, 100, 102–3

Ung Ngoc Ky, 66, 68–69, 78
US Congress: and Vietnam war, 58,
    210–11, 229, 231
USA: at Geneva conference, 30–32;
    its support for Diem, 33–34,
    37, 39, 44, 46–47, 52, 73; its
    policies in Vietnam, 34, 55,
    62, 90–91, 191; enters war,
    58–59, 101; NLF aims
    concerning, 71, 86–87, 209–16;
    and Cambodian invasion,
    182–83, 211–12; undermines
    NLF, 205–9; loses war,
    250–54; Third World hatred
    for, 252–53. See also Anti-war
    movement (in USA);
    "Vietnamization"

Urban unrest, 64–65, 88–101, 103–7,
    111, 203. See also Buddhists;
    Saigon/Cholon/Giadinh zone;
    Youth Liberation Association

Vanguard Youth, 7–8, 42, 105
Van Tien Dung, 251–52, 254, 257,
    262, 264–65
Van Vi, Michael, 69–70
Vietcong. See NLF

Vietminh: their war against France, 9–10, 20, 28; at Geneva Conference, 30; hunted down by Diem, 38, 64; and Albert Thao, 43, 46; and the NLF, 64, 66, 68

Vietnam: author's goals for, 20, 35–37, 71, 248–49, 273, 281; partitioning of, 30–31, 35–36; differences between South and North, 36, 254, 283–86; status and loyalty in, 102, 135–38; reunification of, 226, 262–67, 269, 283–90; in Sino-Soviet relations, 247–49. See also Colonialism; Nationalists (Southern); North Vietnam

Vietnamese Association, 19–20, 23, 25

Vietnamese Communist Workers' Party. See Lao Dong

"Vietnamization," 145–47, 189, 200–1

Vo Nguyen Giap (General Giap), 30, 191, 197, 248

Vo Van Hai, 37, 39, 83

Vo Van Kiet, 82–84, 129, 167, 235, 261, 265–66, 293–94

Vo Van Mon, 85

War in Vietnam. See NLF: its three-pronged approach; Political war

Westmoreland, William, 90–91

White Book, 246

Workers' Party. See Lao Dong

Xom Giua, 76, 82, 83, 147n

Xuan, General, 52

Xuan Thuy, 194, 248, 259

Yao Wen Yuan, 249

Young People's Association of Vietnam, 106–7

Youth: and NLF, 88–101, 103–7, 111

Youth Liberation Association, 103, 105, 235

Zhou En-lai, 31